# The University of Chicago Press

## REVIEW COPY

### Ostrannenie

**Edited by Annie van den Oever**
Published by Amsterdam University Press
Distributed by the University of Chicago Press

Domestic Publication Date: February 15, 2011
Paper $29.95 ISBN 978-90-8964-079-6

For more information, please contact Liz Fischer by phone at (773)702-7490,
by fax at (773)702-9756, or by e-mail at efischer@press.uchicago.edu

Please send a PDF of your published review to: **publicity@press.uchicago.edu**
Or, by mail to: **Publicity Director, THE UNIVERSITY OF CHICAGO PRESS**

1427 E. 60th Street, Chicago, Illinois 60637, U.S.A. Telephone 773-702-7740

D1239797

# ORDERING INFORMATION

**Orders from the U.S.A., Canada, Mexico, Central and South America, East and Southeast Asia, and China:**
The University of Chicago Press
Chicago Distribution Center
11030 S. Langley Avenue
Chicago, IL 60628
U.S.A.
Tel: 1-800-621-2736; (773) 702-7000
Fax: 1-800-621-8476; (773) 702-7212
PUBNET @ 202-5280

**Orders from the United Kingdom, Europe, Middle East, Africa, and West and South Asia:**
The University of Chicago Press
c/o John Wiley & Sons Ltd. Distribution
Centre
1 Oldlands Way
Bognor Regis, West Sussex PO22 9SA
UNITED KINGDOM
Tel: (0) 1243 779777
Fax: (0) 1243 820250
Email: cs-books@wiley.co.uk

**Orders from Japan can be placed with the Chicago Distribution Center or:**
United Publishers Services Ltd.
1-32-5 Higashi-shinigawa
Shinagawa-ku
Tokyo 140-0002
JAPAN
Tel: 81-3-5479-7251
Fax: 81-3-5479-7307
Email: info@ups.co.jp

**Orders from Australia and New Zealand:**
Footprint Books Pty Ltd
1/6A Prosperity Parade
Warriewood NSW 2102
AUSTRALIA
Tel: (+61) 02 9997-3973
Fax: (+61) 02 9997-3185
Email: info@footprint.com.au
http://www.footprint.com.au

**For Information:**
International Sales Manager
The University of Chicago Press
1427 E. 60th Street
Chicago, IL 60637
U.S.A.
Tel: (773) 702-7898
Fax: (773) 702-9756
Email: sales@press.uchicago.edu

Ostrannenie

**The Key Debates**

Mutations and Appropriations
in European Film Studies

*Series Editors*
Ian Christie, Dominique Chateau, Annie van den Oever

# Ostrannenie

On "Strangeness" and the Moving Image
The History, Reception, and Relevance
of a Concept

Edited by Annie van den Oever

Amsterdam University Press

The publication of this book is made possible by grants from The Netherlands Organisation for Scientific Research (NWO), and the Mulerius Foundation.

Cover illustration: Dziga Vertov's *The Man with a Movie camera*, 1929

Cover design: Neon, design and communications | Sabine Mannel
Lay-out: JAPES, Amsterdam

ISBN       978 90 8964 079 6
e-ISBN   978 90 4850 795 5
NUR       670

# Contents

## Part III
## Cognitive and Evolutionary-Cognitive Approaches to *Ostranenie*
## Perception, Cognitive Gaps and Cognitive Schemes

## Part IV
## Discussions
## On *Ostranenie*, Différance, and the Uncanny

# Editorial

Thinking and theorizing about film is almost as old as the medium itself. Within a few years of the earliest film shows in the 1890s, manifestos and reflections began to appear which sought to analyze the seemingly vast potential of film. Writers in France, Russia and Britain were among the first to enter this field, and their texts have become cornerstones of the literature of cinema. Few nations, however, failed to produce their own statements and dialogues about the nature of cinema, often interacting with proponents of Modernism in the traditional arts and crafts. Film thus found itself embedded in the discourses of modernity, especially in Europe and Soviet Russia.

"Film theory," as it became known in the 1970s, has always had an historical dimension, acknowledging its debts to the pioneers of analyzing film texts and film experience, even while pressing these into service in the present. But as scholarship in the history of film theory develops, there is an urgent need to revisit many long-standing assumptions and clarify lines of transmission and interpretation. The Key Debates is a new series of books from Amsterdam University Press which focuses on the central issues that continue to animate thinking about film and audiovisual media as the "century of celluloid" gives way to a field of interrelated digital media.

Initiated by Annie van den Oever (the Netherlands), the direction of the series has been elaborated by an international group of film scholars, including Dominique Chateau (France), Ian Christie (UK), Laurent Creton (France), Laura Mulvey (UK), Roger Odin (France), Eric de Kuyper (Belgium), and Emile Poppe (Belgium). The intention is to draw on the widest possible range of expertise to provide authoritative accounts of how debates around film originated, and to trace how concepts that are commonly used today have been modified in the process of appropriation. The book series may contribute to both the invention as well as the abduction of concepts.

London / Paris / Amsterdam
Ian Christie, Dominique Chateau, Annie van den Oever

# Acknowledgments

The process of making this book was a truly stimulating and pleasurable experience, since many of the authors contributing to it were already involved in the project *Mutations and Appropriations in European Film Studies* and helped to prepare the new book series *The Key Debates*. Many of the authors as well as the members of the Editorial Board were involved in the making of this book from it's infancy, discussing why we felt we had to revisit Russian Formalism and how we could best rethink its key concept, *ostranenie*. I wish to express my sincere gratitude to both the contributors to this book as well as to the members of the Editorial Board for their enthusiastic and unrelenting support and extremely generous contributions to this book and to the project in every phase of its becoming, from the first meetings and workshops via a long series of discussions and emails to correction suggestions in the very last hours before this first book of the series went into print. I cordially thank Dominique Chateau, Ian Christie, Eric de Kuyper, Laura Mulvey, Roger Odin, Emile Poppe, Laurent Creton, Barend van Heusden, Laurent Jullier, Frank Kessler, Miklós Kiss, András Bálint Kovács, László Tarnay, and Yuri Tsivian. One of the real challenges of this project was to bring an international group of scholars together from a wide variety of countries, speaking different languages, and coming from different academic traditions. The real pleasure was to see all the different inputs come together, challenge and contradict each other, compete and cohere. I am aware this process took up a bit more time than we originally planned and I am sincerely thankful to Amsterdam University Press for their patience and utterly supportive enthusiasm in every phase of this project. I sincerely thank Anniek Meinders, Jeroen Sondervan, Magdalena Hernas, Martin Voigt, Chantal Nicolaes, Marieke Smeenk, and their teams. Moreover, a team of assistants and students have been very helpful and supportive in different phases of the project, including the editorial phase. For their help and support I would like to thank Ruben Allersma, Lotte Kruijt, Emily Ekong, Rein Mulder and Shira Wolff. I would also like to thank The Netherlands Organisation for Scientific Research (NWO), the Mulerius Foundation and the Groningen Research School for the Study of the Humanities for their generous financial support, without which this project would not have been possible. I wish to particularly thank Martin Gosman and Herman Hoen, who as Heads of the Groningen Research School helped to start this project. Furthermore, I would like to thank the staff of Arts, Culture and Media from the University of Groningen for their support to the project from the start, in particular Liesbeth Korthals Altes, and Els Jongeneel, from the field of literature; and Susan Aasman, and Annelies van Noortwijk, from the field of film studies. I would also like to thank the Slavist Sander Brouwer. Last but not least, I sincerely thank Viola ten Hoorn, who has been immensely helpful as an assistant in every phase of the making of this book.

Annie van den Oever
Amsterdam, July 2010

# Introduction: *Ostran(n)enie* as an "Attractive" Concept

Annie van den Oever

Traditional accounts from the field of literature have tried to understand Viktor Shklovsky's "Art as Technique" almost exclusively in relation to literature and criticism for many years and found some of its most basic statements "easy to attack."[1] It seems to me, however, that Shklovsky's fundamental statements on *ostranenie* (or "making strange") in art were first and foremost an urgently required and utterly relevant *theoretical* answer to the tremendous impact early cinema had on the early avant-garde movements in pre-revolutionary Russia. Shklovsky himself was part of all this and it was 1913 (and not in 1919, as is often thought) when he presented his now famous revolutionary statements on perception in art to his Futurist friends in a lecture in Petersburg.[2] That year, 1913, was also the very year the cinema was at the center of public attention in Russia, as Yuri Tsivian would later write in his book on the cultural reception of early cinema in Russia.[3] Tsivian labels this particular period in history as "medium-specific."[4] Read within this specific historical context, "ostranenie" and the art theory in which it is presented regain much of their revolutionary impact as well as their relevance for cinema and media studies, as will be argued in this book. As part of the field of literature, one might easily feel that *ostranenie* and early Formalism are *passé*.[5] As part of the field of cinema and media studies, though, one might rather feel that the texts and the term are underexposed and that they urgently need to be re-read and historicized as part of a "medium-specific" period in history.

It is this book's objective to help restore the revolutionary impact of the concept of *ostranenie* and its relevance for fields of research that reflect on medium specificity and media change, and on medium-specific periods in history like the past and the current one. Moreover, the revisits in this book of the pivotal texts responsible for guiding the post-war discourse on *ostranenie* in specific directions (e.g., the "Jakobsonian" re-introduction of Russian Formalism within the context of French Structuralism)[6] will to a certain extent depart from the earlier re-readings of Russian Formalism and the research agenda's underlying them. As such, the current revisits may open a new research agenda for cinema and media studies, and may provide new ways to re-evaluate the "birth" of the cinema as well as the perceptual and cognitive impact of new optical technologies and artistic techniques and the responses to those developments by the avant-garde movements.[7]

Only within such a new framework of thinking, it may become fully obvious how deep the impact of the experience of the movies as a "new medium" must have been in its first decade. The question remains: how *exactly* did the historical avant-garde movements (Shklovsky and the so-called "Russian Formalists" were part of them) respond to the new techniques – not only *after* but also *in the very moment* of "numbness" that is typically triggered by a new medium, as Marshall McLuhan already indicated in the 1960s at the end of his introduction to *Understanding Media*; here, he pleads for the "examination" of the origin and development of new media, "preceded by a general look at some aspects of the media [...] beginning with the never-explained *numbness* that each [new medium] brings about in the individual and society [my italics]."[8] So we might ask ourselves whether *ostranenie* was indeed instrumental in shattering the baffled silence of the early avant-gardes, by breaking the glass window of tradition that blocked their theoretical thinking.

## About the title of the book

The concept of *ostranenie*, coined by Shklovsky, is now almost a century old. It is a neologism and an "attraction" in itself, similar to many of Sergei Eisenstein montages, which is to say: it is puzzling and weird, yet put forward by Shklovsky in a brash, even provocative and slightly aggressive way, typical for the manifestos of those days. Throughout his career Shklovsky revisited and reconsidered the concept, the (aesthetic) principle and the techniques of *ostranenie* many times, not only in "Art as Technique" but also in a dazzling diversity of works such as *Theory of Prose*, *A Sentimental Journey*, a memoir written for his Futurist friend Vladimir Mayakovsky, *Mayakovsky and his Circle*, *Literature and Cinematography*, the many contributions on the cinema in *Poetika Kino*[9] and in his book on Eisenstein, and so on and so forth. It was not until 1983, however, that Victor Shklovsky reflected on that very moment  seventy years earlier, when he introduced the term *ostranenie* and unleashed a revolution in thinking about the arts, that he remarked he "could now admit to having made a spelling mistake" as he had *erroneously* spelt ostranenie "with one n."[10] That is how the word entered the history books, with a single n, to roam about like "a dog with a ragged ear," as Shklovsky would have it. The spelling mistake did not prevent the term from being translated worldwide as "making strange" (or as defamiliarization, deautomatization, alienation, estrangement, and so on), as if he *had* written *stannyi* (strange). Yet he had quietly changed the word once again. So now let *Ostrannenie* be the title of this book, with that unfamiliar double *nn*, to once again estrange us from what may now have become a word too familiar to us, a buzzword, if you will, in art, literature, and film studies since the 1970s.

## About the contributions to this book

The book is structured in four parts, each of which deals with the concept or aesthetic principle of *ostranenie* from a different angle. The first part focuses on early cinema and the avant-garde period as a phase in which this revolutionary new theory of art was formed. The second and third parts explore the ways in which the term has come to resonate deeply in art, film and media studies and has entered (or enters) into dialogue with corresponding concepts from various disciplinary fields, the relatively new fields of cognitive and evolutionary–cognitive research among them (in the third part). Focusing on the appropriation and mutation of the concept of *ostranenie* within diverse epistemological traditions means revealing the prolific range and depth of a concept that has helped shape the trajectory of theoretical inquiry from 1913 onwards.

The book opens with a contribution by Yuri Tsivian dealing with *ostranenie* as a term and an artistic technique which may be closely associated both with early cinema as well as with the avant-garde in art. In "The Gesture of Revolution or Misquoting as Device," Tsivian begins a search for the relation of *ostranenie* to what the Russian writer Aleksey Tolstoy named "the gesture of revolution," a phrase that encapsulated the essence of art by Russian Formalists and the avant-garde of the 1920s. Tsivian's starting point for his quest is Dziga Vertov's KINO-EYE (1924), or more specifically, that one odd shot; the rotated street. The road of discovery Tsivian sets out for his readers, takes him through the writings of Viktor Shklovsky and Anton Checkov and their reflections on the art of their times (Levitan, Kandinsky, Rodchenko), and leads him back to Eisenstein and Vertov and the defamiliarizing artistic technique of rotation, or turning things upside down, as the gesture of revolution.

In "*Ostranenie*, 'The Montage of Attractions' and Early Cinema's 'Properly Irreducible *Alien* Quality,'" I historicize and contextualize Viktor Shklovsky's "Art as Technique" as a true avant-garde *manifesto*. I argue that its main objective is to radically re-think art from the perspective of technique, of *new* techniques and their impact on perception, as the manifesto's title in fact properly indicates. Furthermore, I argue that Shklovsky was deeply embedded in the Futurists' re-thinking of the perceptual powers of new artistic techniques, and their sudden and strong impact on audiences. Thirdly, I argue that this avant-garde project, with which early Russian Formalism was so closely connected, was *itself* a crucial part of what we have come to understand as the tremendous cultural impact of early cinema in pre-revolutionary Russia. This particular context raises some new and urgent questions: if Shklovsky's manifesto was part of the avant-garde's cultural response to early cinema, then how must we exactly situate and understand its basic premises and characteristics in relation to its historical and cultural context, e.g., its radical opposition to the practice of interpretation and to traditional concepts; its abduction of the "muddled notion of form" (replaced by the notion of "technique"); its key terms: *ostranenie, art, technique*; its implications for the study of the arts, film, and media (history)?

Part two of the book is dedicated to the investigation of the various mutations and appropriations of the concept in its post-war reception. Four essays trace the history of the adjustments and modifications of the concept of *ostranenie* within particular contexts, disciplinary fields, and theoretical frameworks. In *"Ostranenie, Innovation and Media History,"* Frank Kessler concentrates on the way in which the concept (or principle) of *ostranenie* can be made or has been made productive in the fields of film- and media history. He argues that even though the concept was first applied in the field of literature, right from the very beginning its scope was directed towards a general aesthetic principle, and as such *ostranenie* has been adopted by the so-called *neoformalist approach* elaborated on by Kristin Thompson. Kessler's historical and historiographical perspective clearly shows that the concept of *ostranenie* has proved itself valuable to several disciplinary fields, and has influenced artistic theory, even if some scholars indebted to Shklovsky's ideas did not always acknowledge it, as Kessler indicates.

In "Knight's Move: Brecht and Russian Formalism in Britain," Ian Christie explores the processes by which Russian Formalism and Brechtian "alienation" became powerful influences on the intellectual regime of Great-Britain during the 1960s and 1970s. Christie sketches how, in those two decades, *ostranenie* and *alienation* were introduced to, and appropriated by, British theater, cinema, and most specifically the critical writings of the British Film Journal *Screen*, which devoted special issues to Russian Formalism in the early 1970s. Echo's of Shklovsky and Brecht can be found in critical contributions to *Screen* by Stephen Heath, Peter Wollen, Laura Mulvey, and others. Christie argues that in the 1960s and 1970s, both Viktor Shklovsky's *ostranenie* and Bertolt Brecht's *Verfremdungseffekt* formed part of an "assertive new vocabulary," embraced by a generation "keen to declare their intellectual, and indeed political, independence." Moreover, he argues that to lay claim to concepts that originated in Russian and Marxist culture was in itself a significant gesture of revolt in those days. He shows that the reception of both Shklovsky and Brecht was in fact part of a wider movement of "revolt against the mendacity and manipulation of the Cold War," which also affected the practice of film making as well as film studies.

In Dominique Chateau's *"Ostranenie* in French Film Studies: Translation Problems and Conflicting Interests," the complications of the adoption and appropriation of *ostranenie* into a foreign language and established theoretical framework take center stage. Chateau argues that in the 1960s, during a revival of interest in Russian Formalism, French Structuralists (Todorov and Genette among them) incorporated several Formalist concepts into their theories, but quite remarkably, Shklovsky's *ostranenie* was blatantly disregarded. Chateau shows that the introduction of *ostranenie* into French Structuralism and French Film Studies was fraught with complications as the prevailing intellectual atmosphere of criticism in France did not allow for a favorable reception of Shklovsky's theories mainly due to reverence towards Roman Jakobson. Chateau may be said to have deepened the knowledge of the processes of appropriation of Russian Formalism by French Structuralism as directed by a "Jakobsonian research agenda," a problem already signaled by Meir Sternberg in 2006, as Chateau indicates.[11]

Whereas Dominique Chateau was invited to focus on the translation problems of *ostranenie* and its appropriation in the more general context of French Structuralism and Film Studies, Emile Poppe was invited to specifically focus on Christian Metz as a film theorist who, it may be argued, might have (re)discovered and possibly even appreciated Russian Formalist theory within the context of his own theorizing on film in the 1960s in France. In "Christian Metz and the Russian Formalists: A 'Rendez-Vous Manqué'?" Emile Poppe indicates, however, that factors such as the popular debate of the days and the inaccessibility of Russian Formalist works, as well as different and incompatible research affinities and scholarly agendas, seem to have kept the two parties away from a successful engagement.

Part three of this book deals with cognitive and evolutionary-cognitive approaches to *ostranenie*. It explores what the current cognitive approaches have to say about the question of perception as initiated by Shklovsky in the field of art studies almost a century earlier. In the first contribution to this section, "Should I see what I believe? Audiovisual Ostranenie and Evolutionary-Cognitive Film Theory," Laurent Jullier argues that in order to study the process of *defamiliarization* (or deautomatization), it is necessary to first examine the way *familiarization* (or automatization) works on a cognitive level. Yet before being able to know what defamiliarization is in a film (or in the cinema), one has to first ask whether the whole cinematographic process itself is not defamiliarizing, as he argues. Jullier devotes three separate sections to audiovisual *ostranenie*, based on three common distinctions in perception psychology: (1) defamiliarizations dealing with the processes of automatic recognition of visual forms (bottom-up); (2) defamiliarizations dealing with the routines associated with the exploration of the environment by the whole body; (3) defamiliarizations dealing with high-level cognitive processes such as opinions and beliefs (top-down). Interdisciplinarity being at the core of his study, Jullier adds an epistemological preamble to clarify what cognitive psychology has to say about the more general question of perception. For readers not yet fully familiar with cognitive or evolutionary-cognitive approaches to film,

Jullier's preamble offers a good start to get acquainted with the approaches in this part of the book.

One of the most comprehensive, if not the biggest, challenge that film theory has to answer to these days is posed by the new digital technology in film production, as László Tarnay states in his "On Perception, *Ostranenie*, and Specificity." In his contribution to this book, he constructs *a possible lineage* (as he calls it) of the concept of *ostranenie* in aesthetic and film theory from the Russian Formalists to the present day. His objective is to define a golden thread for the conceptual labyrinth that would lead from Shklovsky's idea – both theoretically and historically – to what he takes to be a fundamental challenge to the theory of the moving image, namely the arrival of the newest (computer simulated) digital imagery. His approach is primarily conceptual. With regard to the perceptual process of *ostranenie*, he indicates that our cognitive system resorts to "specificity recognition" (as opposed to category recognition), a so-called bottom-up process that *renews* our awareness of the medium or object and thus defamiliarizes the perception. This line of thought, Tarnay argues, is upheld in several 20th century aesthetic theories, from Viktor Shklovsky, to Walter Benjamin, to Gilles Deleuze; there are several interesting references to Vivian Sobchack as well. Tarnay shows that they all argue for the uniqueness and singularity of the art object, something which may be considered particularly remarkable and relevant in our current digital age of technological renewal.

In "Estrangement and the Representation of Life in Art," Barend van Heusden states that Viktor Shklovsky, who considered "estrangement" (or "ostranenie") to be the basic function of art, "was right, but for the wrong reasons." Van Heusden argues that in "Art as Technique," Shklovsky mingled three theoretical perspectives: a theory of perception, a theory of semiosis, and a theory of abstraction. In his step-by-step analysis of Shklovsky's discourse, Van Heusden gives a detailed insight in the current knowledge of artistic (perception and) cognition, and in the shifts and changes that took place in the field of art studies. In passing he points out that in the course of roughly one century, the study of the arts has moved from the study of artistic forms, via the study of artistic meaning, to the study of artistic cognition. His basic statement is that the concept of *ostranenie* can and should be reassessed in contemporary art theory. Moreover, he argues that to keep the concept "alive" in contemporary criticism, we will have to take this changed context of research into account and treat *ostranenie* accordingly, "as a concept that refers to a crucial dimension of human semiotic cognition."

The last essay in this section of the book, "The Perception of Reality as Deformed Realism" deals with the question "what, exactly, does *ostranenie* deautomatize?" In this contribution to the book, Miklós Kiss re-evaluates Shklovsky's highly progressive intuition (as he labels it) on the cognitive distinction of "perceiving" as a *bottom-up* and "knowing" as a *top-down* logic. In his exploration of this opposition, Kiss highlights the discrepancy between the *reality* of perception and comprehension on the one hand, and the *realism* of representation on the other hand. Kiss' objective is to demonstrate and explore the consequences of Shklovsky's "cognitive hunch," which seems to have led him towards introducing the concept of *ostranenie* as part of his radically new theory of art. Kiss starts his argument with a motto taken from Jarmo Valkola, saying that "Our eyes may move like a camera, but our attention jumps like editing." By focusing on film narration and the cognitive and perceptual processes it triggers, Kiss argues that the non-linear cognitive processes with which we perceive reality as well as film are so similar that watching a film that represents its story events out of chronological order should not be an incentive for deautomatization since it does not alter our built-in non-linear perceptive and comprehensive operations.

Part four of this book contains two Conversations in the French tradition of the *Entretiens*: the first one with András Bálint Kovács, and a second one with Laura Mulvey. These Conversations are meant to round up the debate in this book. The first Conversation, between András Bálint Kovács and Laurent Jullier, focuses once more on the cognitive aspect of *ostranenie* in relation to film narration. Weighing the pros and cons of several theoretical paradigms in Film Studies, the Conversation between Kovács and Jullier primarily stresses narrative defamiliarization and denounces the theory that defamiliarization is easily obtainable by means of distorting narrative techniques. Instead, Kovács argues that associative rules other than causality are just as easily applied by the viewer to make sense of the narrative since people have a built-in tendency to find coherence in narratives. Viewers tend to resort to associative rules such as similarity or repetition to make up for a lack of causality that only briefly defamiliarizes the narrative, he argues. Other aspects of defamiliarization discussed between Kovács and Jullier in this Conversation pertain to the "knowledge" acquired through defamiliarization as an alternative to theories by Derrida (*différance*) and Deleuze (*répétition*) and some concluding thoughts on the interdisciplinary nature of *ostranenie* and the most productive ways to approach the concept.

The second Conversation, between Laura Mulvey and myself, aims at gaining more insight into the disruptive and uncanny nature of the early movie-going experience, deemed highly relevant for the re-reading of Shklovsky's "Art as Technique" within its historical context. The powers of the new optical and cinematic techniques to "make strange," and thus to trigger a sudden and strong, *uncanny* feeling of defamiliarization in the viewer are here explored by means of revisiting the past; that is to say, re-reading the seminal texts by Viktor Shklovsky on *ostranenie*, and by Sigmund Freud on the *uncanny* (or *Unheimlichkeit*). As different as these two texts (and authors) may be, it can be argued that they both deal with disruptive perceptual processes in that very particular medium-specific moment in time in which they both were written. One of the objectives of this Conversation is to bring the ideas of "uncanniness" and "estrangement" into some kind of shared framework, in an attempt to better understand the disruptive impact early cinema had on the modes of perception of the viewer and on the way the "uncanny" experience of a world "made strange" by the new mass medium may have been an important factor in the shaping of the way people experienced the modern.

# PART I
## Theory Formation

# *Ostranenie*,
# the Avant-Garde and
# The Cinema of Attractions

# The Gesture of Revolution or Misquoting as Device[1]

*Yuri Tsivian*

## The Primal Gesture

First of all, I would like to comment on an expression used in the title of this article. The phrase "gesture of revolution" is not mine. I have borrowed this word combination from Aleksey Nikolaevich Tolstoy's series of articles "Vozmozhnosti kino" (The Potential of the Cinema) written in 1924, shortly after his return from emigration to Moscow.[2] On his return, the writer concluded that all was not well in the new Soviet literature and the emerging Soviet cinema. Literature was in thrall to an unreflecting fascination with adventure, while cinema was ruled by the febrile American style of editing.

Let's follow the reasoning of Tolstoy's article. Here is what he has to say about literature:

> The contemporary (revolutionary) art, negating 'psychologism', affirms activity instead. But here an error, and often nonsense, creeps in. Let's take a contemporary short story set during the years of the Revolution. What a subject! But you start reading, and what you get is glimpses of little people, objects, fragments of events and so on. Forward, forward, at any cost. People, objects, events, going round and hurtling by...[3]

And here is what Tolstoy thinks of the Soviet cinema and its tendency towards a rapid succession of short shots:

> And it's the same in the cinema: a fascination with American film editing. A mad race of shadows on the screen, not even a promise of something better to come, you're just sitting there, getting dumber by the minute; where are you going to get to by going faster?[4]

Where is the solution? In the new Russia, according to Tolstoy, the old psychological prose and the old psychological cinema should be replaced not by the American montage technique, nor by a mindless literary equivalent of action films, but by a third option – a gesture:

If the image passing in front of me on the screen, however wonderfully produced, however super-American in its editing, full of tricks and so forth, if in this succession of human shadows I fail to discern the endless, faithful, human gesture, my gesture, I shall remain indifferent.[5] We should not begin with speed and motion, nor with the triumph of object over spiritual movement, but with the primal gesture. A human gesture.[6]

Of course, Tolstoy warns the reader, not all gestures are alike. This is not about everyday gestures, "mendacious, duplicitous, nervously lewd."[7] Whoever finds the primal gestures will pave the way for the new cinema and new literature. This qualification – primal[8] – is a recurring motif in Tolstoy's article. What sort of gestures are they, and how are they different from ordinary movements?

Those are gestures preceding thought and feeling, fundamental gestures, *animal* gestures. A cock grouse during the mating season fans his tail out in a particular way and struts around, all puffed up, close to where the hen is sitting. I assure you that the cock's train of thought at that moment is certainly not 'Fine, I shall fan out my tail and pass by proudly, and surely the hen will fall in love with me'. No, this is decadent psychology. The cock grouse opens his tail and puffs himself up and it is *from* this gesture that he feels a surge of amorous courage.[9]

Tolstoy transposes this law of nature to art:

Primal gesture is the starting point for art. The maker of art engaged in the creative process searches speculatively within himself for those primal gestures. They excite him, and they and only they open the bone casket of the human skull to his eyes.[10]

But the artist should look for the primal gesture not only within himself but also in his times, since this gesture, according to Tolstoy, will be consonant with whatever determines our era. It is precisely here that the expression "the gesture of revolution" comes in. Tolstoy introduces it, as Shklovsky would say, through the device of a riddle. It is still a mystery to us just what sort of gesture it will be, but Tolstoy has already given it a name:

The revolution has done away with garish outfits and painted blushes. We see man in his primal gesture. Art must find the gesture of revolution.[11]

It is this last phrase of Tolstoy's article that has given me the title for mine. And now a few words on the content and purpose of the latter. Its main characters are Dziga Vertov, Viktor Shklovsky and Aleksandr Rodchenko. It would be hard to assume that any one of them paid attention to a newspaper call of a former émigré who had fast changed his flag of convenience on return to the Soviet Union. Nonetheless, some of the devices observed by the art and scholarship of the 1920s can be regarded as possible solutions of the task set by Aleksey Nikolaevich Tolstoy.

I will thus deal with Shklovsky the theoretician; the director/documentary-maker Dziga Vertov; and Rodchenko in his photographer's hat. As for all the apparent heterogeneity of material, there is a shared quality in the manner in which Shklovsky used his sources and how Vertov and Rodchenko used theirs – if we allow ourselves to use the literary term "source" to denote whatever finds its way on to the documentary film tape and the lens of an amateur's camera.

## The Device of Rotation: An Act Quintessential to Art

To any Russian native speaker, the word *ostrannenye* (making strange) which Shklovsky derived from *strannyi* (strange) looks odd indeed. It is instantly tempting to familiarize it by dropping one of the two n's in the middle. Spelt this way, *ostranenye* appears to be derived from *storona* (side) and sounds more like "marginalization."

Most of the time, *ostranenye* has been spelt with just one n, and Shklovsky himself takes the blame for this. In 1983, when speaking of the past, Shklovsky divulged the following secret:

> And then I coined the term *ostranenye*; as nowadays I can admit to having made spelling mistakes, I wrote it with only one n. I should have written down *strannyi* first.
> And so off it went and has been roaming the world ever since, like a dog with a torn ear.[12]

We shall return to Shklovsky's mistakes in due course, but let's begin with cinema, and not literature. In Dziga Vertov's film KINO-EYE (1924) there is an odd shot which, without context, it would be easy to dismiss as a technical fault – an incorrectly printed positive. On screen, we see a Moscow street, but shown not as it should be, but rotated sideways, with the road going up vertically.

This, of course, is no production defect and no mistake. The rotated street is preceded by the following shots: the intertitle "On the Tverskaya Street"; then a general view of a street on a sunny day with passers-by, cars and trams speeding along (fig. 1). Then the intertitle "The same street viewed from a different camera set-up" (fig. 2). And only then are we shown the same street, with the same trams and people, but filmed sideways (fig. 3). Nothing except the intertitle anticipates this turn, and nothing in the rest of the film explains it.

But even the intertitle hardly explains it all. What is the meaning of this artistic device, and is it right to speak of meaning and art in this instance? I shall put forward a few possible answers to this question.

So how should we deal with the rotated image? It seems to me that there are three possible approaches. First, we can dismiss it as simple trick for trick's sake as, on occasion, did the critics, even those most devoted to Vertov, who not without reason regarded Vertov and his cameraman Mikhail Kaufman as incorrigible trickomaniacs. Second, it is entirely possible that the frame with the flipped street might make sense in the context of the 1920s theories, for instance, in the context of the theory of the avant-garde or of the Russian Formalist pronouncements about the revolutionary nature of all art. Third, we can connect this odd shot to Constructivist photography, to see if we can find something in Rodchenko's photographs that would explain Kaufman's ways with the film camera.

Let us, for interest's sake, dismiss the first option. This leaves us with two explanatory scenarios: Formalist poetics and avant-garde art on the one hand, and Constructivist photography on the other. Let us explore the former avenue first. I can think of three instances (each of which could have easily come to Vertov's attention) where the gesture of rotating a picture – putting it on its side or turning it upside down – was recognized and interpreted as an act quintessential to art. The first features Shklovsky, Chekhov and Levitan, the second, Vasily Kandinsky, and the third, Chekhov and Shklovsky once again, this time without Levitan.

The first instance: in a late edition of O teorii prozy (On the Theory of Prose), Shklovsky cites Anton Chekhov's letter to his cousin who, like himself, was a friend and admirer of that extraordinary Russian landscape painter Isaak Levitan. The aim of the quote is to show that the connection with a theme or motif in the artist's work is more a hindrance than help. Shklovsky quotes from the letter from memory:

> Chekhov said: I'm tired, I've written a lot, and I'm already forgetting to turn my stories upside down, as Levitan turns his drawings to get rid their meaning and to see only the relationships between patches of color.[13]

Shklovsky's explanation does not entirely conform to our notions of the Russian art and literature of the second half of the nineteenth century. Not an art historian, I am not qualified to discuss the tricks of the trade which Levitan might have used in his studio. However, going by what Levitan's pupils and contemporaries wrote about him, we know that he would roam forests for days and days in pursuit of the right plein-air, and that it was Levitan who invented the notion of the "Russian landscape"; and now we hear that for Levitan, meaning and motif only got in the way. Furthermore, Shklovsky attributes this assertion to Chekhov, a writer whose own object-ness inspired much scholarship.

Let us turn to Chekhov's letter of 24 November 1887. It does indeed mention Levitan's custom of turning his paintings on their side, but Chekhov expresses differently what Levitan had hoped to achieve by that: "I'm ill. My life is dull, and I'm beginning to write badly because I'm tired and can't, like Levitan, turn my pictures upside down in order to distance my critical eye."[14]

There is nothing here about removing meaning or the pure relationship of colors. More likely, it is about self-editing. There is no doubt that both Chekhov and Levitan represented a type of person we would today call perfectionist, and as every perfectionist knows, before a piece of work – a painting, a story, or just an academic article – is handed over, it needs to be put aside for a while ("to distance the critical eye") in order to reveal its shortcomings. "Sometimes it's very difficult to finish a painting," B. Lipkin, a pupil of Levitan's, recalled his master's words. "Sometimes you're afraid to ruin the picture with one brushstroke. So they stand, 'ripening,' turned against the wall."[15]

However it was, Chekhov had hardly meant what Shklovsky saw in Levitan's actions; otherwise, it would be difficult to explain what Chekhov wanted to say by drawing that parallel between writing a story and painting a picture.

## Kandinsky: Discoverer of Abstract Painting

If Shklovsky did indeed see in the example from Chekhov's letter evidence that for the artist, the motif is no more than external motivation, this explanation did not come to him via Levitan, but through the history of art after Levitan; more specifically, the direction given to art at the beginning of the twentieth century by non-representational painters, in the first instance, Kazimir Malevich and Vasily Kandinsky.

There is, indeed, a similar episode cited in Kandinsky scholarship, for the first time in his autobiography. As is generally known, Kandinsky had his own score to settle with realism. In 1911 he blamed the idols of his generation, Chekhov and Levitan, for excessive attachment to nature and object instead of making art see the invisible and the spiritual.[16] Shortly afterwards, in a book called Stupeni. Tekst khudozhnika [Steps. An Artist's Text] published in 1918 in Moscow, Kandinsky wrote about himself as the original discoverer of abstract painting and, as is the custom of discoverers, recounted what precisely became his Newton's apple. Here is the relevant passage from Stupeni:

Much later, already in Munich, I was charmed on an occasion by an unexpected sight in my own studio. It was getting dark. I was about to go home having finished a study, still engrossed in my work and in dreams of how I should be working, when suddenly I saw in front of me an indescribably beautiful picture, glowing with an inner fire. At first I stopped short, but soon I walked towards this mysterious painting, totally incomprehensible in its external content and consisting exclusively of spots of color. And then I found the key to this mystery: it was my own painting, standing against the wall on its side.[17]

Could this be why Shklovsky thought Levitan's habit of turning his unfinished paintings upside down was a way of seeing them as abstract? For what Shklovsky wrote Chekhov had meant to say about Levitan fits well with what Kandinsky says about himself, "Generally, I realised beyond doubt that day that object-ness harmed my paintings."[18]

## Shklovsky and the Rotated Shop Sign

This is the second parallel to the instance of a rotated street as flipped by Vertov. Like the first, it comes from representational art or, to be more precise, from the theory thereof. One more passage from Shklovsky's book *O teorii prozy*, this time from an early edition, will add to our collection of paintings turned on their side. Here it is not a turned painting, but rather rotated words.

In the early version of the book, Shklovsky also quotes Chekhov, and again from memory. This time it is not a letter but an idea for a short story found in Chekhov's *Zapisnye knizhki* [Sketchbooks]. Chekhov's idea, if we were to believe Shklovsky, was about the eye-opening effect of a rotated shop sign. Shklovsky refers to this unborn story to illustrate that the effect of defamiliarization, which as we remember from Shklovsky, is at the heart of all art.

According to Shklovsky, only displaced objects truly reach us. Art is the knowledge of how to displace things:

> In order to transform an object into a fact of art, it is necessary to detach it from the domain of life, to wrest it out from the web of familiar associations, to turn over the object as one would turn a log in the fire.[19]

In prose and poetry, Shklovsky continues, the word is the object that needs turning:

> Someone walks along a certain street for 15 years or maybe 30 years. Each day he reads the sign that hangs above a certain shop: "Nectars of varied colors" and each time he passes it he asks himself: "Who needs nectars of varied colors?" Well, one day the shop sign is taken down and put on its side against the wall. It is then that he reads for the first time: "Neckties of varied colors."[20]

Turning the shop sign on its side, Shklovsky continues, is the quintessence of art. The artist treats objects in the manner of a revolutionary building a barricade:

The poet takes down all the shop signs, the artist is always the instigator of a rebellion of things. In poet's hands, things rebel, discarding their old names and assuming a new appearance with new ones.[21]

As we can see, the gesture of turning is a welcome guest in Shklovsky's theoretical trope-kit. It is all the more instructive to compare Shklovsky's account of the shop sign with the original. Here is Chekhov's idea in *Sketchbooks*:

'A wide selection of nectars', so read X, walking every day along the street and continuing to wonder how anyone could trade in nectars alone and who needed them. And only thirty years later, he read correctly, carefully, 'A wide selection of neckties.'[22]

Those who in their day paid their due to puzzle pages of children's magazines will easily see how Chekhov's original idea differs from Shklovsky's account. All the elements of the story's subject are there, except Shklovsky's key one. In Chekhov's notebook no one takes the street sign down and turns it on its side. Shklovsky's memory sneaked into Chekhov's plot a detail from Kandinsky. According to Chekhov, it is enough to look more carefully at a thing in order to see it; according to Shklovsky, you need to turn it.

The street turned on its side in Vertov's film KINO-EYE (fig. 3) can also be explained by the belief in defamiliarization. In order to demonstrate it, let's turn to the third version of events, according to which that particular frame should be viewed with the avant-garde photography of the 1920s in mind.

## The Revolution of Our Visual Thinking

Mikhail Kaufman, brother of Dziga Vertov, was the cameraman in KINO-EYE. Before he became a cameraman, Kaufman experimented a lot with the photographic camera. Even afterwards, many regarded him as a photographer: at times, stills from Kaufman's films were reproduced as independent photographic work. The Constructivist artist Aleksandr Rodchenko, known for his bold experiments in photography, was a good friend of Kaufman's. Both men were often berated for their attachment to an unusual point of view of the camera. In their defense, they would say that in order for the camera to see its object, you can't take a picture from the "belly-button level," you need to rotate it.

"Belly-button level" was Rodchenko's term for the usual point of view, in common use in photographic studios, as well as in amateur photography. "I find writing difficult, I think visually, my thoughts come in separate pieces,"[23] complained Rodchenko in an article "Puti sovremennoy fotografii" (The Paths of Contemporary Photography). I shall quote two excerpts from that brilliantly written article:

Fig. 1: Still from Dziga Vertov's film KINO-EYE (1924). Tverskaya street on a sunny day with passers-by.

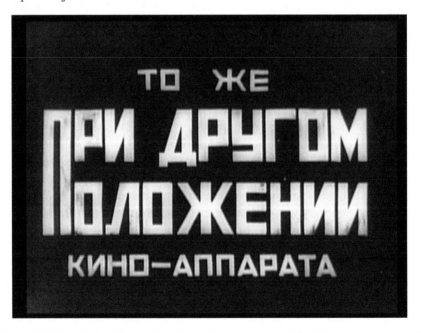

Fig. 2: Still from Dziga Vertov's film KINO-EYE (1924). Intertitle: "The same street viewed from a different camera set-up."

Fig. 3: Still from Dziga Vertov's film *Kino-Eye* (1924). The rolated street.

Fig. 4: Novyi Lef *cover photo by Rodchenko.*

Fig. 5: Rodchenko, "Passers-by. A street" (1928).

Fig. 6: "Mystery of the Street," 1928. Photo by Umbo (Otto Umbehr).

We do not see what we look at.

We do not see remarkable perspectives and positions of objects.

Accustomed to seeing the ordinary and the inculcated, we must open up the world of the visible.

We must revolutionise our visual thinking.

We must let the scales called 'belly-button perspective' fall from our eyes.

Take pictures from any point of view except from the belly button until all points of view have been accepted.[24]

[...]

To sum up: in order to teach people to see from new viewpoints, it is necessary to photograph ordinary, familiar objects from completely unexpected points of view and to photograph new objects from different points of view in order to give them their full representation.[25]

One of Rodchenko's photographs, reproduced on the cover of the same issue of the *Novyi Lef* magazine which featured the article (fig. 4), is the best illustration of this manifesto. If we hold the journal normally, it is not easy to recognize in the photograph a multi-storey building with a fire escape at the front. In order to see the building, we need to turn the journal counter-clockwise. The recognition has been hindered, but it is to the advantage of the object. Pure defamiliarization.

Sometimes, a Rodchenko angle (a term used both in photography and cinematography) was crowned with a visual pun. Such is his photograph "Passers-by. A street" (1928), taken vertically, from top down (fig. 5). This angle turns shadows into pedestrians and reduces pedestrians to tiny pedestals at the "shadows" feet.

As high-rise dwellers could observe such scenes every sunny afternoon, it was only to be expected that the idea might occur to more than one photographer, and indeed, it so happened that in the same year, a former Bauhaus student Umbo (Otto Umbehr) took two similar photos (fig. 6). Apparently, the sight of shadows which appeared to be walking all by themselves reminded the German photographer of the fantastic worlds imagined by Freud or Adelbert von Chamisso, for he named one "Uncanny [Unheimliche] Street" and the other "Mystery of the Street."

Yet if there was a photographer who could have claimed to be the first to discover this visual trick (or sight gag, as such tricks are sometimes called in films), it was Mikhail Kaufman. Let's look again at the rotated street from Vertov's 1924 KINO-EYE (fig. 3). Here, too, shadows walk erect with pedestrians prostrate at their feet. There was hardly anything uncanny or unreal about Kaufman's or Rodchenko's walking shadows, however: for a true left-wing filmmaker, as for a Constructivist, to see a street in a strange – defamiliarized – way was tantamount to making it more real.

Sergey Eisenstein, who alternated filmmaking with research and lectures, became famous among his students for an assignment involving composition of a film sequence. Beginning with a sketch of a quiet street, the task was to turn the quiet street into a revolutionary one without drawing in sailors or armored cars. The solution involved a simple displacement of objects already in the picture: what was low became high, high became low, the distant came to the fore, and the near receded into the background.

Eisenstein's second favorite assignment involved choosing the right gesture. According to Eisenstein, when actors search for the best gesture to express this or that emotional state, they should begin their search with a well-chosen word, not a movement. And why the word? It would do well here to remember once again Aleksey Tolstoy's essay on the primal gesture of revolution, from which I quoted at the beginning of this article. In the essay, among other things, Tolstoy speaks of words as existing in an evolutionary dependency on gestures:

> The first person made the first gesture, and only then attributed meaning to it. The word, a spoken sound, was the consequence of the gesture of the facial muscles, perhaps hands, head and body. The fundamental gestures slumber in our bloodstream, in our consciousness, in our muscles.[26]

Like Aleksey Tolstoy (and like many before and after Eisenstein and Tolstoy), Eisenstein believed that the language of words evolved from the language of gestures. And if this were the case, Eisenstein would say during his lectures on biomechanics, let's look for the word that has retained the imprint of the gesture that gave birth to it:

> However you represent revulsion, at the basis of it there will always be a motion of turning away, to the point where you have turned your back on what is revolting to look at. This word is the same in all languages, *aversion* in French, *Abscheu* in German.[27]

Let's follow Eisenstein's advice and begin the search for the gesture of revolution in etymology. According to the dictionary, the word "revolution" comes from the Latin *revolvere*, to turn. Eisenstein would add that this word is as much a fossil as revulsion – the gesture that gave rise to it is clearly visible in the word. While the word "revulsion" retains the imprint of shrinking away, the word "revolution" bears the impression of turning, as in "turning the picture." In Eisenstein's words, a tram on its rails is a means of transport, while a tram lying on its side becomes a barricade.

Shklovsky, we may recall, spoke of exactly the same thing: art is a rebellion of things. We need to turn the log for it to burn better. I think that this is precisely what Shklovsky did with his sources: he did not misquote them, he turned them so they would burn.

*Translated by Magdalena Hernas*

# Ostranenie, "The Montage of Attractions" and Early Cinema's "Properly Irreducible *Alien* Quality"

*Annie van den Oever*

> "Art, perhaps, is measured by its capacity to provide evidence for the falsification of whatever theories we arrive at."
> – Geoffrey Galt Harpham, On the Grotesque. Strategies of Contradiction in Art and Literature, 2006.

## Prologue

For quite some time now, it has been apparent that the dominant post-war re-reading of Russian Formalism within the context of an immanent approach to literature created a serious misreading of some basic terms, notably "ostranenie," and "technique."[1] It was only while preparing this book, however, that it became clear to me that Viktor Shklovsky's "Art as Technique" is not the proto-structuralist treatise on art as "form," that many have been eager to suggest.[2] On the contrary, "Art as Technique" is a true "manifesto," in the best of avant-garde's traditions,[3] and its main objective is to re-think art from the perspective of technique, or *as technique*, as the title clearly indicates. The manifesto proclaims a revolutionary shift in the way art should be studied: *from the perspective of techniques and their perceptual impact, and not as a form to be interpreted*. I came to understand that this was an attempt to rethink the problem of art from the new and "radically unconventional" (Eichenbaum)[4] perspective of perception. Shklovsky's "brash irreverence" (Erlich) towards tradition[5] was really deeply embedded in the avant-garde's re-thinking of the perceptual potential of new technologies and techniques, their evocative and revolutionary powers, their sudden and strong impact on audiences. Even more, I came to understand that this avant-garde project, with which early Russian Formalism had been so closely connected,[6] was itself a crucial part of what we have come to understand as the tremendous cultural impact of early cinema in pre-revolutionary Russia. Early cinema studies has contributed considerably to our knowledge from this period.[7] However, an urgent and new question not posed by avant-garde studies or early cinema studies so far is: If Shklovsky's manifesto was part of the avant-garde's cultural response to early cinema, then how must we exactly situate and understand its basic premises and characteristics in relation to it, e.g., its radical opposition to traditional concepts and practices; its new "theoretical principles" and the implications for arts studies; its key terms: *ostranenie, art, technique* – the last term was used to replace the "muddled term" of "form," as Boris Eichenbaum already wrote in his retrospective overview of 1926.[8]

"Art as Technique" was written December 1916 and was first published in 1917.[9] Some crucial passages on perception were already written and published in 1914.[10] The essential issues raised in "Art as Technique" were already presented by Shklovsky to his Futurist friends in a lecture in The Stray Dog in December 1913.[11] That was the very year "the general craze for cinema reached its peak in Russia," as Yuri Tsivian has noted.[12] This provided a very specific context with a general craze for cinema, and a particularly strong Futurist's response to it (they mimicked the techniques of "distortion") as well as a strong and enduring appreciation for the new (optical) techniques, perhaps more lasting in pre-revolutionary Russia and later in the USSR than in the USA, with a re-editing culture as nowhere else in the world (Hagener).[13] Re-read within this very specific context, it instantly becomes clear that "Art as Technique" is not a sort of research manual, presenting a "formal method" to enhance interpretation, as post-war readers might have come to think.[14] It also becomes clear that it is relevant and necessary to reread and re-evaluate "Art as Technique" as a manifesto, written in a medium-specific period in history, not unlike the current one, which means that not artworks or story worlds but rather the new techniques themselves and their impact in the perceptual process take center stage, as we can now more easily understand, perhaps, than readers of "Art as Technique" in the 1960s and 1970s.

To historicize the notion of *ostranenie*, I will re-read "Art as Technique" here in its historical context. This almost automatically means *defamiliarizing* it from its long history of misreading – appropriately in the context of this book. "Misreading" here, however, does *not* express deprecation, but an acknowledgement that each re-reading – including this one – has a function in its own context and time, and that we, passers-by in a medium-specific period of history ourselves, are perhaps better placed than post-war readers in the wake of classical narrative cinema, to appreciate early cinema's "properly irreducible *alien* quality," which, according to André Gaudreault, "traditional film historians have always tried to paper over."[15]

"Art as Technique" needs to be excavated from under that older version of Film History, which, in keeping with the demands of the institution "cinema," rejected and repressed early film's *alien* quality – yet this is a quality that we may assume was still more or less center stage in Russia in 1913, when Shklovsky presented his thoughts on *ostranenie* for the first time (the term is often translated as *alienation, estrangement,* or *defamiliarization,* but here it will simply be translated as "making strange"). The excavation of "Art as Technique" is meant in part as a contribution to a New Film History. It is also meant to contribute to the contemporary desire to integrate Film, Media, New Media, and Avant-Garde Studies. By historicizing this crucial part of (art) theory, the texts on *ostranenie* may regain much of their revolutionary impact and contribute to a contemporary convergence of media theory and practice.

## Medium-Specific Period in History

Film historians have pointed out, quite correctly, that the cinema and its prehistory are too deeply imbricate, ideologically and technologically, for an abrupt 'birth of the cinema' to be conceptually valid. But from the perspective of the uncanny, the arrival of celluloid moving pictures constitutes a decisive moment.
– Laura Mulvey, *Death 24x a Second. Stillness and the Moving Image.*

To understand the tremendous impact of the new viewing experience, one needs to understand the deeply *alienating* experience a visit to the movies was for most in those days. Many described the experience as exciting and strange at the same time. The new medium provided *movement* and thus a sudden taste of the animated, of life, of the real. Yet seeing this mute, two-dimensional world in a rather bleak black and white made all this seem slightly ghostly and *uncanny*, animate and inanimate at the same time. All was familiar, yet it was "made strange" by the new "cinema machine." This seems to be at the heart of the *disruptive* early movie-going experience, as Laura Mulvey has argued.[16] Remarkably similar observations can be found in many descriptions (turn-of-the-century) of the movie-going experience, as Yuri Tsivian has pointed out.[17] As Maxim Gorky famously put it in his often cited *critique* of 1896, and it is constructive to cite him once again, in an attempt to evoke the taste of an experience of stupor and excitement at seeing the first moving images, since 21st-century movie-goers have inevitably lost contact with this moment in time:

If you only knew how strange it felt. There were no sounds and no colours. Everything – earth, trees, people, water, air – was portrayed in a grey monotone: in a grey sky there were grey rays of sunlight; in grey faces – grey eyes, and the leaves of the tree were grey like ashes... Silently the ash-grey foliage of the trees swayed in the wind and the grey silhouettes of the people glided silently along the grey ground, as if condemned to eternal silence and cruelly punished by being deprived of all life's colours.[18]

After more than a century of film, the medium has stabilized into a mimetic tradition. In retrospect, it is very hard, almost impossible, to understand such experiences and exclamations when viewed from our current perspective, because not only film itself, but also the viewing practices have changed radically since 1896. Judging from the responses of those early movie-goers, it seems that for them seeing moving images ("movies") was an uncanny experience, "astonishing" (Gunning) and often even *stupefying*.[19] That these early viewing experiences as confrontations with the completely "new" were *stupefying* did not strictly mean that the viewers were silent *all the time*. Laura Marcus commented on the "silencing" effects of the cinema in its early phase in an interesting way. She quotes Virginia Woolf who, relatively late in life, wrote in her notebooks: "A new art comes upon us so surprisingly that we *sit silent*, recognising before we take the measure."[20] Marcus comments:

> It suggests that the "relative" silence of Woolf and her Bloomsbury contemporaries on the question of the new art of film is to be understood as a necessary pause – a reticence in the face of the unfamiliar. It by no means connoted indifference.[21]

On the contrary, Marcus concludes, the cinema may have resonated throughout Woolf's life and writings. Moreover, the Bloomsbury group[22] was only *relatively* silent: they were *silenced* or stupefied in the first moment of awe, as one may assume, but they were rather loud in the hours thereafter: pronounced enough to be noticed by their contemporaries, who have described their notable presence. That one was silent in the first moment, yet loudly and vividly talking in the next, did not necessarily mean one had already found the right words to "frame" the new experience, as Woolf indicates. In fact, they seem to have needed years before they could get to terms with the new optical technique and the new experiences it triggered. Of course the most interesting part of this story is how the impact of early cinema on Woolf and the Bloomsbury Group may be understood in relation to the *modernist* revolution in literature and the arts of their days, a revolution in which Woolf and her group were obviously leading figures.

Within the context of this book, it is interesting and even striking to see that similar words to the ones expressed by Virginia Woolf in the 1920s were expressed by Viktor Shklovsky in a memoir dedicated to his friend, the revolutionary poet Vladimir Mayakovsky, a leading figure in the early Russian Futurist movement, who died in 1930 (he was born in the same year as Shklovsky, 1893). In *Mayakovsky and His Circle* Shklovsky, like Woolf, noted that the "new" cannot be "seen" (understood, verbalized, labeled) in the first moment of confrontation, but this does not mean that the "new" has, or had, no impact. Ordinarily, it is only later, as Shklovsky states, that the "new" turns out to have had a *revolutionary* impact, which is to say that it had a truly profound and disruptive impact, turning tradition upside down. Perhaps this was what the "birth" of the cinema did with tradition, it shook its very foundations.

As Tsivian has shown in his *Early Cinema in Russia and Its Cultural Perception*, film in these early days triggered a true cascade of descriptions and reflections by poets and novelists on the medium and the new viewing experiences. Interestingly, the "film shows" not only offered a fascinating experience, they also provided a *shared* experience: the masses flocked together to see the new technology. One may argue that the very fact that it was a *shared* experience in most cases may well have deepened the cultural impact of the new medium, much the same as large strikes, revolts, coups, earthquakes or draughts may be experienced more fully and may leave a deeper imprint in memory and in the culture, since they not only affect larger parts of society but may also trigger debate on a massive scale.[23] Movie-going *as a shared experience* – the going together; the sitting together; the excited atmosphere of expectation, experienced together – may well have given these early movie visits the character of an "event." Moreover, since it was a shared experience, it also provoked group discussion and public debate, even more so as the movie experience was in many cases a slightly destabilizing experience. According to Ian Christie and Richard Taylor, it was after the revolution and after Lenin's proclamation of the cinema as the most important art "for us" of all the arts[24] that the cinema in the Soviet Union became an ideal battleground for often very heated debates on all sorts of political and artistic issues. Cinema, backed by Lenin, could take such a central role in the cultural debate precisely because it could be turned into a "mass medium," and *as such* the cinema could feed most of the "debates that raged in the 1920s." In the words of Christie and Taylor:

> Cinema's central position in Russian and Soviet cultural history and its unique combination of mass medium, art form and entertainment industry have made it a continuing battle for conflicts of broader ideological and artistic significance, not only for Russia and the Soviet Union but also for the world outside.[25]

The years after the Russian revolution was the period in which the cinema was turned into an institute with the help of the state, which chose to put all its revolutionary powers behind it. About two decades earlier, *before* World War I and the Russian revolution, the cultural panorama was quite different. Those were the years in which, like elsewhere in the Western world, the introduction of the cinematograph took place. However, in the 1910s, the debate on the cinema was not yet "shaped" as it was in the 1920s. The cinema in these very early days triggered an immense outpouring of reactions in strong and significant ways, clearly in response to the cinematograph itself as "a new medium." The responses in Russia are in many ways indicative of "the period of the discovery of the cinema"

(Gunning)[26] as a "medium-specific period in film history" (Tsivian),[27] with a "medium-sensitive film viewer," that is, a viewer who:

> went to see a film show in order to experience the new medium more than to see a specific film. In other words, the earliest period of film reception foregrounds the attraction of filmgoing itself often over the specific story or content of the films shown, which may serve as little more than pretexts for a trip to the cinema.[28]

Within the broader context of the impact of early cinema on culture in Russia, several parties and individuals may be singled out as having had an impact on the debate of the time, some of whom, it may be said, have had a lasting impact in the field of art (and film) studies:

> the Symbolists (with Andrei Bely as a leading figure);
> the Futurists (with Velimir Khlebnikov and Vladimir Mayakovsky as leading figures);
> OPOYAZ (or the Russian Formalists, with Viktor Shklovsky as a leading figure).

Shklovsky was part of the Russian avant-garde, more specifically the Russian Futurists. He was also a member of OPOYAZ and LEF, a group of Formalists and Futurists, initiated and organized by Mayakovsky in 1923, with its own magazine, *Lef*, well-known for its publications by the leading figures of the avant-garde, Mayakovsky and Shklovsky among them. Ground-breaking essays by the young Sergei Eisenstein such as "The Montage of Attractions" and "The Montage of Film Attractions" were published for the first time in *Lef*, in 1923 and 1924, respectively.

In the following section, I will argue that "Art as Technique," as the manifesto of OPOYAZ, and *ostranenie*, as the manifesto's most significant term, can best be contextualized and understood (e.g., its implications for the study of the arts) within this particular context; that is, within the context of several, partly successive avant-garde groups in St. Petersburg and Moscow. Moreover, I will argue that for a good understanding of this very specific historical context, it is essential to see Shklovsky as part of the avant-garde and to see the avant-garde as a crucial part of the cultural reception of the cinema in Russia in its early days. The avant-garde shared and cherished the disruptive and evocative impact of the early cinema experience. Avant-garde poets immediately made use of what the cinema had to offer by mimicking the fallacies and specialties of the new optical techniques, in order to produce similar effects. To construct my argument, I will situate the avant-garde responses to early cinema within the broader context of the cultural reception of early cinema in Russia.

# "Birth" of the Avant-Garde in a Medium-Specific Period in History

## The Symbolists

One of the interesting points of Tsivian's book on the cultural reception of early cinema in Russia is that it shows how the Symbolists, a group that was already well-established in society as well as in literary tradition when the cinema arrived in Russia, may be said to have played a decisive role in the cultural reception of early cinema in these days. They dominated the public debate that it triggered. One may argue that they were in the right position to help shape the discourse which helped to frame the experience that in itself lacked a distinct "form" because at that specific point in time no one had yet formulated a distinct framework or the appropriate words to describe what most found "strange," if not astonishing or stupefying. The Symbolists, as Tsivian has convincingly argued, responded to that "unfamiliar" and rather "ghostly" silent world in black and white that the cinematograph presented by describing or labeling the viewing experience in terms of an "absence," "death" or "(dual) identity" and other well-known motives in poetry and literature. The Symbolists, like all other movie-goers in those days, were medium-sensitive viewers; that is, the medium itself triggered their attention initially. The scratches on the reel; the unusual ("deadly") silence surrounding the moving and animate figures on the screen; the grayish ("ghostly") tones of the world on the screen, bathing in a rather bleak black and white; the changing size and scale of figures or things moving towards the camera, abnormally enlarged; seeing oneself on the screen or a reversed projection, presenting a reversed course of events: all that was new and unusual to these viewers who were not yet used to moving images was linked to a thing or theme they did know. One could say that they "thematized" the technical fallacies and specialties of early cinema: "death" would turn up as a theme when the moving images looked less animated; "doubles" and "double identity" when one saw a familiar face yet presented in an unfamiliar way, and so on and so forth. Thus, the typical *shock effects* of the new, soon to be *exploited* by early cinema, were channeled and smoothed along thematic lines and motives one knew *all too well*. In ascribing a *meaning* to "this or that feature of the cinema," as Tsivian argues, the Symbolists tended to stay well within "the dominant cultural pattern of the epoch."[29] This seems to indicate that the "early film reception" *worked*, at least on this specific group of medium-sensitive viewers, "by putting new life into old literary clichés," as Tsivian put it. "Whatever its immediate cause, more often than not the first shock of seeing images in motion assumed the form of recognizable cultural patterns." He labeled these patterns the "tropes of film reception" and concluded that these "patterns (or tropes) formed a buffer zone between film and culture."[30]

This was the way in which the "Symbolist mentality shaped the reception of cinema in Russia, at least among the urban classes," as Gunning wrote.[31] In many ways the Symbolists were in charge of the public debate in this first phase of its cultural reception. They were the dominant group in the landscape of literature, and as such they were destined to "frame" the discourse on the new in this first phase. As the dominant group in literature to speak up, they were also destined to become the nemesis of the avant-garde. They were OPOYAZ's "hostile neighbours," as Shklovsky would later write in his memoir on the Futurist poet Mayakovsky, *Mayakovsky and His Circle*.[32]

## The Futurists

The Russian Futurists, among them the poets Khlebnikov and Mayakovsky, were an essential part of the very early avant-garde movements in Europe, and as such they had a strong impact on the later avant-garde movements in their own country and in the rest of the continent. In many ways they were comparable to Filippo Marinetti's Futurists in Italy, who manifested themselves from 1909 onwards.[33] Their response to the cinema in its early days was quite different from the Symbolists' response, and their role in the public debate was also radically different: more disruptive, more captivating, more memorable.

Whereas the "cultural reception" of the Symbolists stayed within the realm of literary tradition – and sometimes well within its margins, as the word "clichés" used by Tsivian already indicates – the Futurists broke with tradition in a rather brisk and bewildering way.[34] They entered the scene with great turmoil in 1913, the very year Russia's "general craze about the cinema" peaked.[35] They indeed caught public attention after having presented one of their stunningly aggressive manifestos, *A Slap in the Face of Public Taste*, in an almanac with the same title published in December 1912.[36] The Futurists chose to bully "public taste," and shocking an audience in a direct address was one of their specialties. Provoking and creating disturbance was an essential part of their poetics and performances. They wanted to trigger a strong audience response and often succeeded, as newspaper articles of the time can attest to. According to an influential conservative newspaper, for instance, the Futurists stood out as "a bunch of half-wits," in that "crazy" year when the cinema was also most impressive.[37]

So by 1913, the Futurists were closely identified with the cinema, and the reception of two separate, *new* phenomena overlapped and formed a single image in the eye of the public, as Tsivian argues. Both cinema and Futurist poetry were associated with something feverish and vague, with something "incoherent, spasmodic, senseless," with the "[u]ngrammatical, asyntactic," and last but not least, with that icon of modernity, "the increasingly feverish pulse of the big city." Tsivian concludes, "these are only some of the features that Futurists and cinema were found to have in common."[38]

Contrary to the Symbolists, who "thematized" the unfamiliar aspects of the viewing experience by attributing *meaning* to them, the Futurists responded to the new optical *technique* itself and to the radically new and disturbing perceptual experience it created, and mostly with great appreciation for the shock effects. Technology and optical, visual and audio techniques and their impact on perception became themselves the real focus of their attention. *These* were the elements they took from the new practice of early cinema in order to build a new poetical practice, one they themselves helped to create. *Techniques* and the perceptual *experience* played a central role. Contrary to the Symbolists, the Futurists' attention was caught by the very techniques which had such a strong and sudden impact on the imagination. They noted that *accidental* techniques which automatically came with the new "cinema machine" were able to work strongly on audiences. That is, *dumb* techniques with no ingenious intentions behind them whatsoever proved to be no less *evocative*, or *poetic*, or *effective* than the symbols the Symbolists carefully constructed in their poetry with the utmost care. This made the Futurists re-think and reframe technology and techniques, which they now approached from a *perceptual* perspective. Moreover, the disturbing and evocative potential of technique (verse), and of techniques in art in general, became a new and very basic interest for the Futurist poets and for avant-garde artists, eager to renew their use of techniques and to reconsider and change their potential powers over the perceptions and the imagination of their audiences. According to Andreas Huyssen:

> [N]o other single factor has influenced the emergence of the new avant-garde art as much as technology, which not only fueled the artists' imagination ...,
> but penetrated to the core of the work itself. [39]

It is obvious that the same goes for the Futurists and the "old" or historical avant-garde movements of the beginning of the 20th century. As such, the Futurists could be seen as part of "the avant-garde of technical visioning in history," to use Siegfried Zielinski's phrase,[40] since their imagination was indeed fuelled by utopian visions of technology.

In response to the strong perceptual impact the Futurists had experienced in the cinema (such as strange distortions of vision and other forms of deformation of the visual, well into the grotesque),[41] Futurist poets tried to trigger similar effects in their poetry by inventing a whole series of poetic techniques one would, in retrospect, indeed consider to be typically avant-garde. One may think of their use of the ungrammatical and asyntactic (which were privileged techniques in the poetics of the Italian Futurists, too) and also of their preoccupation with the visual aspects, graphics and typography of language, as part of their program of emphasizing the *autonomous* powers of the "self-oriented word" either spoken or printed, as Vladimir Markov signaled.[42] The Futurists experimented with a maximum variety of letter types and size of letters, and with the equivalent in speech, such as variety in pitch and loudness. Mayakovsky reciting his poems was a phenomenon described by many as a true "event."[43] In short, one can say that they experimented with new forms of addressing the viewer, listener, or reader to awaken the "static," "stupid voyeur" of the traditional art forms (Marinetti).[44] An amount of emotional and psychological disorientation and shock effect – not unfamiliar to the early cinema spectator – and even an amount of face-to-face aggression might well have been part of this. Futurist poets *sought* the confrontation and were after creating instant and sudden effects, much the same as early cinema, to purposefully shock and thrill their audiences once the first accidental effects of the technical novelties started to wear off, as Tom Gunning argued.[45]

*Sergei Eisenstein, six years younger than Shklovsky and Mayakovsky.*

One may argue that the Futurist poets provided examples for Sergei Eisenstein's own art and functioned as a model for his "attractions" because Eisenstein also meant to "aggressively" attract the spectator's attention with any element that might subject the spectator to "emotional or psychological influence" and "produce specific emotional shocks in the spectator."[46]

"I believe that, without Mayakovsky's LEF, there would not have been such a phenomenon as Eisenstein," Shklovsky wrote in *Mayakovsky and His Circle*. "LEF's poetry pointed the way for art."[47] Shklovsky wrote this in direct relation to the "attractions" in Eisenstein's THE WISE MAN, STRIKE, and THE BATTLESHIP POTEMKIN, which he seemed to consider as an "attraction" in its entirety:

> After *The Wise Man*, he directed *Strike*, which still had many disconnected attractions; then *The Battleship Potemkin* – a film that holds together, expressed in one breath. Here art deals directly with reality instead of propping reality up on attractions which bear approximate resemblance or parody resemblance to reality.[48]

In fact, Shklovsky saw Mayakovsky as a tremendous example for many, not only for Eisenstein, though it may have been of some importance that Eisenstein was six years younger than Mayakovsky and Shklovsky, who both started off in different ways in 1913, when they were both twenty. The Eisenstein of the montage film, starting in the 1920s, was really part of a different era altogether. The cinema in the Soviet Union was now institutionalized with the help of the state, and it had an obvious political and ideological intention, and Eisenstein, too, *as he was supposed to have*: "These shocks [intended by the montage of attractions] provide the only opportunity of perceiving the ideological aspect of what is being shown, the final ideological conclusion," he wrote at the end of the paragraph on "attractions."[49] By then, Eisenstein was part of an art circle that was, and was supposed to be, effectively *political* and produced art suited for consumption by the masses, whereas most, if not all, Futurists had no such intention at all in the 1910s. On the contrary, they were after creating absolutely nonsensical and incoherent shocks, the way Marinetti was. They experimented with perceptual impact – full stop. What *they* expected from "attractions" and appreciated in them was a *dumb* and *sudden impact on the imagination*, they sought and valued, in Mayakovsky's words, "die dumme Plötze der Vorstellungskraft."[50]

Mayakovsky and other Futurist poets may be said to have tried to "theorize" the experience and effects of the sudden, the surprising and the stupefying, and they did so in their poems as well as in their infamous avant-garde *manifestos*.[51] But were they good at theorizing? There can be no doubt, however, as to whether Futurist manifestos had an impact or whether their performances were successful – if only as scandalous successes. They were unpopular, and they were seen as "rascals" by many, yet they *were* seen and heard. Hence, one may well argue that they, like the Symbolists, had an impact on the public debate of their time and, at some point, even with some dominance. Of course, 1913 stands out as *their* year. The Symbolists were dominant slightly earlier. The Futurists' impact and performance were radically different from the impact and performance of the ones they chose to see as their "hostile neighbours." However, one may argue in retrospect that *they*, the "rascals," the Futurists, far more than the Symbolists, helped to provide a discourse to frame the new "cinema experience" as a truly new and modern experience: one of disorientation and disruption. One may even argue that perhaps, in the long run, they thus provided a new model to frame the utterly disorienting, disturbing, and even deeply traumatic experience of the Russian revolution and the grave crises following the revolution (hunger, starvation, loss, exile). One may argue that there is in fact a recursive principle at work here, where the new "cinema experience" (a shared experience) offered a new, modern model to frame the new, modern experience of poetry/art (as a disorienting and shared experience), which offered a model for the much larger and even traumatic experience of the revolution. But to follow this argument through would be an excursion far beyond the scope of this article.

Viktor Shklovsky, c. 1913. Drawing by the famous Russian painter Ilya Repin.

## "Art as Technique" as an Avant-Garde Manifesto

In 1913, a young Viktor Shklovsky also responded to the "alienating" experiences triggered by both early cinema and the Futurists. His response, however, was much more appreciative and sharply articulated than the blunt one that an influential conservative newspaper provided ("craze," "half-wits") in 1913.[52] In the year the Futurists "bullied" public taste, this "brilliant" young scholar made his "debut" in The Stay Dog as a "pink-cheeked youngster in frock coat and high collar" and presented his revolutionary theoretical insights to his Futurist friends.[53]

During the years immediately preceding World War I, the prominent artists of Petersburg frequented an avant-garde cabaret known as The Stray Dog. It was there, in December 1913, while known as a freshman at the University of Petersburg, that Shklovsky read a paper entitled 'The place of Futurism in the History of Language'. In his talk he maintained that futurist poetry emancipated words from their traditional significance and *restored them to perceptibility* by calling attention to their sounds.[54]

*Vladimir Mayakovsky, "Pro Eto" [About that]. I am at the top. Illustration – photomontage made by Alexander Rodchenko, 1923.*

In retrospect, Shklovsky may be said to have provided the theoretical framework for explaining the impact of such new techniques from the revolutionary new perspective of perception. It may be argued that Shklovsky came up with the theoretical framework the Futurists themselves were not able to provide. It has been argued by Markov that the Futurists quarreled too much and theorized too little[55] – and that they were not half as accomplished as the Symbolists at that point in time. As Richard Sheldon wrote: "Only Khlebnikov had some training in linguistics."[56] The Futurists were glad to now have a connection with the Department of Philology at the University of Petersburg, via Shklovsky, which, in effect, made him an even more interesting "ally." One may argue that Futurist poetry was powerful and effective, but that their poetical reflections were not half as competent as the best-known works by the Symbolists, whose approach dominated the thinking on poetry and art of the day. It may also be argued that, in the 1910s, the Futurists were not yet ready to theorize their own radical poetic experiments – which of course does not imply that their experiments were not interesting, effective, or successful. From Shklovsky's own notes on the period (in his memoirs on Mayakovsky, in *Sentimental Journey*, and so on), it is obvious that it was his great friend Vladimir Mayakovsky, whose presence, poetry, and poetics had a tremendous, and even crucial, impact on him as on many others (Eisenstein would be included in this circle ten years later).[57]

Shklovsky's intervention in December 1913 took place exactly a year after the publication in December 1912 of the almanac *A Slap in the Face of Public Taste*, of which Markov wrote:

> The aggressive tone of the manifesto and its attacks on everyone from Puškin to its contemporaries distracted attention from a more important fact. The idea of the 'self-oriented word' (*samovitoe slovo*) was proclaimed here for the first time, though at that time its implications and long-range significance were probably not realized, even by those who coined the slogan. For them it primarily meant creation of neologisms, but it also implied that "the word as such" was becoming the main protagonist of poetry, that it was ceasing to be merely the means to express ideas and emotions and that, ultimately, poetry could grow directly from language.[58]

Language (words, sounds) could *shock* just like the movies, one did not *need* meanings in poetry to effectively have an impact: this was the discovery the Futurists presented and labeled here for the first time. In his 1926 retrospective, Eichenbaum commented on this crucial point in time – crucial to understanding the development of Shklovsky's thinking

> Even before the formation of the *Opoyaz* in 1914, at the time of the public performances of the Futurists, Shklovsky had published a monograph, *The Resur-*

*rection of the Word,*[59] in which he took exception partly to the [Symbolists'] concepts set forth by Potebnya and partly to those of Veselovsky [...] to advance the principle of perceptible form as the specific sign of artistic awareness [...][60]

*Group of Mayakovsky's friends, from left to right: V. Mayakovsky, O. Brik, B. Pasternak, S. Tretyakov, and V. Shklovsky; (sitting) E. Triolet, L. Brik, and R. Kushner.*

It was in his *The Resurrection of the Word* that Shklovsky more fully explored and explained his thoughts on "the perceptibility of form," though it must be added that Shklovsky's rhetoric was not very didactic most of the time: he preferred to write *manifestos* on the topic, quite in line with the needs of the time. In *The Resurrection of the Word* he wrote:

> We do not experience the commonplace, we do not see it; rather, we recognize it. We do not see the walls of our room; and it is very difficult for us to see errors in proofreading, especially if the material is written in a language we know well, because we cannot force ourselves to see, to read, and not to "recognize" the familiar word. If we have to define specifically "poetic" perception and artistic perception in general, then we suggest this definition: "Artistic" perception is that perception in which we experience form – perhaps not form alone, but certainly form.[61]

Realizing that most contemporary readers might easily misunderstand Shklovsky's thoughts, Eichenbaum added an explanatory note to the word *perception* in his 1926 overview – when they were already misread as "Formalists," a term they themselves refused to use without quotation marks.[62] Eichenbaum's explanatory note shows that they were aware that the new approach to art, *from the perspective of perception*, was revolutionary and in fact simply implied the abduction of the traditional notion of "form."

> *Perception* here is clearly not to be understood as a simple psychological concept (the perception peculiar to this or that person) but, since art does not exist outside of perception, as an element in art itself. The notion of "form" here acquires new meaning; it is no longer an envelope, but a complete thing, something concrete, dynamic, self-contained, and without a correlative of any kind.[63]

Shklovsky had a tendency to rephrase certain problems over and over again, sometimes in slightly varying formulations. It seems to me that he did so not so much to repeatedly stress the same point, but rather because it was part of his unfolding thinking process, which (like Nietzsche) he presented in his work *as such*: as something open, never finished, and in connection to life itself. He kept returning to one or two fundamental problems in particular: the problems of "form" and "ostranenie."

In his memoir on Mayakovsky, there are some interesting retrospective notes on the question of what made him (or them) *start* to think of the problem of art in terms of perception/ostranenie as well as on the question of what theories were of help to them at that point in time. Halfway through *Mayakovsky and His Circle*, Shklovsky recalls the first meeting of OPOYAZ:

> The first conference of OPOYAZ took place in the kitchen of the abandoned apartment on Zhukovskaya Street. We used books to make a fire, but it was cold, and Pyast kept his feet in the oven.[64]

He adds that "Mayakovsky was already living in Moscow" and "came to Leningrad only occasionally" and that his good friend, the linguist Osip Brik, "used to come, too." They discussed collections of writings "by Potebnya's last pupils," *Problems of the Theory and Psychology of Art*:

> In these collections, direct references were made to Avenarius. Avenarius and Mach dominated the minds of those days. This is what Avenarius wrote on *the principle of economy*:

'If the soul had inexhaustible power, then, of course, the quantity spent from this inexhaustible source would hardly matter – except perhaps in terms of the time necessarily spent. But since its power is limited, one must assume that the soul will strive to carry out its *apperceptive processes* in the most expedient manner, that is, with a relatively minimal effort or, in other words, with a relatively maximal result.'[65]

This *was* of interest to them at that point in time, since they were already quite aware that they, the Futurist poets, were after something very different in art than their "hostile neighbors [...] the Symbolists and the Machists."[66] As Shklovsky wrote:

> In opposition to the Symbolists, the poets Khlebnikov, Mayakovsky and Vasily Kamensky put forward a different kind of poetics.
> They [the futurists] required of a thing not so much multiple meaning as *perceptibility.* [...]
> Part of the work of OPOYAZ was connected with this new poetics. *The theory of "defamiliarization"* [ostranenie] *was put forward in its name.*
> This theory originated from an analysis of Tolstoy's realistic art. *In Mayakovsky's own poetics, there was something that suggested to us the search in that direction.*[67]

Several notes must be added here. First of all, it is unusual that two remarkably different authors, Lev Tolstoy and Vladimir Mayakovsky, were both topics under discussion because most people perceived them as hardly comparable. Tolstoy was Russia's single most-esteemed and best-read novelist of the 19th century, while the Futurist poet Mayakovsky was part of the "half-wit" break with tradition. The search in the direction of perception and *ostranenie* was suggested by "something" in Mayakovsky's poetics, as Shklovsky states. That "something," I would like to argue, is what at the time was so hard to put into words, precisely because it still needed phrasing and framing: it still needed a new theory in order to get to grips with these completely new and different phenomena in the work of Mayakovsky. That "something" in Mayakovsky's work was part of the Futurist response to the cinema in those days. One needed a theory to frame something as daringly different as this. It seemed that the "something" could be framed from the perspective of *ostranenie*: in art, as *in the cinema of the day*, things were "made strange." This became OPOYAZ' central statement. Mayakovsky's work indeed pointed in this direction. His work as well as the available theories of perception helped them understand the general role of technique in the perception of art. It is important to note, however, that, in Shklovsky's words, only "[p]art of the work of OPOYAZ" was connected with Mayakovsky and the new poetics of the Futurists. What they did in their research in this very early phase was *use literary work* to test their new theory of art; Eichenbaum made this perfectly clear in his 1926 retrospective too:

> At this time, the Formalists quite naturally used literary works only as material for supporting and testing their theoretical hypotheses; we had put aside questions of convention, literary evolution, etc.[68]

In the earliest meetings of the OPOYAZ group, it must have been Tolstoy, a life-long favorite of Shklovsky, who could well withstand the first testing of their hypotheses. In other words, the first research on Tolstoy within the context of re-thinking art from the perspective of perception and *ostranenie* turned out to be a successful attempt to generalize about the perceptual impact of techniques "making [things] strange" in art. As such, the work on Tolstoy may well be said to have provided the *theory* of "defamiliarization" or, in Shklovsky's words: "This theory originated from an analysis of Tolstoy's realistic art." Nevertheless, it seems to me that the "something" that drove them to explore art from the perspective of perception and *ostranenie* was found in Mayakovsky's work. The "something" was disruptive and "strange": it was a response to the unsettling, new optical technology and techniques the avant-garde proved to be highly sensitive to.

## OPOYAZ and the Early Avant-garde's Rethinking of Technique

OPOYAZ and Shklovsky should *not* be regarded as part of the later avant-garde of the 1920s, but rather as part of the early avant-garde with its focus on the reassessment of technique and technology triggered by the very experience of the uncanny and the strange in the first decade of the century. In this *early* project of reframing technique and its role in art, the Futurists played a crucial role. Central to the *early* avant-garde's reconsiderations and experiments was a fascination with the perceptual potential of optical techniques to "estrange," distort, disrupt, disorient, and in general, work strongly on the imagination and *transform experience*: "Avant-Garde discourse on technology responds to transformations of experience technology offers," as Tom Gunning puts it.[69]

In retrospect, it is rather obvious that Shklovsky and the group assembling under the name OPOYAZ (soon Brik and Eichenbaum were among its members, Jakobson would follow almost a decade later, in 1921, and soon after leave for Prague)[70] were part of the *early* avant-garde which responded to the "attractions" of the new cinema machine. On the one hand, they thought as *avant-gardists*, responding primarily to the strong perceptual impact of the new technology, reflecting on it from every possible angle. On the other hand, they responded by *theorizing*, something they did exceedingly well. Perhaps, it may be argued, they did so well because Viktor Shklovsky, avant-garde's best theorist, was among them. He explained *why and how technology and techniques transform experience*.

*Mayakovsky (seated) with Lily Brik, Boris Pasternak (left) and Sergei Eisenstein when they were all members of the Lef group.*

Whereas Mayakovsky and his Futurist friends created a revolutionary practice, Shklovsky and his OPOYAZ friends provided the conceptual space for framing and explaining the impact of the new disruptive techniques in the form of a theory the Futurists themselves were unable to formulate. Shklovsky, OPOYAZ's "gadfly,"[71] filled the niche: he successfully theorized on the "sense perceptions" (Tsivian)[72] triggered by new techniques in a revolutionary and polemic way from his lecture in The Stray Dog onwards. Mayakovsky is said to have accepted the new theoretical input gracefully, while also being puzzled and surprised by it.[73] The Futurists were indeed aware that the "theory" put forward in their baffling manifestos was "largely inferior, both quantitatively and qualitatively, to that of their predecessors, the Russian Symbolists."[74] It is important to note that the new and revolutionary Futurist *practice* preceded the theoretical phase instigated by OPOYAZ by several years.[75] The Futurist *practice* came into being well before 1910, and well before they presented such manifestos as "A Trap for Judges" (1910) or their better-known manifesto "A Slap in the Face of Public Taste" (1912).[76] The Futurists' project emerged early enough in Russia to consider them *early* avant-garde, just like Marinetti's Futurists in Italy who manifested themselves from 1909 onwards.[77] What fuelled the *early* avant-garde's (the Futurists' and OPOYAZ's) imagination was the acute, disruptive experience of the world transformed by technology, or to use Shklovsky's words: a world "made strange," thus made visible.

*Making the world visible once again by making the world strange (alien, de-familiar), using techniques in art which disturb and delay our perceptual process:* this was the central statement Shklovsky presented in 1913 and 1914. His friends in OPOYAZ and LEF would repeat this in the 1920s (e.g., in *Poetika Kino*). Then, at last, the new phenomenon had obviously lost enough of its "newness" to explicitly attract their attention. Now they were made to write their essays on the cinema's techniques of "deformation," its "photogenicity," and so on. One may argue that the 1913 idea of "making visible" by "making strange" (*ostranenie*) actually described what most contemporaries at that point in time already experienced. Shklovsky helped shape and frame the experience. Obviously, they needed time to let it sink in. Almost a decade later, the idea had grown into "a leitmotif of film criticism in the 1920s," as Francesco Casetti wrote:

> Stupor, appreciation, expectation. Since its invention, film has provoked debate about its significance and much speculation about what it might contribute to the new century. The conviction soon emerged that *film could make us look at the world anew.* It taught us not only to take a second look at the world, but to look in a different way. Film set our sense of vision free, restoring it to us with an invigorating potential. [...] Bela Balázs summed it up in a formulation that would become popular: 'From the invention of printing, the word became the principal channel of communication between men...in the culture of words, the spirit – once so conspicuous – became almost invisible... Now film is impressing on culture a change as radical as that of the invention of the press. Millions of people each night experience with their own eyes, sitting before the screen, the destinies of men, their personalities and feelings, states of mind of every sort, without needing words... Man will go back to being visible.' Balázs said it clearly: film restores human visibility, and gives reality back to the gaze.[78]

Regardless of the genealogy of the idea, and whether or not it can be traced back from film criticism in the 1920s to Shklovsky's reflections on *ostranenie* in the 1910s, it may be argued that he was *the* avant-garde theorist of the decade. His thinking seems to have affected many of his contemporaries, from the Formalists and the Futurists to Eisenstein and Rodchenko. Moreover, by theorizing on the relation between technique and art in a radically new way, he envisioned novel ways of studying art.

## Rethinking Art from the Perspective of Technique

If anything, "Art as Technique" is a *manifesto*, in the tradition of the Futurists: scanty, brazen, and provocative by its very generic nature.[79] With brashness,[80] Shklovsky presented his new ideas to the outside world on behalf of a group,

ANNIE VAN DEN OEVER

*Alexander Rodchenko, "Steps" – photo, 1929.*

OPOYAZ, that was close enough to the Futurists to also be considered as "half-wits," but they did not seem to care. With great polemic ardor, Shklovsky as OPOYAZ's leading figure presented his (or their) thoughts in the form of a radical attack on the traditional premises held by the Symbolists and on their idealist poetics. Characteristically, the manifesto is evocative as well as provocative, although not very didactic or impressively coherent. The argument presented is found wanting and hard to follow, though some parts are solid and of lasting value, in particular the part on "making strange" and its perceptual impact. The examples Shklovsky came up with have been studied over the decades with some puzzlement and, at times, even downright irritation.[81] No doubt, some of his arguments are "harsh," a fact for which Shklovsky himself apologizes, if only in one particular case.[82] They were taken almost exclusively from the fields of literature (including the folktale) and linguistics, the two fields the members of OPOYAZ were most familiar with. The choice of examples comes across as rather grotesque and incomprehensible in several ways. They were said to be chosen almost randomly, to test their theory, as Eichenbaum wrote.[83] In "Art as Technique" they are inserted to merely *illustrate* his point, as Shklovsky states: "Here I want to illustrate a way used by Leo Tolstoy repeatedly [...]."[84] However, these examples also seem to be chosen to incite and shock the readers, perhaps also to amuse and entertain them, bombarding them with a bunch of remarkably incompatible examples, taken from Tolstoy and Puškin as well as Gogol; from a collection of erotic riddles as well as the *Decameron* and *War and Peace*. One example is taken from folk literature and features that memorable passage in which a peasant tortures a bear, a magpie, and a horsefly, while pretending to do something else to them, next thing we know he is torturing his wife, trying to "shove a stick up [her] rump," or so the horsefly assumes, but readers are of course supposed to know better (the abbreviated versions of "Art as Technique," available in text books and on the internet, were keen to leave these examples out). Other examples are chosen from great literature, and many from Tolstoy:

> In *War and Peace* Tolstoy uses the same technique in describing whole battles as if battles were something new. [...] Anyone who knows Tolstoy can find several hundred such passages in his work. His method of seeing things out of their normal context is also apparent in his last works. Tolstoy described the dogmas and rituals he attacked as if they were unfamiliar, substituting everyday meanings for the customarily religious meanings of the words common in church ritual. Many persons were painfully wounded; they considered it blasphemy to present as *strange and monstrous* what they accepted as *sacred*. Their reaction was due chiefly to the technique through which Tolstoy perceived and reported his environment.[85]

All examples prove to have an essential point in common: they are all ambiguous, and they show that, as Shklovsky states:

> [ostranenie] is found almost everywhere form is found. In other words, the difference between Potebnya's [and the Symbolists'] point of view and ours is this: An image [form] is not a permanent referent for those mutable complexities of life which are revealed through it; its purpose is not to make us perceive meaning, but to create a special perception of the object – it *creates a 'vision' of the object instead of serving as a means for knowing it.*[86]

For many reasons, "Art as Technique" could be considered hard to interpret: its examples are baffling; it is an exploration of something new; it turns traditional thinking upside down.[87] In fact, "Art as Technique" is easier to understand and appreciate once one perceives Shklovsky's manifesto as part of a series of avantgarde manifestos, written in the context of that *early* medium-specific period in history, a typical phase of destabilization of form/referent relations similar to our current one. The new medium clearly presented a challenge to the traditional notions of "form" and "form/content."[88]

All the examples in Shklovsky's quirky text have precisely this in common: they are all ambivalent and indeterminate in many ways, and thus they may easily trigger a sudden and radical shift in interpretation (e.g., from sacred to monstrous).

All of Shklovsky's examples expose the potential "ontological instability of all mimetic representation"[89] in the same way new technologies might: they allow for an uncanny "re-animation" of the sense of instability that underlies mimetic tradition. Within this context, it may be argued that the era which made Gorky stress "the uncanny effect of the new attraction's mix of realistic and non-realistic qualities"[90] signaled a crisis in the mimetic functioning of the cinematograph *as a new medium*. Understandably, the new optical technology (the "cinema machine," to use Laura Mulvey's phrase)[91] had not yet established a firm and stable relation to mimetic tradition, and the new "machine" did not yet function as a proper *medium*, that is, as a technological *means* that can properly transmit meanings, as I have argued elsewhere.[92] Yet proper forms with proper and stable relations to referents: *that* the machine in its infancy could *not* provide. On the contrary, the technological novelty mostly provided *monstrous* forms, at least in the first phase of its monstration (and roughly in the first decade of the last century).[93] Hence, the new optical techniques easily caused ruptures in the viewer's relation to the seen and to mimetic tradition, because the new "machine" was not yet functioning properly *as a medium*, and as such it more or less accidentally *destabilized* mimetic tradition, making all that was seen appear "alien" or "strange" (note that almost all examples given by Shklovsky indeed somehow deal with *seeing* and the *seen*). In effect, the cinema machine may be said to have caused an epistemological crisis, a crisis for which the cultural explosion of discourses on the *shared* disruptive experience may well be said to have been symptomatic. Within this era and context, "Art as Technique," stressing the "strange" quality of the seen and its impact on perception, in fact hardly stands out as original. *Making strange* is basically what the new medium in its first "primitive"[94] phase *did* in the experience of most of its spectators. In many ways it provided not only a strong and striking, but also a shared *revolutionary* experience, in the very sense of the word Tsivian reconstructs in this book, following Shklovsky, Rodchenko, Eisenstein, and their avant-garde contemporaries: it turned things upside down. But the new medium itself being revolutionary, given its impact on culture in the century that followed, does not make the labeling of the experience as "alienating" revolutionary in itself. "Art as Technique," I would like to argue, is *revolutionary* for different reasons. Truly revolutionary, it seems to me, were the implications Shklovsky envisioned for art studies. They are rather brilliantly thought through and still surprisingly relevant for art studies today. Starting with what seems an epiphany on how *techniques* in general "worked" on audiences perceptually – by "making (the seen) strange" – Shklovsky launched both an attack against the assumptions held by traditional scholars on "form" and argued for the removal or "abduction" of the unfortunate dichotomy of form and content from the field of art, replacing the muddled notion of "form" by the notion of "technique" (*priom*).[95] Furthermore, he presented a *plea* for the "autonomous" study of *techniques* in art, a radically new approach in art studies, in which *technique* (technology) and *art* are in fact made synonymous. This may be considered truly revolutionary and indeed surprisingly relevant for Film and Media Studies today, as it creates the conceptual space for studying the responses to, and the (cultural) impact of, new techniques from the perspective of perception. Interestingly, artistic techniques and the technology that simply comes with the new medium are approached within one and the same conceptual framework. Their impact may be analyzed, regardless of the fact whether triggered intentionally by an artist or accidentally by a *new* technology that *has not yet established a stable position in mimetic tradition as a medium.* Note, moreover, that *new techniques* and *art* may be opposed to *old techniques* and *media* because the last two *have*, and the first two *have not*, established firm and stable relations to mimetic tradition. Conceptually speaking, "Art as Technique" thus opens new ways to reconsider the impact of the "new" in culture. If ever there was a field that might profit from the abduction of the traditional ("clumsy") concept of "form" and its replacement by "technique" apart from the field of art studies, obviously, it must be the field of film and media studies, because "Art as Technique" opens up new ways to frame the impact of the *new* in culture.[96] The notion of "technique" creates a conceptual space to analyze the effects of both hardware and software, of technology and (artistic) techniques. This is exactly what makes the term productive and suitable for studies in the field of the arts and media, in which technology profoundly interferes with the creation and development of the arts. Shklovsky provided the conceptual tools to describe and analyze the process of appropriation of new techniques in culture, and he brought to light that the genealogies of art and technique are intertwined because they are inherently connected.[97]

## Epilogue

"New phenomena accumulate without being perceived, later they are perceived in a revolutionary way."[98] Shklovsky wrote these words in his book on Mayakovsky. On another occasion, Shklovsky wrote that "the new arrives unnoticed."[99] As we have seen, Virginia Woolf also spoke of how the "new art" came upon her and her Bloomsbury friends so surprisingly that they *sat silent* when it happened – to only comment on it much later. The "new," as Gunning argued, needs a *discourse* to be perceived.[100] Hence, very often the "new" cannot be "seen" in its first moment of confrontation. Only much later can we begin to fully understand the extent of its *revolutionary* impact. This also seems to have been the case with Shklovsky, who nevertheless may be said to have helped provide the discourse to frame the new and "uncanny" (cinema) experience back in the 1910s by labeling it as essentially "strange." Mayakovsky and his Futurist poetry and poetics clearly had a strong impact on Shklovsky, as his *Mayakovsky and His Circle* can attest to. That the cinema also had a revolutionary and "modernizing" impact on him (as it had on Woolf and her Bloomsbury contemporaries) is confirmed by his *Hamburg Account*, published in 1928. Looking back on the previous decades, Shklovsky writes that the cinema and his work on the cinema "probably modernized me."

> Cinematography got rid of my exclusiveness, simplified and probably modernized me. In my cinematography I see how form is created, how invention is created out of contradictions and mistakes, and how the consolidation of accidental change turns out to be newfound form.[101]

Still from Sergei Eisenstein's THE BATTLESHIP POTEMKIN.

Shklovsky wrote this almost a decade and a half after his lecture in The Stray Dog. The cinema modernized his vision on technique. In the 1920s, he wrote that to him, coming from the field of literature to now *make* films, all was "new" and unfamiliar at first. Thus, he could experience, at first hand, how "form" is something that is "created" *from something* (and not just out of thin air, as tradition would have it). He simply saw how artistic inventions were accidentally created from "contradictions and mistakes" in their dealings with the new techniques, and how these accidental changes nevertheless could find their way into history as "newfound form" in a simple process of "consolidation." This experience "simplified" him, as he wrote. One may well understand here that he discarded the traditional (and highly romantic) idea of the "exclusiveness" of the artist as a creator and a genius who, like God, creates out of nothing, an idea which was deeply embedded in the tradition and in the arts.[102] The process of *modernization* of the arts and art studies may perhaps, in part, be seen as a process in which artistic creation was now understood in new and modern terms, due to the confrontation with the new optical technology and techniques of the cinema.

# Part II
# Mutations and Appropriations

# Alienation Theories and Terminologies

# *Ostranenie*, Innovation, and Media History[1]

*Frank Kessler*

There are, undoubtedly, many ways in which Viktor Shklovsky's concept of *ostranenie* can be used in a variety of fields. Even though the concept was conceived with regard to literature, right from the very beginning its scope was that of a general aesthetic principle, and thus, *ostranenie* has also been adopted by the neo-formalist approach elaborated by Kristin Thompson (1981 and 1988). In this essay, I would like to concentrate on the way in which the concept (or principle) can be made or has been made productive for work in the domain of film history and, by extension, for media history in a larger sense, independently of whether or not the scholars referred to here do indeed acknowledge any debt to Shklovsky's ideas.

## Ostranenie – An Inherently Historical Concept

As I have tried to show elsewhere,[2] Viktor Shklovsky's concept of *ostranenie*, which he introduced in his 1917 essay "Art as Technique,"[3] works on various levels. It is used to explain mechanisms of perception and attention as well as the functioning of art with regard to everyday experience, the way in which specific devices operate within a given work of art, and finally, it even opens up towards a theorization of stylistic change. In his famous statement: "And art exists that one may recover the sensation of life; it exists to make one feel things, to make the stone *stony*," Shklovsky condenses, as it were, his aesthetic *credo* and, by the same token, somehow camouflages its complexity.[4] Building his argument, Shklovsky first defines the purpose of art, which is "to impart the sensation of things as they are perceived and not as they are known,"[5] and then he explains how this goal can be achieved: "The technique of art is to make objects 'unfamiliar,' to make forms difficult, to increase the difficulty and length of perception because the process of perception is an aesthetic end in itself and must be prolonged."[6]

These basic statements need to be explored further in order to fully understand their implications. When Shklovsky describes the purpose of art in terms of an opposition between "things as they are perceived" and "things as they are known." he actually introduces a temporality, or diachronicity, which it is important to recognize as being the very foundation of the concept of *ostranenie*, or defamiliarization. While "things as they are perceived" refers in the first instance to an experience that takes place *hic et nunc*, the "being known" of things depends upon a process that precedes that act of perception, and in the course of which the "knowledge" about the object in question has been accumulated. This is the process that Shklovsky calls "habitualization" or "automatization." Or, in other words, defamiliarization necessarily presupposes familiarization. This means that in the course of time, the things that surround us have grown so familiar to us that our perception of them is automatized as it were, and thus, in a certain sense, they have become "invisible." When art's technique has as a result "to make objects 'unfamiliar'," this implies that the artist must have gained some kind of understanding of the automatized way in which the object is usually perceived, so that the chosen devices can actually work against this. One step further yet, it becomes possible also for the critic to recognize in what way, at what level, in what respect, and in what sense such a familiarization or a habitualization has occurred and how it has been defamiliarized.

Shklovsky's statements with regard to the purpose of art and the techniques it employs in order to achieve its goals thus implies a complex diachronic process in the course of which perception has become habitual or automatized. Consequently, an artist has reached a level of understanding of this process that makes it possible to work against its grain and to achieve a defamiliarization that undoes the habitualization. It is important to underscore the fact that this theoretical construction firmly roots artistic creation in History, which makes it by definition impossible to have a purely immanent conception of a work of art and, more specifically, its form. This latter concept is introduced as a specification of the technique of art, which consists in making "forms difficult, and to increase the difficulty and length of perception." In fact, by orchestrating this shift that makes the perceptual dimension of the process dependent on the formal qualities of the work of art, Shklovsky's theory moves from a psychological realm – the fact that we do not really "see" what we have become used to and thus have taken for granted – to an aesthetic one. To be even more precise, one needs to take the discussion of this process one step further: Shklovsky's starting point is the automatized perception of objects in our everyday surroundings that art has the task to undo by means of strategies that "make forms difficult" and thus intensify, deautomatize, our perception of them. The dynamics of this process, however, do not come to an end here. Within the aesthetic realm, the formal means by which defamiliarization was achieved can themselves fall victim to habitualization, because otherwise there would be no need for change in the domain of the arts, and thus there would be no art history. So artistic techniques – devices – can also become automatized and will then no longer be able to fulfill their aesthetic function. This, however, would unavoidably lead to a standstill, which in its last consequence would mean the end of Art – and so techniques that have become automatized need to be defamiliarized, or else others have to take their place.

Form, thus, ultimately is an inherently historical category, and Shklovsky's explanation of the way in which *ostranenie* functions already implies, albeit in a more or less embryonic way, a conception of formal change. Not only is there a necessarily diachronic development taking place that leads to a habitualization of certain formal strategies, but there is also a specific historical context with regard to which formal defamiliarization has to be achieved. There is no form outside History.

## Ostranenie and Historical Poetics

This historical dimension, which as we have seen is fundamental to Russian Formalist theory, made this tradition particularly interesting to the project of a Historical Poetics sketched out by David Bordwell in the early 1980s. In a programmatic article, published in 1983 in the first issue of the journal *Iris* that aimed to map the "current state of theory," Bordwell highlights the following aspect:

> It is evident that from the start Russian Formalist theory is grounded in history: the conception of background and foreground, the emphasis on the literary environment, the openness to the vagaries of the work all refute the common notion that these critics were ahistorical.[7]

Along with Kristin Thompson's neoformalist approach, presented in her analysis of Sergei Eisentein's IVAN THE TERRIBLE, as well as in her subsequent collection of analyses,[8] David Bordwell's project, already inaugurated in his 1979 study on *The Films of Carl Theodor Dreyer*, constitutes an important and influential strand of thinking in the field of Film Studies. The work by these two writers can also be considered the most consequent – and the most consequential – attempts to make Russian Formalism productive in Film Studies, precisely because of its fundamentally historical orientation.

Given the status the work of Kristin Thompson and David Bordwell has acquired in the field of Cinema Studies over the last quarter of a century, considering also the sometimes fierce discussions and controversies their writings have provoked, it may seem superfluous to look back into their roots. However, it is important to emphasize the significance of the scholarly gesture here, aiming at bridging the gap between "theory" and "history" that continues to exist, even today, in spite of this and many other efforts. The way in which Historical Poetics and Neoformalism refer to Russian Formalism is admittedly selective, privileging in particular a number of key concepts, including *ostranenie*, but also *syuzhet* and *fabula*, background and foreground, the dominant, system, or function,[9] are significant.[10] These concepts are linked to a series of basic assumptions about the nature of the work of art, constructional principles, and the activities of both the spectator and the artist that lead to the "one approach, many methods" governing the analyses elaborated within this framework.

In Kristin Thompson's methodological reflections, the concept of *ostranenie* plays a rather central role. On a first and, in a certain sense, strategic level, it allows her to eschew what she calls a "communications model of art," proposing instead an approach that places the artwork in a realm that is different from other cultural phenomena because it must be perceived in a specific way.[11] This is an important methodological choice, as it blocks both an interpretation of the work in terms of its "message" (and thus also the form/content split) and the use of linguistic methods and metaphors in the analysis. Quoting the well-known passage from Shklovsky's essay "Art as Device," Thompson concludes: "Art defamiliarizes our habitual perception of the everyday world [...]."[12] She also follows Shklovsky in his reasoning that the perceptual requirements of art are the result of making form difficult through defamiliarization.[13] So, on a second level *ostranenie* becomes a central concept for the analysis of artistic form. However, form is an inherently historical concept, as we have seen, and thus defamiliarization is, thirdly, important for the neoformalist approach in that it makes it necessary to look at the individual artwork in its historical context in order to be able to appreciate the way in which it defamiliarizes habitualized formal patterns and devices.[14] Hence the importance of understanding the norm against which the artist works in creating forms.

While in David Bordwell's Historical Poetics the concept of *ostranenie* plays a considerably less prominent role, the importance of looking at individual works against the broader background of historical norms is already highlighted in his study on the films of Dreyer. In this respect he appears indeed to follow Tynyanov's precept that "one cannot be certain of the structure of a work when it is studied in isolation."[15] In order to identify what is unique in Dreyer's work, he argues here, it is necessary to set it against a background allowing the characteristic difference of Dreyer to be defined and appreciated.[16]

> This book examines Dreyer's work as a set of deviations from some historically defined norm within the same medium. If films frequently jostle our aesthetic perception, the disturbance often arises from a clash between the film and dominant practice. That is, our background set can be some other film style. Although several choices are possible here, I shall pick a background set which I shall call "the classical Hollywood cinema."[17]

The implicit reference to Shklovsky's concept is clearly discernible here: the terms "deviation" and "disturbance" in fact illustrate the two-sidedness of defamiliarization as a constructional strategy and an effect produced at the level of reception. Furthermore, this passage demonstrates that the choice of the classical Hollywood cinema as a background is a heuristic one, in the first instance. Bordwell motivates this as follows:

> Why this construct? Historically, it is at once proximate and pertinent, central to a knowledge of the development of cinematic forms. If there is an "ordinary cinematic usage" for the fifty years of Dreyer's career, it is the narrative and stylistic principles of the American cinema. This book attempts to show the value of situating a filmmaker in relation to a model of typical traits of narrative feature films between 1920 and 1960.[18]

The heuristics are thus grounded in a historical reflection on the relative dominance of the stylistic and narrative devices developed within the Hollywood film industry and the fact that this dominance was a given throughout Dreyer's career. Bordwell continues by explaining that the "classical Hollywood cinema" he refers to is indeed an abstraction, and in this respect one might say that the monumental project he undertook with Kristin Thompson and Janet Staiger, resulting in their seminal book on this subject,[19] is also an attempt to give an empirical foundation to this abstraction (in addition, of course, to the many other merits of this study).[20] There is a risk, however, that a background/foreground constructed in that way might become itself "automatized." Taking Hollywood as a norm seems an obvious and convincing choice, but one that might also block an understanding of other logics at work in the construction of a given film, or group of films. Explaining the guiding principles of Historical Poetics in his 2008 book, Bordwell explicitly addresses this point, stating:

> By positing alternative norms, our work becomes comparative in a rewarding way. Instead of the couplet *norm-deviation*, we can posit competing systems of principles, operating at roughly the same level of generality. We find varying norms of narration and style in Hollywood cinema, "art cinema," Soviet montage cinema and other modes. [...] Although it may be momentarily helpful to characterize art cinema narration as a "deviation" from Hollywood principles, it's more enlightening to characterize it positively, as possessing its own fairly coherent set of storytelling principles [...]. Recognizing that we are engaged in a comparative exercise allows us to give equal weight to one norm and another.[21]

Here the sometimes mechanistic tendencies, at least in appearance, of the background/foreground construction are countered by a more generalized comparative approach. Apart from being a good illustration of the openness towards corrections and revisions claimed by Bordwell for his as well as the neoformalist approach, these reflections raise the question of to what degree this critique of the norm-deviation perspective concerns the concept of defamiliarization as a whole.

To begin with, one could argue that Neoformalism and Historical Poetics share with the structuralist semiology of Christian Metz the idea that the system of every film is constructed on the basis of codes that a filmmaker either adopts, trans-forms, or works against,[22] even though Bordwell and Thompson would hardly express this in such terms. The main difference here is, however, that the (neo) formalist analysis proceeds by historicizing the various manifestations of what Metz describes as codes, and also the way in which the code (the norm) is being defamiliarized. However, at its most elementary level, Metz in his observation underlines the fact that every filmic system is by definition singular, and this in a way also explains the problem that Kristin Thompson had to face when she was looking for an "ordinary" or "average film" she could use to demonstrate the complexity of even a standardized movie.[23] And indeed, even though the film she studies here, TERROR BY NIGHT (Roy William Neill, USA 1946), a Sherlock Holmes adventure, can hardly be considered to be noteworthy in any way, her analysis teases out the efficiency it deploys in telling the story, building up at least some kind of suspense, etc. Similarly, although in a completely different perspec-tive, Thierry Kuntzel's meticulous analysis of THE MOST DANGEROUS GAME (Irving Pichel, Ernest B. Schoedsack, USA 1932) reveals an unsuspected density in the opening sequence of an otherwise little known adventure movie.[24] Inde-pendently of the relative artistic value one may or may not ascribe to these films, what both Kuntzel's and Thompson's studies show is that a well-conducted ana-lysis can, literally, make a film appear "out of the ordinary." As Kristin Thompson puts it:

> Ordinarily, the average Hollywood film is largely automatized, remaining part of that undifferentiated mass that we have come to think of as the classical cinema. In such a case, the critic's job could be to re-defamiliarize the film – indeed, to defamiliarize it more than it would have been at its first appear-ance.[25]

In this case, the concept of *ostranenie* takes on yet another meaning, i.e. defami-liarization now becomes an analytical strategy. This move, however, raises the question of whether its function to distinguish art from non-art can still be up-held. If the analysis can defamiliarize an object, and that would actually mean: any kind of object, then one might say that an acknowledgement of its specific aesthetic qualities lies, as is often said with regard to beauty, "in the eye of the beholder." As a critique of the neoformalist approach, this is in fact only a minor point, as its purpose can be reached by other means: there are many ways in which one can avoid a communications model of art. And with regard to this point, it seems to me the approach via the concept of *ostranenie* is actually not necessarily the strongest one. However, and more importantly, Thompson's productive analysis defamiliarizing an average, or ordinary, film does point out the usefulness of the concept as a heuristic methodological principle.

There is indeed one dimension of the concept of *ostranenie* that tends to function in a more or less schematic way, especially when it is conceived of in terms of the norm-deviation couplet critiqued by Bordwell in the context of his Historical Poetics. Considered in such a fashion, *ostranenie* appears in fact to be too much of a "mechanical" concept; according to an insightful study by Steiner,[26] the central metaphor in this historical phase of Russian Formalism is the machine, the artwork being considered in this period by Shklovsky as the sum of the devices that constitute it. The process of defamiliarization would then function in an equally mechanical way: the automatized parts of the machine are being replaced by fresh ones for which, once they themselves have become habitualized, other substitutes have to be found. However, as we will see in the next section, Shklovsky's own conception of this process turns out to be much more complex than that, in spite of his seemingly mechanistic views on the formal construction of an artwork.

So rather than using *ostranenie* as a concept functioning in absolute terms, it appears not only more prudent, but also much more productive to use it as a heuristic principle, with regard to both historical and textual analyses (though the Neoformalists definitely would not use the latter term). Constructing a background against which a film is situated and analyzing it in a basically comparative perspective can indeed yield interesting results, provided that the choices made can be convincingly supported. As a heuristic principle, this is not only valid for cases such as the ones discussed above, where an apparently "average" or "automatized" production is shown to be constructed in an actually rather sophisticated way, but can also serve as a starting point for an investigation into films that at first sight appear odd, unskillful or even failed.

In my own work, I have tried to make use of such a strategy in order to gain a better understanding of the rather peculiar way in which text elements are used in the Dutch film EEN TELEGRAM UIT MEXICO (Louis H. Chrispijn, NL 1914). Here the sheer quantity of written material is indeed amazing: there are 27 shots, 13 intertitles and 7 inserts presenting letters, telegrams and newspaper articles. The overabundance of these largely expository elements could be seen as some sort of incapacity of the filmmaker to tell his story without the help of linguistic crutches. However, a closer look and a more detailed formal analysis show otherwise, as I have attempted to demonstrate elsewhere.[27]

The film tells the adventure of a young Dutch colonist in Mexico, who becomes involved in the troubles of the Mexican revolution (indeed, a contemporary topical event). His mother and blind father back in Holland anxiously await news from him, following the reports published in their local newspaper. One day the young man decides to leave his farm and head home. He wants to inform his parents, but the messenger simply throws the telegram away. On his way, the hero is attacked and pursued by the rebels. At this point, the narration returns to the parents. A telegram arrives and upon reading it, the mother faints. The father, unable to read the message, presumes that it is bad news and almost goes mad with grief. Right at that moment, the door opens and the son enters, safe and sound. The telegram announced his arrival at the port of Rotterdam.

When compared to the use of written messages in other contemporary films,[28] it is not only their quantity that is surprising in EEN TELEGRAM UIT MEXICO but also the fact that in several cases the various letters or newspaper articles shown as textual inserts are more or less redundant because of intertitles that precede or follow them. They do have an obvious expository function, but hardly contribute to the film's narrative economy. They slow down the flow of the action, interrupting it time and again by textual elements, which only partly provide the viewer with new information. Compared to another thriving story pattern of that period, which presents a similar narrative situation, namely films where a last-minute rescue occurs thanks to helpers being called by telephone,[29] it is quite clear that both the distance separating the son from his parents and the frailty of the latter indicate that EEN TELEGRAM UIT MEXICO tells a different tale.

This Dutch film therefore appears to depart from existing norms, but in such a way that the deviation is taken as a shortcoming at first sight. However, once the seeming incompetence of the filmmaker is identified as a strategy, it becomes obvious that the focus of the story is not the young colonist, but rather his parents. The film is not about the adventure, but about the wait, about the hope and the despair of those who are longing for news from the loved one overseas. The insistence on the efforts to communicate rather than on the communication itself is functional *for* the narrative precisely because it appears dysfunctional *within* the narrative.

Here *ostranenie* could serve as a guiding principle for the analysis, insofar as it allows us to conceive the "strangeness" of EEN TELEGRAM UIT MEXICO not as a flaw, that is as a failed attempt to comply with a historically existing norm of efficient narration, but as an effort to tell a different kind of story. The reversal of the traditional perspective assessing films in terms of their appearing "advanced" or "retarded" with regard to an assumed general development of cinematic means of expression thus helps us to adopt a more nuanced view on film style.[30] Using *ostranenie* as a heuristic principle, in other words, is by no means linked to a conception of film history as governed by a process of progression. Quite the contrary, the concept, when used accordingly, can also lead to an assessment of stylistic features in terms of their historically embedded functions within a given film.

## Ostranenie and the Historiography of Cinema

When approaching *ostranenie* as an inherently historical concept, it should have become clear by now that this by no means entails reasoning in terms of a simple norm-deviation mechanism. Shklovsky, it seems, was very well aware of the dangers that a view on the history of the arts driven by an ongoing process of defamiliarization might bring about. When talking about historical evolution in "Literature without a Plot: Rozanov," he proclaims that literary evolution does not follow the lineage "from father to son" but "rather from uncle to nephew" (and of course a number of other lineages are conceivable when one lets go of the inherent gender bias: "from uncle to niece," "from aunt to nephew" or "from aunt to niece"). The important point here is, according to Shklovsky, that in the history of literature, often formerly marginal or sometimes also archaic forms are taken up and can then become central aspects in a later period. So Aleksandr Blok "canonizes the themes and rhythms of the 'gypsy song'," or Dostoyevsky "raises the devices of the cheap novel to the level of a literary norm."[31] In terms of a historical development, in other words, there seems to be a shift, or rather a qualification, with regard to the process of defamiliarization. While in his general definition the focus lies on the simple fact that habitualized forms are made strange in one way or another, the introduction of a diachronic perspective demands a more precise characterization of the means by which historical change is brought about. The answer Shklovsky proposes in this – very brief – allusion to literary history is remarkable in so far as he actually roots innovation in tradition. The innovative act then consists mainly in turning to a *different* tradition, in appropriating forms or devices that may be automatized in their original context, but become both defamiliarized and defamiliarizing when transplanted into another realm.

In a certain sense one might argue that in the realm of film history, the French *Nouvelle Vague* could be seen as a prime example for a historical development of the kind Shklovsky evokes. Rejecting the lineage that the dominant French film industry could offer, namely the so-called *tradition de la qualité*, the *Cahiers du cinéma*'s Young Turks not only severely criticized the aesthetic principles of Claude Autant-Lara and his scenarists, Jean Aurenche and Pierre Bost, but also created their own family tree based on the *politique des auteurs*. François Truffaut's famous polemical article, "Une certaine tendance du cinéma français," and the subsequent interventions by himself and his fellow critics at the *Cahiers* represented a twofold provocation in fact. On the one hand, these young writers attacked those who were perceived as being the most prestigious and successful French filmmakers, denying them all artistic and moral merits; on the other hand, they praised a number of Hollywood directors for their creativity, for the coherence and originality of their world view and for the way they translated their ethics into film images. The future filmmakers of the Nouvelle Vague, in other words, chose for themselves the filmic forms "from the lower stratum of society" (but not exclusively, as Jean Renoir or Robert Bresson also figured prominently among the references evoked by Truffaut in his manifesto, even though one could argue that at that point at least, both filmmakers were marginalized within the French film industry) they wanted to bring to the fore as their main artistic reference "to replace the old ones."[32] So here we have a case where, to use Meir Sternberg's formulation, it is not "the uncle [who] bequeaths his art to the nephew, [but] more exactly the nephew looks back to the uncle for his patrimony."[33] The line of tradition is in fact one that is quite consciously – and strategically! – constructed rather than being a given, thus permitting us to polemically reject the then dominant forms of cinematic style.

Quite obviously, this is but one version of the story, it is but one way to frame the rather complex historical developments that led to the emergence of the Nouvelle Vague. In fact, it also leaves out quite a number of aspects pertaining to the broader socio-cultural environment in France in the late 1950s, the organization of the French film industry, the internal tensions in the field of French film criticism, etc. So in this respect the caveat formulated by David Bordwell needs to be taken into account, and could even be broadened towards these other factors I just mentioned:

> Moreover, we don't have to postulate every historical change as a deviation from a norm. I have already suggested that we can often think of changes as driven by problems, some inherited from tradition, others devised by the filmmaker. There are as well many ways to realize norms, some obvious, some subtle. The most striking stylistic changes in film history often don't stem from absolute innovation, but rather from a recasting of received devices. Welles' deep-focus staging in CITIZEN KANE is a famous instance, but we could say much the same of Godard's cutting in BREATHLESS [À BOUT DU SOUFFLE] (1960), which recasts orthodox continuity principles (matching on movement and eyelines) into new patterns, to new effect. An innovation is not necessarily a deviation.[34]

Historical change is indeed a multi-causal phenomenon, and so its complexities clearly should not be simply boiled down to a mechanics of norm and deviation. In fact, one of the strengths of Shklovsky's notion of historical development in terms of a complex interaction between dominant and minor traditions is the avoidance of a linear model of historic progression. On the other hand, however, it is clear that the knight's move – to quote Shklovsky's famous metaphor – cannot provide a universal principle of literary or art history either. Yet, the theory of innovation that emerges out of the concept of *ostranenie* is worth taking a look at.

The conception of innovation inherent in the process of defamiliarization is indeed a complex one. It rests upon an interplay between the perceptual realm and certain conscious formal choices the artist makes. Perceiving a device, a type of narrative construction, a configuration of elements as having become habitual presupposes a familiarity with them that necessarily reaches back into the past. This is the fundamental diachronic dimension governing the process. But the choices made by the artist do not imply something like a *creatio ab nihilo* but rather, as Shklovsky's remark on the historical evolution of literary style shows, a taking up or appropriation of features that are part of a tradition, albeit a minor, or "lower," and non-canonized one. Or even, as Bordwell's comment on Godard's À BOUT DU SOUFFLE [BREATHLESS] suggests, canonized devices can be recast by a filmmaker in ways that defamiliarize them (even though one might add here that Godard's take on continuity editing is in any event also shaped by his own film historical erudition acquired in ciné-clubs and at the Cinémathèque française, he looks at it, as it were, through an experience of half a century of editing practices).

It may indeed be the case that the Shklovskyan model is interesting in particular with regard to such moments of historical change that are in a way overdetermined by political or generational ruptures, since artists joining ranks in order to precipitate change generally look at such times for a lineage that suits their purpose. The young directors of the Oberhausen Manifesto, and more generally the rather diverse group of filmmakers labeled New German Cinema, not only declared the death of papa's cinema, but actively searched for points of reference elsewhere: in German film and literature of the 1920s from Murnau to Brecht, in the work of Hollywood directors understood as *auteurs* such as Douglas Sirk or Nicholas Ray, and clearly also in the stylistic and narrative experiments of their Nouvelle Vague contemporaries. Similarly, the young Soviet filmmakers made a clean break with the mise en scène practices and the slow editing pace of the directors from the Tsarist period such as Jevgenij Bauer or Jakov Protozanov, turning instead to the fast editing rate of the American cinema, emblematized in the father figure of David Wark Griffith (a father figure from whom they also distanced themselves in terms of politics and ideology).[35]

While offering at least a number of insights into the way a historical current or movement constructs itself discursively against a previously dominant one (obviously, such denominations are anything but innocent and also require a thorough historical critique), this is evidently a limited perspective. There are important other factors that stay outside the scope of such an approach, as the economic, political, social, legal or institutional environments that frame and shape, promote and support, enable and channel such developments, and of course also the technological conditions that provide opportunities and open new possibilities or, as in the case of the young Soviet cinema, force us to look for alternatives and stimulate experimentation in a situation where there is a general shortage of equipment and material.

So, looking at the history of style in terms of lineages, following Shklovsky's suggestions, can offer an interesting but necessarily very limited perspective that, in addition, does not provide an equally productive approach in all cases of historical change. Even so, this again reveals the potential productivity of the concept of *ostranenie* as a heuristic tool. With regard to a diachronic perspective, it thus not only focuses on stylistic innovation as such, but also takes into account the origins of the new forms coming out of a different tradition, and specifically out of the undercurrents of popular culture, which often escape the attention of conventional historical inquiry. In that respect, one might add, such an approach is almost inherently a non-teleological one.

From such a point of view, one could even claim that in the historiography of film (or, for that matter, of any art or medium), scholars will often have to defamiliarize the dominating and canonized versions in order to open up new fields of inquiry, to look at phenomena in the light of new questions, or to shift focus. This may take many forms, as the so-called New Film History of the 1980s has amply demonstrated. Moving from the groundbreaking highlights and masterpieces to the anonymous mass production – as Bordwell, Staiger and Thompson[36] did with regard to Hollywood, or Michèle Lagny, Marie-Claire Ropars and Pierre Sorlin[37] did in their large-scale study on French cinema of the 1930s – is part of such an enterprise, as are the various initiatives to write film history from the viewpoint of marginalized or neglected groups, or the manifold investigations into early cinema that were launched at an international level after the Brighton FIAF conference in 1978.

This latter body of work is particularly interesting when looked at in the light of Shklovsky's concepts. Traditional historiography saw early films as "primitive" and was interested only in those features that could be seen as forerunners announcing the artistic potential of the medium that would be realized many years later in both classical narrative cinema and the European art cinema of the 1920s. This way of looking at the beginnings of cinema only changed in the 1980s and 1990s, when scholars such as Noël Burch,[38] Tom Gunning[39] or André Gaudreault[40] took a different approach and tried to understand the formal features of early films in light of the 1960s and 1970s avant-garde practices or the dys-narrative experiments of modernist films. Schooled by such viewing experiences, they did not look for the first manifestations of the narrative conventions of classical film (they abolished altogether, in fact, the quest for "firsts" that drove traditional historiography to a large extent), but rather tried to understand the logic proper of these films, a logic that was then described in terms of a specific "Primitive Mode of Representation" by Burch, or a "cinema of attractions" by Gaudreault and Gunning. The relationship between early cinema and the later avant-garde worked both ways, in fact, as demonstrated by the reworking of early films by experimental filmmakers (TOM, TOM, THE PIPER'S SON by Ken Jacobs, EUREKA by Ernie Gehr) as well as by the lectures given by Stan Brakhage on Georges Méliès or David Wark Griffith.[41] So looking at early cinema from the viewpoint of the avant-garde, in spite of the anachronistic perspective that this might engender, proved to be rather productive for an understanding of the specific difference, or otherness, of this mode of representation even though, obviously, there is always a whole bundle of factors that come into play in such a process.[42]

With this kind of consideration, Shklovsky's original concept seems rather distant. This does point, however, to the fact that the fundamental principle (or "bedrock idea," as Meir Sternberg calls it)[43] of defamiliarization can take a variety of shapes, and that it can be used as a strategic or heuristic tool with regard to a whole range of issues. Here it appears, to be more precise, as a specific – and in a way voluntaristic – kind of foregrounding, a term coined by the Czech structuralists that Sternberg sees as one of the "resurgences" of *ostranenie*.[44]

So it may be less surprising that one can indeed observe a reappearance of this principle in more recent attempts to theorize processes in media history in light of the developments brought about by the new digital media and their various manifestations.

## Ostranenie and the Historiography of Media

So, how can the idea of defamiliarization be made productive when looking at the history of media? Several authors such as Tom Gunning, Jay David Bolter, Richard Grusin, and Isabelle Raynauld approach the question of the historical development of a medium by distinguishing two different logics that appear either alongside each other or in a diachronic sequence, namely one that foregrounds the technology and one that foregrounds the "content." This latter type of functioning is in fact often addressed as "transparency," that is, as a form of experiencing a medium where the process of mediation itself is not perceived as such and thus has become "invisible." Obviously, this so-called transparency of a medium is actually always a constructed one (or to use the terminology of a period when this issue was a centerpiece of film theoretical debates: a coded one). And here the concept of *ostranenie* as defined by Shklovsky does reappear, in particular its inherent historicity. The transparency, which cannot manifest itself in ways other than a "having-become-transparent," indeed implies that the use of the medium as such has become "evident," thus presupposing a diachronic dimension in the very core of such a logic.

Proposing a historical approach to old technologies by "re-newing" them, that is, by looking at them from the viewpoint of their once having been newly emerging technologies, Tom Gunning chooses not only a somewhat defamiliarizing perspective on media history as such, but also considers the deconstruction of the processes of habitualization in the functioning of a medium as a crucial starting point for its historical appreciation.[45] In terms astonishingly similar to Shklovsky's formulations, Tom Gunning remarks: "When a tool works, we pay no attention to it; it seems to disappear."[46] This leads Gunning to an analytical perspective that somehow resembles Kristin Thompson's strategy with regard to the so-called "ordinary film" discussed earlier. He calls here, in other words, for a defamiliarization of a technology that has become familiar:

> To imagine an old technology as something that was once new means, therefore, to try and recapture a quality it has lost. It means examining a technology or device at the point of introduction, before it has become part of a nearly invisible everyday life of habit and routine. But it also must mean examining this move from dazzling appearance to nearly transparent utility, from the spectacular and astonishing to the convenient and unremarkable.[47]

Looking at old technologies as devices or media from the viewpoint of their once having been experienced as novelties is indeed an important methodological choice. It means looking at their potentialities not in retrospect, from a position where their future has already been realized, but as a set of promises, or potentialities, which the contemporaries projected into them. But even their normal functioning in itself is not something that is taken for granted. Quite the contrary, it provokes what Gunning calls "a discourse of wonder [that] draws our attention to a new technology not, simply as a tool, but precisely as a spectacle, less as something that performs a useful task than as something that astounds us by performing in a way that seemed unlikely or magical before."[48] For those who witness the manifestations of a new media technology in the period of its emergence – it being put to use in what Charles Musser with regard to cinema has called its "novelty period" – the simple fact that it does or shows what it is supposed and announced to do or show is a marvel.[49]

It is in this respect that Gunning remarks that, as far as the cinema of attractions is concerned, one can state that the technology itself constitutes the main attraction for the first viewers of the various devices presenting animated photographies.[50] Similar things can be said about most other media as well: one may think of the voices almost "magically" travelling along telephone lines or through a space interestingly referred to as ether, or of television with its possibility to transmit live images from events elsewhere. And even the rather recent introduction of the mobile phone showed signs of this phenomenon, even though this technology became a habitualized tool in a very short time. How else can we explain the story (perhaps fabricated) of people in Italy walking around with wooden dummies pretending to partake in the wonderful universe of mobile communication.

Jay David Bolter and Richard Grusin discuss the two ways of experiencing a technology presented by Gunning in terms of a historical configuration that occurs diachronically, moving from wonder to invisibility, as two synchronic "logics of remediation," one of which they call "immediacy," the other "hypermediacy."[51] The first one aims to make the medium "disappear," while the other one stresses mediality, that is, it foregrounds the processes of mediation in one way or another. For Bolter and Grusin, however, this is not a matter of a medium's functioning being perceived differently over time. These logics of remediation are conceived of as modes which are inherent to a medium or, to be precise, as certain specific uses that media are put to. According to them, all sorts of "immersive" media inherently strive for immediacy. The viewer or user is supposed to no longer perceive the fact that there is a technology that makes communication or various forms of experience and interaction possible. Hence the statement: "Virtual reality is immersive, which means that it is a medium whose purpose is to disappear."[52] Bolter and Grusin also use the term "transparency" to describe this phenomenon. Obviously, a medium never simply disappears. Its technological design, its affordances, but also its limitations clearly shape the ways in which the viewers, or users, can experience or interact with it. So there is always a level at which the mediality manifests itself. Hypermediacy, on the contrary, refers to a visual style refusing a unified representational space. Bolter and Grusin's example here is the "windowed" computer interface or the multi-layered information streams that run across the television screen in news programs such as those offered by CNN. The viewer or user is continuously confronted with different forms of mediations, often appearing simultaneously, so that there is no way these can all become merged into the experience of a closed and homogeneous representational universe.

Bolter and Grusin thus conceive immediacy and hypermediacy as two different strategies in media history, both of which are based on remediation. Contrary to the conception presented by Gunning, the transparency effect of immediacy is not due to a process of habituation, automatization or canonization, but rather one of two possible ways in which media do function. Both are in fact equally valid, their relationship is neither one of familiarization and defamiliarization, nor one of norm and deviation. They are not even to be taken as characteristic manifestations of a medium. While television may sometimes strive to achieve a maximum effect of immersion by presenting itself as a direct-access medium to an event happening simultaneously or by inviting forms of para-social interaction between the viewers and people on the screen, other formats display hypermediacy, such as the CNN newscasts in combination with stock market and other information running across the bottom of the screen and maybe even additional windows showing an anchorperson addressing a journalist.[53]

Nevertheless, the concepts used by Bolter and Grusin are useful in our context in so far as they show that what is at stake here is not so much a general development of media from hypermediacy to immediacy, or from wonder to invisibility, but rather the issue of specific forms or uses to which media can be put. These, too, are subject to historical change, often because of an older medium's confrontation with an emerging new one, which may change the entire mediascape and bring about new forms of intermedial relationships. Television in the age of the internet does look different from television in the 1950s, and this also affects the medium's use of forms of immediacy and hypermediacy. However, in the definition of a medium that Bolter and Grusin give, there seems to be a certain privilege accorded to the reality effect associated with immediacy:

What is a medium?

We offer this simple definition: a medium is that which remediates. It is that which appropriates the techniques, forms, and social significance of other media and attempts to rival or refashion them in the name of the real.[54]

It is not quite clear in how far such an appropriation of a medium by another one "in the name of the real" entails that representational strategies which foreground hypermediacy are in fact to be considered less central to such a process. In any event, introducing the "real" as a teleological category here does suggest exactly this to some extent.

In an article drawing upon both Gunning and Bolter/Grusin, Isabelle Raynauld discusses what Gunning calls a "move from dazzling appearance to nearly transparent utility"[55] in terms of "opacity" and "transparency":[56]

We thus state that, following the ideas of Grusin, Bolter, and Gunning, an emerging medium has to go through a period of opacity during which its materiality is so visible that, literally, it makes the content disappear. However, as the viewers or users become more competent, this opacity is reduced and ultimately turns into a transparency that allows the content to become fully visible.[57]

Again, the way in which Raynauld describes the phenomenon she undertakes to deal with appears quite similar to Shklovsky's formulations on *ostranenie*. Again, it is habituation, here associated in an interesting way also with the users being increasingly competent in the manipulation of a device or the interaction with a medium, that leads to its becoming, or at least appearing, more and more transparent. In Raynauld's analysis, however, this does not concern artistic devices or styles, but – in accordance with Gunning's ideas – the process an emerging medium undergoes, from flaunting mediality to striving for transparency. According to Raynauld, this process is reflected also in the different textual forms media adopt, as she illustrates with examples from early films and from multi-media CD-ROMs.

So bringing these ideas together, one could argue that the media historians referred to here do see transparency, or invisibility, as the result of a diachronic process of familiarization with the workings of a technology on the one hand, and also a strategy that is particularly important with regard to all forms of viewer or user involvement from simple interactions to immersion on the other. While such transparency is always relative and only functions on the basis of certain codes and conventions, its effects can indeed be observed on many levels. Hyper-mediacy or opacity, then, is either a strategy foregrounding mediality by means of certain formal or technological devices, or it is linked to a specific phase in the development of a medium, namely the period of its emergence. Formulated by Gunning in terms of both a perspective for media historical research adopted deliberately – "to imagine an old technology as something that once was new" – and a characteristic feature of a medium in its "early" period, it seems indeed that technological innovation in the realm of media (but clearly not only there) does produce an effect of "strangeness" that needs to be analyzed.

This, however, is different from the conceptions proposed by Shklovsky, in spite of certain quite obvious correspondences. While the "stoniness of the stone" is revealed afresh through art after having become invisible in a process of habi-tualization, the foregrounding of the "mediality of a medium" is linked to its emergence and then disappears as viewers or users become increasingly familiar with its workings. While ostranenie refers to a diachronic and in essence also his-torical process in the course of which the familiarized becomes defamiliarized through the work of the artist, the media historical perspective seems to work the other way round. The non-familiar, the novelty that characterizes the emerging medium, provokes wonder and dazzles those who encounter it for the first time. Once this effect has worn off, the utilitarian aspect of the media technology comes to the fore, and then it is experienced as some kind of a "transparent" carrier for the semiotic material that it mediates.

So the question arises of whether these two processes are somehow related, or whether they belong to two incommensurable logics. The common denominator here is of course the phenomenon of innovation. In both cases the new is indeed characterized in terms of a specific kind of visibility that is due to its differential quality. But then they seem to part ways. While the differential quality in the case of artistic innovation is the result of a defamiliarization of habitualized forms – however complex this process may be in terms of its relation to tradition, the recasting of existing devices, etc. – it is less obvious in relation to what other phenomenon a media novelty is perceived as. Here the concept of remediation might be a productive one. As Bolter and Grusin state, a medium "appropriates the techniques, forms, and social significance of other media and attempts to rival or refashion them in the name of the real."[58] Leaving aside this last point, which may be too apodictic a formula, this remark opens up the field towards intermedial relationships and the possible diversity of what André Gaudreault has called "cultural series."[59] So here technological innovation should be analyzed with regard to the broader mediascape in which it occurs. And in this respect one could indeed reframe or rephrase Tom Gunning's argument and say that not only the "move from dazzling appearance to nearly transparent utility, from the spectacular and astonishing to the convenient and unremarkable" needs to be examined, but also what one might call – to coin a new phrase for the occasion – "the newness of the new," which means that one also has to defamiliarize novelty itself.[60]

## Ostranenie – To Be Continued

Following the adventures of Shklovsky's concept of *ostranenie*, from literary theory and history into issues of film and media history, reveals both its problems and its potentials, its limitations as well as its merits. When taken as a general principle governing all processes of artistic innovation, there clearly is the danger that it may turn into a mechanistic and axiomatic explanatory instrument. Its strengths, on the contrary, seem to lie in its heuristic qualities. These, as we have seen, can work on a number of levels. To begin with, one may indeed consider defamiliarization a fundamental analytical strategy allowing us to interrogate and to problematize seemingly self-evident or well-understood phenomena. Whether Kristin Thompson studies so-called "ordinary" films or Tom Gunning looks at old technologies from the viewpoint of their once having been novelties, such cases show that defamiliarization results from a choice made by a scholar when deciding how to approach an object. It functions as a research strategy in a slightly different, yet similar way when David Bordwell looks at Carl Theodor Dreyer's films against the background of classical Hollywood cinema. Conceiving of defamiliarization in such a way, however, is quite different from Shklovsky's original definition, which refers to aspects that are immanent to a given work of art and which in fact are an essential feature of its aesthetic quality.

It could actually be argued that Shklovsky's conceptualization of art is indebted to a modernist aesthetics that stresses aspects such as formal complexity, prolonged perception, and the foregrounding of materiality. In that sense, *ostranenie* is fundamentally two-sided, as it resides in the form of the artwork itself, while also needing to produce a corresponding effect during the act of reception. Defamiliarization, in other words, is always "in the eye of the beholder," and by this very token it reveals itself as an inherently historical phenomenon. Any defamiliarizing device is bound to turn into a habitualized one as time goes by, so to the readers or viewers of later generations, it may indeed appear as an utterly conventional feature. And this also means that at its very foundation, it is a relative one. So if there is, as Meir Sternberg affirms, a "bedrock idea" at the core of

Shklovsky's concept that has turned out to be so very successful, one must also accept that it is one that cannot escape historicity and thus relativity.

In any event, for Shklovsky the work of art is anything but a transparent rendering of the outside world, let alone a representation according to the norms of a classic ideal of beauty, as he also points out in his novel *Zoo, or letters not about love*. Here he distinguishes two ways of approaching art: the first one takes the traditional stance of considering art as a window upon the world; the other one, in contrast, sees art as the relation between its formal elements. (One recognizes here his notion that the artwork is a sum or, as he would say later on, a system of devices.) And so he concludes that if art is to be considered as some kind of a window at all, then the only way to do so is to conceive of it as a painted window.

Apart from being a very insightful and elegant description of what is at stake in formalist theory, this remark also points to the very important issue of the ever-present mediality. The critical stance that Shklovsky makes here can serve as something like a constant *memento* with regard to the reflections by Gunning and Raynauld on media history and the concepts of immediacy and hypermediacy proposed by Bolter and Grusin. Obviously – and no one among the authors quoted here says otherwise – conceptions of the workings of a medium in terms of "invisibility," "immediacy" or "transparency" are not meant to deny the fact that mediality never *actually* disappears. However, it is indeed worth remembering that one should never lose sight of the crucial role played by media technology. The window opening on our computer screen may no longer be a painted one, but it is no less artificial.

Rather than a conclusion, I can offer an observation, a question, and a suggestion. First my observation: however critical one can be of Shklovsky's concept – the phenomenon of automatization and *ostranenie* – the problem of transparency and mediality made visible, as well as the processes of normalisation and deviation from an existing norm, obviously still haunts our debates in media history on different levels. The question now is whether a conceptualisation in these terms does indeed help us to understand these phenomena better. My suggestion is then to never cease to defamiliarize defamiliarization.

# Knight's Moves: Brecht and Russian Formalism in Britain in the 1970s

Ian Christie

> I was referring to a production detail when Tretyakov corrected me, remarking: 'Yes, that is an estrangement [*Verfremdung*]' and looked conspiratorially at Brecht. Brecht nodded. That was the first time I had met the expression *Verfremdung*. I must assume therefore that Tretyakov provided Brecht with the term. I think that Tretyakov had reshaped the term originally formulated by Shklovsky, *ostranenie*, 'distancing,' 'alienation.'
> – Bernhard Reich[1]

> The problem is that ideologies of art are forever swamping and waterlogging the distinct practice of art itself.
> – Peter Wollen[2]

Today, the genealogy of the concepts of Viktor Shklovsky's *ostranenie* and Bertolt Brecht's *Verfremdungseffekt* can be traced and compared with comparative ease. Most of the founding texts, originally in Russian and German, have long been translated into French and English, and a large secondary literature exists, continuing to analyse and contextualise them. They have, in Zygmunt Bauman's phrase, "become settled in scholarly and common vocabularies," seemingly on a more or less permanent basis.[3] But it was not always so. In the 1960s and 1970s, both formed part of an assertive new vocabulary that was embraced by members of a generation keen to declare their intellectual, and indeed political, independence. By no means all of this generation would join the "New Left" or mount the barricades of May 1968, but such overtly political phenomena were part of a wider movement which can perhaps now be interpreted as a revolt against the mendacity and manipulation of the Cold War. So to lay claim to concepts that originated in Russian and Marxist culture was itself a significant gesture of revolt.

Bauman's discussion of how once-novel concepts are normalised occurs in the context of his exploring how the shock of the First World War led European thinkers to promote a new study of "generations." That concept continues to be used in scholarly discourse, although without the same immediate reference or urgency as in the years after 1914-18. It has become what he calls an "echo word," reverberating long after the crash that caused it has died down.[4] This reminds us that critical concepts are not merely functional tools, readily available and selected or discarded according to utility. Their introduction is typically circumstantial: announcing a response to new conditions, an attack on the status quo, a new insight or challenge. Later, they may be more carefully analysed, but grasping why *ostranenie* and its cognates ("alienation" and "distanciation" or "defamiliarisation") became so central to a revolution in aesthetics and culture in the 1960s and 1970s is an important contribution to understanding the intellectual regime that produced the one we still inhabit.

It also helps illuminate an important cultural moment when cinema was finally accepted as part of the wider contemporary culture – when films began to be "taken seriously" by a generation to which they spoke more directly than works in the traditional art media. There was indeed a subterranean connection at work. The same "Formalist" aesthetics that originally promoted *ostranenie* had also made a vital contribution to early Soviet film theory and its key concept of "montage" – another *mot clé* that echoed down much of the twentieth century. When the Russian avant-garde filmmakers Lev Kuleshov, Vsevolod Pudovkin and above all Sergei Eisenstein defined their film practice as based on the linking or collision of shots in montage, this was widely understood as a technique, or "device" in the Formalist sense, which challenged the apparent naturalism of the filmic image and so made it capable of artistic composition. But although montage enjoyed considerable cultural prestige in the 1920s and 1930s, in the visual arts and literature as well as film, after World War Two it seemed distinctly less relevant to the new kinds of cinema that had emerged from the war, almost all of which claimed some form of "realism."

Writing in 1955, the French critic André Bazin drew a sharp distinction between the era when "montage was the very stuff of cinema" and what he identified as a new phase that began in the early 1940s, when it became one among other resources in a "revolution in the language of the screen."[5] By the early 1970s, however, this revolution had led to a situation where "realism" itself seemed to have become a debased concept, used "without question or reflection," as an editorial in the British journal *Screen* stated in 1971.[6] To challenge such flaccid notions of realism, it seemed timely to the generation of May '68 to investigate more closely the debates that took place in Russia in the 1920s before "socialist realism" was imposed as the official Soviet aesthetic in the following decade.

> *Screen* has chosen in this number to reproduce the debates and ideas of Soviet artists and film-makers of the 1920s for those debates are reflections upon and struggles with notions of 'realism' which *Screen* regards as crucial to any understanding of the cinema in the past and at the moment.[7]

What we will not find in later, more academic discussions of *ostranenie* is this early sense of discovery, expressing a belief that lessons could be learned from the experiments of the Soviet 1920s that would inform a contemporary "politics of film."[8]

The revolution in cinema that Bazin hailed had entered a new phase around 1960, when a series of formally complex and often reflexive films commanded wide cultural attention. At this climactic moment in international "art cinema" (as it came to be known), a group of mainly French films seemed to focus on issues of narrative and "film language." These included Jean-Luc Godard's prodigious output from À BOUT DE SOUFFLE (1959) to DEUX OU TROIS CHOSES QUE JE SAIS D'ELLE (1966), together with HIROSHIMA MON AMOUR (Alain Resnais/ Marguerite Duras, 1959), L'AVVENTURA (Michelangelo Antonioni, 1960), L'ANNÉE DERNIÈRE À MARIENBAD (Resnais/Alain Robbe-Grillet, 1961), and CHRONIQUE D'UN ÉTÉ (Jean Rouch/Edgar Morin, 1962).[9]

Such films demanded new reference points and a corresponding vocabulary for discussion, which began to be supplied by the emergence of a new strand in the cultural industry of publishing. In addition to the "little magazines" that had formed the backbone of Modernism in all the art-forms since the early twentieth century, and which now included many devoted to film, paperback book publishing expanded rapidly during the 1960s to provide a range of provocative texts that addressed an emerging new market. Eric Hobsbawm[10] noted the dramatic increase in student numbers in Western Europe and the United States during the 1960s which would fuel the revolutionary movements of May 1968. Perhaps less known is how this also created a new mass intelligentsia for whom, as a "media generation," the processes of representation and mediation formed a self-evidently important field of concern. Authors as diverse as Marshall McLuhan, Roland Barthes and John Berger quickly became international figures through innovative ways of presenting their ideas about "mediation." In many cases, they were explicitly reviving ideas that dated from the pre-war era, such as those of Harold Innis, Ferdinand de Saussure and Walter Benjamin. New paperback imprints were quick to enter the field and, in doing so, create a new market for "ideas."[11]

Books about cinema formed an important part of this publishing explosion, many of them dealing with film in terms which would transform the cultural landscape in Europe and the United States. With the cult of directors established by French journals (and by Bazin) and enthusiastically adopted by young British and American cinephiles, series such as *Cinéma d'aujourd'hui* in France and *Cinema One* in Britain provided commentaries on both classic and contemporary directors that drew on a wide range of references – for instance, Hegel was offered as a key to understanding Godard in Richard Roud's 1967 book on the filmmaker, at a time when he was virtually ignored in Anglo-American academia – to elucidate what was claimed with increasing confidence to be "the language of our time."[12]

Without the simultaneous explosion of "new wave" cinema and the accompanying burst of culturally ambitious commentary and publishing that challenged conventional intellectual traditions, the legacy of Russian Formalism may well have remained known only to Slavic scholars.[13] Instead, we find the leading promoter and theorist of "new American cinema," P. Adams Sitney, invoking Shklovsky's "Art as Technique" as the "historical origin" of what he labelled "structural film" in an influential article from 1969.[14] And when Cape Editions published a translation of Vladimir Mayakovsky's engaging pamphlet *How Are Verses Made?* in 1970, this provided an attractive object lesson in Formalist method at the very moment when the achievements of the early Soviet avant-garde were being rediscovered.[15] The delayed influence of *ostranenie*, in fact, became a prime instance of Shklovsky's own concept of the "knight's move" – history following indirect or crooked lines of transmission.[16]

One such detour was the adoption of the Russian Formalists' *ostranenie* by the German Communist Bertolt Brecht in the mid-1930s, and its subsequent emergence twenty years later in advance of any wide knowledge of its origins. What Shklovsky and his colleagues had developed as both a critical and a compositional method in the 1910s and 1920s was taken up by Brecht in 1935 to theorise his concept of "epic" theatre, as recorded by Reis (above). It was then invoked by filmmakers and critics in the 1960s to explain the reflexivity that characterised much "new wave" film. A decade later, in the mid-1970s, with Brecht more fully assimilated in his own right, attention turned towards the Russian avant-garde culture to which the Formalists had belonged, and more of the original Russian texts began to appear in English translation – giving rise to a vigorous debate about the pedigree and implications of *ostranenie*. Much of this centred on the British film journal *Screen*, which has come to be regarded as the crucible of modern Anglo-American "film theory." What would ultimately prove most controversial in *Screen*'s new matrix of "theory" was the adoption of a psychoanalytic orientation strongly influenced by the discovery of Jacques Lacan's neo-Freudian linguistic turn and by Louis Althusser's conception of ideology. But however influential and fashionable they would become, much of the original scaffolding for a new theoretical perspective on cinema came from the earlier appropriation of Brecht and the Russian Formalists, and from efforts to situate these in relation to other Anglophone discoveries of the 1960s and 1970s, notably the early philosophical writings of Karl Marx and the sophisticated Marxism of Walter Benjamin.[17]

What follows here is a closer examination of the processes by which Brechtian "alienation" and Russian Formalism became powerful influences on a new Western critical vocabulary that took shape in the 1970s. The motivation for their revival was not scholarly in the first instance. These concepts had emerged from "struggle" and might therefore serve in another struggle to create art or "work" that would provoke, inspire, teach. The fact that they appeared to be technical, even forbidding, and uncontaminated by association with entertainment or traditional aesthetics was seen as a virtue. And, in the spirit of the times, a "correct" political interpretation was sometimes in conflict with more scrupulous attention to the circumstances of their origins. But such information was sparse in any event, much of it still embargoed by political disfavour and hampered by slow and irregular patterns of translation. (And by looking at the order of reception, we will be abandoning any claim to an objective overview, instead tracing the sequence of ideas backwards and forwards, like Shklovsky's roaming knight.)

## Brecht Reaches Britain

Coming to terms with the legacy of Brecht in post-war Britain was complicated by the Cold War and by severely limited access to both performances and his writings. In the 1930s, there had been a lively appreciation of his work, especially the plays using music, with performances at Sadlers Wells and on BBC radio. But after his arraignment by McCarthy's witch hunting HUAC in America and subsequent return to live in East Germany, an interest in Brecht acquired an almost inescapable political dimension. Behind the scenes, the British government worked hard to frustrate any visits by his Berliner Ensemble to Britain, and the first of these only took place in September 1956, a month after the playwright's death.[18] Yet between this and the company's second visit a decade later, a considerable culture of "Brechtianism" grew up in Britain – no doubt fuelled in part by the appeal of an artist considered politically controversial.

This was probably less due to an intellectual or even political interest than to the desire of theatre practitioners to engage with an almost legendary figure in modern drama, and to experiment with Brecht's ideas about staging and acting. Among radicals, Joan Littlewood had produced Brecht in the 1930s and appeared in *Mother Courage and her Children* in 1955 at her pioneering Theatre Royal in East London. And another left-wing actor-manager, Bernard Miles, staged an equally notable *Life of Galileo* at the Mermaid Theatre in 1960. However, the young producer William Gaskill became fascinated by Brecht's aesthetic and successfully produced *The Caucasian Chalk Circle* in 1962, before delivering a *Mother Courage* at the National Theatre which confirmed many stereotypes of doctrinaire drabness.[19] Not until the Berliner Ensemble's return to London in 1965 would such prejudices be challenged by the evidence of a living Brechtian practice.

But perhaps more significant was a considerable number of new English plays that showed the influence of Brecht in their desire to be "realistic without being naturalistic" – as John Arden described his pacifist "un-historical parable" *Sergeant Musgrave's Dance* (1959).[20] John Osborne, popularly associated with British theatre's "kitchen sink" naturalism after his *Look Back in Anger*, adopted Brecht's epic form for *Luther* (1961). Robert Bolt's highly successful *A Man for All Seasons* (1960), dealing with the trial of Thomas More on grounds of conscience, featured in its original stage version a "Common Man," who acts as a kind of Brechtian chorus. And even Lionel Bart's immensely popular Dickens musical *Oliver!* (1960), strongly influenced by his earlier mentoring by Littlewood, owed much of its initial impact to a striking skeletal set designed by Sean Kenny, which brought Brecht's radically simplified staging to the popular London – and later Broadway – stage.

The influence of Brecht was suddenly apparent in both experimental and mainstream Anglophone theatre, and producers, actors and critics on both sides of the Atlantic were struggling to interpret Brecht's strictures on naturalism and his much-debated "alienation effect." The *Verfremdungseffekt* had become part of Brecht's evolving theory during or immediately after his first visit to Moscow in 1935. There, he had seen a performance by the Chinese actor Mei Lan-fang and been in contact with members of the early Soviet avant-garde, including Sergei Tretyakov and Sergei Eisenstein, who were well versed in Formalist poetics, even though this was now heavily proscribed under "socialist realism." According to John Willett, Brecht admired Mei's "detachment" and his "[making] it clear that he knows he is being observed" and began to theorise his "V-Effekt."[21] Willett's *The Theatre of Bertolt Brecht*, and Martin Esslin's *Brecht: The Man and His Work* both appeared in 1959, and served as valued guides for the first generation of British and American Brechtians.[22]

From the start, English-speaking champions of Brecht had to contend with the problem of translating his *Verfremdung*, an invented word related to *Entfremdung*, which has usually been translated as "alienation" or "estrangement" when used by Hegel and, in his early writings, Marx. In fact, there are two similar terms in German philosophical language, *Entfremdung* and *Entzauberung*: the former often translated as "estrangement" and the latter as "alienation." Thus, for instance, Marx's *Economic and Political Manuscripts* of 1844 appeared in English translation in 1961 with the following usage:

> If then the product of labour is alienation [*Enttäusserung*], production itself must be active alienation, the alienation of activity, the activity of alienation. In the estrangement [*Entfremdung*] of the object of labour is merely summarised the estrangement, the alienation, in the activity of labour itself.[23]

The issue could be further complicated by noting that both of these German words are originally themselves derived from the English word "alienation," used from the fourteenth century onwards in a theological sense (estrangement or separation from God), as was explained by another important thinker of the period, Raymond Williams.[24] But whatever precise meaning or implication is attached to the term since Hegel, in Marx's and indeed Freud's uses, "alienation" has acquired an unmistakably negative implication – a "lack," that which is to be ended or overcome. So although "estrangement effect" may well be closer to the intention behind Brecht's coinage, this has generally been translated into English as "alienation effect," usually with some attempt to explain that the implication was not necessarily intended to be pejorative.

The result was, and perhaps continues to be, a belief that Brecht wanted an artificial and potentially anti-dramatic effect. How much this problematic term and the mystique that grew up around it has coloured attitudes to the playwright should not be underestimated. An otherwise enthusiastic 1962 review of *The Caucasian Chalk Circle* in a popular British newspaper, having found the production genuinely moving, crowed "What price the '*alienation* effect' now?"[25] Similar scepticism or confusion about Brecht's concept has persisted: as recently as 1998 an American review of *The Threepenny Opera* referred to Brecht's "intention to 'alienate' audiences... and implicate them in the crimes of society."[26]

While Brecht had become a live issue in Anglo-American theatre in the early 1960s, his relevance to cinema was initially less obvious. Brecht's own involvement with film had been intermittent, and initially contentious, when he initiated a lawsuit against Pabst's 1930 film of his THREEPENNY OPERA. Only the collaborative KUHLE WAMPE (1932), about a camp of this name for unemployed people on the outskirts of Berlin, fulfilled his aspirations for a politically effective cinema. Living in Hollywood in the 1940s, he had little opportunity to make any equivalent contribution to American film, apart from Fritz Lang's anti-Nazi HANGMEN ALSO DIE (1943). It was initially through allusions by Godard, whose influence was infectious, that Brecht began to be seen as a point of reference for the new reflexive or "distanced" cinema of the early 1960s. From the theatrical tableaux of VIVRE SA VIE (1962) and bare parable style of LES CARABINIERS (1963) to the direct quotation of Brecht by Fritz Lang in LE MEPRIS (1963), Godard did more than anyone to make Brecht a pervasive presence in the "new wave" cinema culture of the 1960s.[27] Even before taking an explicitly political turn in 1967, he was making frequent use of quotations from Brecht – as when Marina Vlady in DEUX OU TROUS CHOSES QUE JE SAIS D'ELLE (1966) recalls "Old Brecht [saying] actors must quote" – and a range of distancing and framing devices intended to translate Brecht's model for "epic" theatre into cinema terms.[28]

When Godard came under the influence of Maoism in 1967-8 and threw himself into the ferment of May 1968 (demonstrations with a commitment to depersonalised "agitational" filmmaking), his avowed model was the observer of "life caught unawares," Dziga Vertov, by then considered more radical and truly "communist" than Eisenstein. Godard's films of these years combined deliberately simplified technique and "non-acting" with highly provocative political sloganeering, and for the most part failed to reach either militants or former admirers of his work. But with his return to feature-length films, the ironically titled TOUT VA BIEN (1972), Brecht was apparently once again the model for a de-mystification of filmmaking within a capitalist society. Indeed, a number of other contemporary filmmakers were now identified as "Brechtian," and the way was open to reassess Brecht's contribution to the cinema of the past, as well as his presence in such current films as Straub-Huillet's HISTORY LESSONS (1972) and Oshima's DEAR SUMMER SISTER (1972). This became part of an ambitious project by the editorial board of Screen during 1973-5, which began with a special issue of the journal, "Brecht and a Revolutionary Cinema" (summer 1974), followed by a conference held during that year's Edinburgh Film Festival, with transcripts of the conference sessions and additional articles appearing in the Winter issue of 1975-6, entitled "Brecht and the Cinema/Film and Politics."

The issue that united these discussions of films and practice from the 1930s to the 1970s was that of *representation* and the treacherousness of different modes of self-proclaimed "realism." Thus, for example, Colin MacCabe argued in his influential 1974 essay "Realism in the Cinema," subtitled "notes on some Brechtian theses," that Brecht had been typically "recuperated" during the Cold War period, and especially in Britain.[29] This meant that he was seen primarily as a satirist of capitalist society, with his "alienation effects" becoming "pure narcissistic signals of an 'intellectual' work of 'art.'" MacCabe proposes the contrast between Lindsay Anderson's O LUCKY MAN! (1973), "an explicitly Brechtian film" that "pretends to offer a tableau of England" while merely providing the spectator with a superior view of national stereotypes, and Godard's similarly panoramic view of France in TOUT VA BIEN, where "the tableaux are used to reflect the contradictions within the society." Here was a case study of productive versus de-politicised Brechtianism; and by way of historical parallel, the same issue of Screen included Walter Benjamin's 1931 attack on the "left-wing melancholy" of the poet Erich Kästner.

The centrepiece of this issue is a group of articles about the then little-known KUHLE WAMPE. But these were followed by an important debate contained in two articles that dealt explicitly with the relationship between Shklovsky's *ostranenie* and Brecht's *Verfremdung*. In the first, Stanley Mitchell set out to "specify the relationship between Shklovsky's notion of *ostranenie* (making-strange) and Brecht's *Verfremdung*, which has immediately the same meaning."[30] He starts from the observation that Shklovsky's original insight was "purely aesthetic," claiming that the proper role of art is to de-routinise, to "make strange" the familiar, and hence to "refresh our perception," a polemic aimed at both the traditional Russian aesthetics of literature as moral guidance and at Symbolist transcendentalism. Nearly twenty years later, after Formalism had been proscribed under Stalin's regime, Brecht would ask, "if the world could be shown differently... could it not be differently made?"[31] What links the two concepts, Mitchell suggests, is that they capture the theoretical imagination because they "strike at their objective homonym, i.e. the alienation of consciousness which is the reflex of capitalism."[32]

Here Mitchell invokes the historical underpinning behind Brecht's term. If, according to Marx, labour under capitalism produces alienation, and if capitalist entertainment seeks to distract from, or domesticate, such alienation, then the "resisting consciousness" seeks to "make alien the alienation." Both concepts, Mitchell notes, were formulated in times of crisis, *ostranenie* during the First World War and on the eve of the Bolshevik revolution in Russia, and *Verfremdung* amid Hitler's "fascist counter-revolution." The former, even if at first "only" an aesthetic position, would effectively be politicised in 1920s Soviet Russia by the Constructivist and Productivist artists of *Lef* and other groups, while the latter was intended to "shock people out of a passive-fatalistic acceptance of authoritarian politics."[33]

Ben Brewster's response to this account, while accepting its general trajectory, sharply challenged the implication that Russian Formalism remained essentially "neo-Kantian" since this would leave it open to the charge of idealism from a Marxist standpoint. Quoting Shklovsky's contemporary and founder of the Moscow branch of the movement, Roman Jakobson, he refutes the charge that Formalism advocated art for art's sake and argues that "the Marxist Formalists were attempting to inscribe their practice within the terms of... cultural revolution, surely an authoritative concept of Marxism-Leninism."[34] The issues at stake here may seem relatively theological at this distance in time, although they reflect the intense doctrinal debates with the Left that followed the disappointment of 1968 and subsequent period of industrial and political turmoil in Britain. What mattered was the vindication of Formalist analysis as a legitimate tradition of work towards "cultural revolution."

## The Return of "Formalism"

Russian Formalism was certainly a topic of lively interest in 1970s Britain after its long history of controversy since the late 1920s. No less than Brecht's "alienation effect," it had acquired a problematic political ballast by the 1960s. Its most frequent use was as a blanket term of condemnation during the Stalin era, applied indiscriminately to any artist or movement deemed to be deviating from the orthodoxy of Soviet Socialist Realism. In 1928, Eisenstein had dismissed Vertov's work in 1928 as "formal trifles and mischief with the camera," implicitly making use of the already prevailing attitude of hostility towards whatever seemed overly concerned with form rather than substance. During the show trials of the late 1930s, it became part of the litany of accusation that preceded many arrests, and Sergei Tretyakov was one of the intellectuals executed on specious charges of espionage in 1937. After the ferocity of the Purge, "Formalism" could not be discussed openly, although Shklovsky's 1940 biography of Mayakovsky – who had become an icon of Stalinist culture after his suicide – boldly argued that "eccentric art could be realistic art" (with "eccentrism" serving as a code for various forms of non-realist art).

After Stalin's death in 1953 and the programme of relative liberalisation under Khrushchev that came to be known as the Thaw, Western interest began to grow in the hothouse of avant-garde activity that preceded and followed the Russian revolutions of 1917. Much of this interest was centred on the visual arts and on film, with the Constructivist and *Lef* groups a particular focus for new scholarship and translation. Translations of texts by Eisenstein and Vertov began to appear in the 1960s, and two of their most obviously "Formalist" films – Eisenstein's THE STRIKE and Vertov's THE MAN WITH A MOVIE CAMERA – started to circulate widely in film societies and colleges, lending substance to the idea of a revolutionary cross-media avant-garde, which saw no contradiction between formal innovation and political agitation. When Godard joined the striking students and workers in Paris in 1968, he and his associates adopted the emblematic *nom de guerre* of the Dziga Vertov Group. In Britain, similar links would be made between contemporary politics and the independent filmmaking groups, such as the Berwick Street Collective, who maintained an interest in Soviet cinema through their association with Chris Marker's SLON and by making an English version of Marker's THE TRAIN ROLLS ON, about the agitational and satirical films of Alexander Medvedkin.

A major exhibition of Russian avant-garde art at the Hayward Gallery in London in 1971 provided a focus for the post-war generation's new engagement with the experimental period of Soviet culture. Work by artists belonging to the rich ferment of groups that included Futurists, Suprematists and Constructivists stimulated broad interest in the Soviet artists who had emerged before the Bolshevik Revolution and who in many cases rallied to support it, before the majority found themselves at odds with the authoritarian regime imposed by Stalin in the 1930s. And a reminder that the Khrushchev Thaw was over came when a number of promised works were withheld by Soviet authorities from the Hayward exhibition. Meanwhile, a film commissioned to accompany the exhibition, ART IN REVOLUTION by Lutz Becker, helped make connections between the Russian visual artists of the 1920s and the filmmakers. Many of them had been well-known internationally since the 1920s – Pudovkin and Eisenstein were by far the most famous of all Russian "revolutionary" artists – and their writings as well as their films had long been available.

However, by 1970 these had long been associated with an unsophisticated support for the Soviet regime – a position that many in the New Left would regard as equivalent to "vulgar Marxism." What began in the early 1970s was a process of exploring the diversity of Russian Modernist culture that would bring to light a wide range of hitherto unknown artists and scholars – including the various Formalist critics, many of whom became involved with cinema, visual artists who were also title and set designers, and pioneering literary theorists. Through translations published in *Screen*, starting with a pioneering special issue on Soviet film in the 1920s that coincided with the Hayward exhibition (12.4, winter 1971-2) [following the special issue of *Cahiers*, "Russie années vingt," 1970] and a later issue largely devoted to the critic and "factographer" Osip Brik and in *Twentieth Century Studies*, a journal more aligned to the visual arts (7-8, December 1972), an important body of early theoretical analysis of cinema became available, and soon fed into the burgeoning activity of contemporary theorists.

Probably the most influential of the newly discovered Russian Formalists was Vladimir Propp, whose *Morphology of the Folktale* quickly became an inspiration for those seeking to apply structural analysis to popular cinema. But essays by Boris Eikhenbaum were equally important in suggesting a new field of inquiry into "inner speech" in cinema.[35] The discovery that Eisenstein had been in close contact with such figures in Soviet psychology as Lev Vygotsky and Alexander Luria, whose work was also belatedly being translated, gave fresh impetus to Eisenstein studies, rescuing him from an association with Stalinist culture that had been fostered by the wide circulation of ALEXANDER NEVSKY during and after the war. In the 1970s, a "new" Eisenstein began to emerge, located at the centre of diverse 1920s avant-garde networks and strongly committed to sophisticated theoretical speculation.[36] As we have noted, however, it was Vertov, the prophet of the "kino-eye," who seemed a more attractive role model than Eisenstein for the revolutionaries of 1968 and their immediate successors, seeking to build a radical independent film practice in the 1970s.

Penthesilea (1974) by Laura Mulvey and Peter Wollen, "posing the question of film as text."

What was the relationship between these exemplary models from the past and current practice? Theorists grouped around *Screen* generally agreed that, in Stephen Heath's words, it was "not a question of defining an essential 'Brechtianism' and then casting around for films that might agree with it."[37] Rather, the aim should be to use "the emphases of Brecht's theory and practice as a means of grasping, understanding, helping to resolve difficulties related to the artistic and ideological intervention of film."[38] Despite the wish to avoid setting up exemplary works as models, there was clearly an unofficial pantheon – Godard, Straub/Huillet, Oshima – with a number of historic works associated with key foundation figures also subject to privileged exegesis, including the newly validated early Soviet works and KUHLE WAMPE. But were there British examples to set alongside these?

## Distanciation in Practice

Two films in particular showed the impact of "theory" in mid-1970s Britain. Indeed, neither would be fully comprehensible without some knowledge of what shaped their much-debated "difficulty." THE NIGHTCLEANERS (1975) had begun as one of a number of films linked to the emerging Women's Liberation movement, in this case supporting a campaign to secure better conditions for office cleaners. But having gathered interviews and clandestinely shot footage of the cleaners at work, the Berwick Street Collective did not produce a cinéma-verité style portrait of the cleaners and their struggle but a feature-length work that refused overall narrative and fragmented its material.[39] Techniques used included refilming (to produce a grainy "second-order" image), retaining footage normally discarded, such as the clapper-board, and the repetition of shots. The most striking compositional technique is the use of black spacing to separate individual images. Two of the film's leading supporters, Claire Johnston and Paul Willemen, discussed this in their presentation at the Edinburgh "Brecht and the Cinema" event:

> The black spacing re-focuses our attention on the editing work, but the alternation between image/black spacing/image also serves as an analogy for the composition of the image band itself, for this consists of a series of separate images. The 'blind spots' between them, normally invisible [...] are re-introduced by the marked interruption of marked groups of images.[40]

Developing this analysis of the semiotic implications of the black spacing, Johnston and Willemen went on to suggest that it strikes at the usual "plenitude" of the film frame, which is the basis of its claim to transparency, to present an analogical "truth" about the world ("the truth 24 times per second," as Godard had said in his pre-Marxist period). By interrupting this "illusion of homogeneity," the filmmakers were, they claimed, "re-introducing contradiction into the frame" and were also alluding to the "absent" images that could not be filmed. Above all, they argued, such strategies gave the spectator "an incentive to think."

In Edinburgh, THE NIGHTCLEANERS fulfilled an important role as a putative British "Brechtian" film, which was itself an issue of lively debate. Johnston and Willemen drew attention to the film's Brechtian treatment of the workers it shows, "not only as a member of a class but also as an individual" and to "the use of what Brecht called 'quotable gestures,' such as the slow motion gesture of the black woman hoovering an office," which is repeated.[41]

Brecht had become the touchstone for a contemporary political cinema, as he had been for theatre in Britain a decade earlier. But the "devices" used in the film could equally be considered a revival of those used by Soviet avant-garde film-makers in the 1920s, which had attracted the attention of Formalist critics seeking validation of their theories in revolutionary practice. Screen had already published two unfilmed scenarios by Mayakovsky in the "Soviet Film 1920s" issue in 1971,[42] which were introduced by Peter Wollen, whose influential Signs and Meaning in the Cinema had first brought Brecht and a "reinvented" Eisenstein together as models for a Modernist political cinema. Mayakovsky's scripts made extensive use of fil-mic tricks, ranging from reverse motion to animation combined with live action, to "defamiliarise" what he saw as cinema's automatism. Wollen stressed the po-tential to "learn from Mayakovsky as we can learn from Eisenstein or Dziga Vertov"[43] and would soon put this advice to good use in his own practice. Mean-while, the complex reworking of the image in THE NIGHTCLEANERS also bore a considerable formal similarity to the work of such American avant-garde film-makers as Stan Brakhage, Ken Jacobs and the "structural filmmakers" identified by Sitney, albeit few of them would have claimed any left-wing political motive for their "defamiliarisation." And it was American independent film that would influ-ence the period's other exemplary film.

PENTHESILEA (1974) marked a deliberate blurring of the difference between creative and critical activity and a first step into production by the critics Laura Mulvey and Peter Wollen, made while they were working in the United States. The film's ostensible subject is the legend of the Queen of the Amazons, but this is no more than a starting point for a series of five tableaux, each presented in a different filmic form, which simultaneously explore the myth of the Amazons as strong, militant women, and the history of forms of representation that make speaking about/by women possible. Thus, after the first tableau showing Hein-rich von Kleist's play PENTHESILEA performed by a mime troupe, later sections include painted images, archive film, video and direct address to camera. Unlike THE NIGHTCLEANERS, PENTHESILEA had an explicit ambition to bring to-gether the widest possible range of cultural references and practices, including anthropology, psychoanalysis, film theory and feminism, to present them in a "diagrammatic" form. In a 1974 interview with the filmmakers in Screen, Wollen spoke of PENTHESILEA as "posing the problem of film as text rather than as pure representation"[44] and argued for their film as a contribution to theory, intended primarily for a "cadre" or initiated audience, as distinct from what would have been appropriate in an agitational or propaganda film.

Wollen was already one of the British film theorists most involved with reassessing early Soviet culture and Mulvey had been writing feminist art criticism before they became filmmakers. In doing so, they opened the way for a rapprochement in the mid- and late 1970s between avant-garde filmmakers, who were in some cases also theorists, and their more Hollywood-oriented contemporaries, now influenced by the radical turn taken by Godard and *Cahiers du cinéma*. In 1975, Mulvey's celebrated Lacanian essay on "Visual Pleasure" ultimately called for a re-orientation towards new pleasures, beyond those of traditional Hollywood, however cleverly this might be "deconstructed" or read against the grain. And in the following year, Wollen's essay "The Two Avant-gardes" invited adherents of both the Modernist tradition and the Brecht-Godard-Straub/Huillet camp to consider their common interest in foregrounding the conventions and material of film, in a spirit that directly evoked the original Formalist links with Futurist and Constructivist artists in Russia. In another creative superimposition, like that of "alienation," "materialism" became a common issue for avant-garde and political radicals. Mulvey and Wollen would continue their parallel careers as critics and filmmakers, making RIDDLES OF THE SPHINX (1978) and AMY! (1979) after PENTHESILEA, both continuing to put into practice a range of neo-Formalist strategies. The films were highly reflexive and "literalist," drawing attention to film language and technology, combining fiction and documentary, and making use of mimetic forms and devices to "retard" and defamiliarise the perception of the everyday and of history.

Artist filmmakers associated with the London Filmmakers' Co-operative, such as Malcolm Le Grice, Peter Gidal and Lis Rhodes, already familiar with the canons of Modernism and Conceptualism, directly addressed aspects of film form and materiality/"textuality" in their work during the 1970s and early 1980s. Le Grice made three highly reflexive feature-length films between 1977 and 1981, which explored the construction of filmic space, time and identification, focusing attention on the production of narrative out of perceptual paradoxes.[45] The fact that these shared an English suburban setting, rather than the more exotic locations of L'ANNÉE DERNIÈRE À MARIENBAD (LAST YEAR AT MARIENBAD) or the American wilderness of Brakhage, aligned them with the Modernist literary tradition of Joyce and Woolf. Feminism also became a distinctive influence on British avant-garde filmmakers, in works as diverse as Lis Rhodes' structuralist LIGHT READING (1978), Sally Potter's deconstructed melodrama THRILLER (1979), and THE SONG OF THE SHIRT (Sue Clayton and Jonathan Curling, 1979), an epic exposé of the exploitation of women in the nineteenth-century garment trade that mingled genres in Brechtian style.

Although little of this work offered easy identification or traditional pleasures to viewers, many of the texts and films would become part of the foundation corpus of the new academic discipline of film studies. The cultural politics of the 1960s and 1970s frequently invoked doctrines and conflicts of the interwar years as a touchstone of revolutionary purity. Thus, the Russian Formalist critics and the avant-garde artists linked to them had to be defended against charges of idealism or a failure to grasp Marxist principles. Equally, the fact that many of these critics and artists were denounced and persecuted in the USSR – and especially by Stalin's opponent, Trotsky – had to be explained in such a way that did not simply reinforce Cold War anti-Sovietism.[46] By the late 1970s, however, a major revision of traditional interpretations of the early Soviet era was underway, which went some way towards recognising the relative autonomy of the aesthetic that had been asserted by both Marx and Engels. The films and writings of Eisenstein and increasingly Vertov continued to dominate, but in 1979 a retrospective of Soviet "Eccentrism" at the National Film Theatre in London opened up new perspectives on the relationship between Formalism and early avant-garde filmmaking.

This series included films by the FEKS group, led by Grigori Kozintsev and Leonid Trauberg, by Lev Kuleshov and members of his workshop, including Boris Barnet, by the long-despised pre-revolutionary veteran Yakov Protazanov and by Alexander Medvedkin. Many of the films were comedies, or included comic elements, and parody was also a recurrent feature. This display of "another kind of Soviet cinema," as the season's planner John Gillett described it, challenged the monolithic view of Soviet montage cinema and showed films that were interacting with contemporary reality, and with a wide range of other texts, from both past and present. To accompany the season, a booklet of translations was published, FEKS, Formalism, Futurism: 'Eccentrism' and Soviet Cinema 1918-36,[47] which included writings by filmmakers and critics of the time, as well as the introduction to a French translation of the 1927 booklet Poetika Kino.[48] Not only was this alternative canon of Soviet cinema welcomed as a corrective to the traditional canon that had been established in the 1920s, but the articles by Shklovsky, Tynyanov and others made clear what had passed between filmmakers and critics in the 1920s.

Kozintsev recalled the FEKS group's experience of working with Tynyanov on The Overcoat:

For us this project became vitally important. A strange thing happened to us; at a time when we were exclusively devoted to the cinema... we plunged into Gogol's stories – and found it impossible to tear ourselves away. Immersing ourselves in a book written at a time when cinema did not exist, we discovered something new about the expressive possibilities of the screen... We were learning one of the most complex procedures in the art of the filmmaker – how to read that art.[49]

In later years, both Kozintsev and Trauberg, understandably, would play down the influence of Formalism on their work. But in 1928, Shklovsky provided a clear rationale for Eccentrism as, effectively, Formalist poetics in action:

> Eccentrism is based on the selection of memorable moments, and on a new, non-automatic, connection between them. Eccentrism is a struggle with the monotony of life, a rejection of its traditional conception and presentation.[50]

Another contributor to the 1928 anthology, Vladimir Nedobrovo, carefully distinguished the FEKS group from the "Eccentrism of the music hall and the variety theatre," which is associated with Marinetti's Italian Futurism. Instead, he argued, using Shklovsky's terminology:

> The FEKS try to convey the sense of an object 'through vision and not through consciousness.' Their Eccentric concept is one of 'impeded form.' Impeded form extends the period of time taken by the audience to perceive an object and complicates the whole procedure of perception.

> The FEKS work on the alienation of the object. Alienation – the extraction of an object from its automatic state – is achieved in art by various methods [which] Shklovsky has demonstrated in his Theory of Prose.[51]

Narboni's preface to the French translation of Poetika Kino acknowledges the differences between various Formalists, notably Jakobson and Shklovsky, leaders of the Moscow and St. Petersburg groups, respectively. But it also stresses the continuing value of the fabula/suzhet distinction, here construed as "material" and "construction," and links Eikhenbaum's ideas about film and inner speech with Christian Metz's then-contemporary conception of film as "signifying practice." Narboni quotes Tynyanov to explain this process as a way of rebutting Bazin's charge against montage cinema:

> The film's 'play' enables the spectator to read it: s/he has been 'introduced into the action,' as Tynyanov says, and is thus 'edited.'

> In spite of loose terminology and mentalist presuppositions, this is a very long way from the idea of the cinema (and particularly a cinema of 'montage supreme' and 'sovereign manipulation' [Bazin's phrases]) as hammering home to the impotent and passive spectator its univocal (and of course politically 'directed') significations.[52]

Leaving aside the internecine controversies of the period (between Cahiers and Cinéthique, and Cahiers and Positif), what remains clear is the leading part played by the rediscovery of Formalist writing about the cinema in moving beyond Bazin to create a new kind of discourse about film.

The 1980s would see widespread and varied uses of Formalist approaches to the filmic text, as the writings of Shklovsky, Jakobson, Tynyanov and Eikhenbaum were assimilated. Much of this influence would be mediated through French theorists, notably Roland Barthes, Christian Metz and Gerard Genette, who had been among the first avid readers of the Formalists in translation during the 1960s. The many full-scale semiotic analyses of single films that appeared during the 1980s, and the studies of narration and its historical modes in Hollywood by David Bordwell and Kristin Thompson, can all be counted as descendents of the key Formalist insights of the 1910s and 1920s – insights which had to wait for a later historical conjuncture to achieve their wider impact and development.[53]

*Brecht and Eisenstein, a photograph taken by Sergei Tretyakov in 1932.*

When Shklovsky gave the title *Knight's Move* to a collection of occasional writings in 1923, he explained the significance of the title: "The knight is not free – it moves in an L-shaped manner because it is forbidden to take the straight road."[54] Formalism was forced underground, or into emigration, to be rediscovered, along with Marx's early writings and the shrewd dialectics of Benjamin and Gramsci, at a time when Western intellectual life needed new bearings, new ways of understanding the rising tide of post-war "mass communications."[55] Near the end of his life, Brecht argued that "fake solutions in the arts must be combated as fake social solutions" – to which he added, "not as aesthetic mistakes," since he was writing in 1953 to protest against the continued stigmatizing of "Formalism" by the Stalinist leaders of the GDR.[56] Formalist analyses, like Brecht's advice on showing "how things really are," were not prescriptive formulae but invitations to demystify and to experiment. They also offered hope, as did Benjamin and Gramsci, to a generation that felt stifled by resurgent consumerist capitalism that cultural struggle *mattered*.

# *Ostranenie* in French Film Studies: Translation Problems and Conflicting Interests

Dominique Chateau

When one thinks of the use of a concept in a given context, like the corpus of a discipline, one refers either to the linguistic sign (word or expression) which denotes this concept or to the conceptual content which is embedded in the sign, and perhaps even to the ideas the term evokes. If, moreover, the question is about importing the concept into a foreign language, it complicates matters further: we not only have to consider the occurrence of the original word in the new context, but also its translations as far as they are explicit. In our case, the French Film Studies form the context in which the concept *ostranenie* will be explored. Even though the context is narrow, the body of written texts on the subject of film is rather extensive. Remarkably, these writings do not refer to *ostranenie* as such, or so rarely that using this word seems to be superfluous, when we focus on the word itself, and infinite, when we consider the series of more or less close translations. To give an extensive analysis of this subject is far beyond the scope of this paper, and I shall therefore restrict myself to a few relevant observations.

## French Discovery of Formalism

First of all, the absence or the rarity of the word *ostranenie* in French Film Studies has something to do with the general characteristics of a French habitus. One must be wary of clichés, but it is clear that French culture has a strong centripetal tendency which manifests itself in the difficulty with learning foreign languages. We may presume that this is because the genius of the language offers a kind of resistance to alteration based on an old political centralism.[1]

Nevertheless, the concept behind *ostranenie* found a place in several French books, primarily in works on literary criticism, but the word itself was rarely used in reference to the concept. As a result, there was a proliferation of proposals for the translation of the word: *défamiliarisation, estrangement, singularisation, differenciation,* and so on. With regard to this proliferation, contradictory ideas come to mind. If just one word could involve so many linguistic variations, it is probably because its original semantic content is vague or ambiguous. But the reverse is also true, in so far as we can surmise that the dispersal of the French translation proceeds from the exclusion of the original word.

In the narrower context of French Film Studies, we once again see this kind of dispersal. An obvious reason which explains why there was such a dispersal of linguistic variations is that the writings in this field were influenced by the extent of knowledge the authors had about Russian Formalist theories, which was not first-hand but second-hand knowledge, refracted by the choices of translation. It was Tzvetan Todorov who provided the French with the first translation of Viktor Shklovsky's "L'art du procédé" ("Art as Technique"), and thus set in motion a process of translation that would prove to be anything but simple and straightforward. In his anthology of Formalist texts entitled *Théorie de la littérature* (1965), Todorov chose the word *singularisation* without clarifying his choice of word.[2] Previously, in the passage of "La théorie de la 'méthode formelle'," where Boris Eichenbaum refers to Shklovsky's conception, we find only a very short footnote attached to the first occurrence of the French word *singularisation*.[3]

The French word *singulier* has several meanings that we can translate in English by odd, strange, remarkable, rare, unique, singular or single. As an abstract word, *singularité* denotes a quality of uniqueness or signifies that which is rare, strange, and original. The verb *singulariser* means to be distinguished from others, while *se singulariser* means to be noticed by some uncommon or strange character. It follows that the neologism *singularisation* is ambiguous: it can refer to both an effect of uniqueness or strangeness. In a way, something strange can also be considered unique, but the contrary is not true: fingerprints are unique but not strange. Moreover, according to Shklovsky's definition, *ostranenie* means an effect of strangeness produced by the transformation of a common object, and by a device applied to its form. The result is that perception becomes compromised because it forestalls interpretive closure; it is difficult to make sense of what we are seeing. Todorov's anthology lacks the kind of critical elaboration in which the translation of *ostranenie* by *singularisation* would have been justified. Such an elaboration would have been beneficial for a better understanding of the word and for the discussion about the ambiguous nature of the concept. To fully understand *ostranenie*, one has to accept that ambiguity is an essential part of the equation: a part that, in effect, keeps stirring up various debates surrounding the concept.

Knowing the difficulties Todorov is faced with in translating *ostranenie* into French, it stands to reason that other languages might encounter the same problem. Comparing different languages and their choices of translation could indeed be fruitful for the debate on the concept. According to Pere Salabert from the University of Barcelona,[4] the Spanish translation of *ostranenie* is *extrañamiento*, which means: what has the condition to be or to feel (*ñamiento*) on the outside, or alien (*extra*). In this case, the ambiguity of translation leaves room for ontological overtones. For example, *te extrañado* means "I missed you," or more literally, "you remained outside of me." These derivations also call to mind figures of speech in which a word or a phrase is often used that diverges from the normal or literal meaning. It is well known that figures of speech are sometimes designed to clarify the thought while, at other times, they render it ambiguous through the interplay of literal and figurative meanings. Whether in French or in Spanish, the translation of *ostranenie* defies explicitness of meaning; acknowledging its ambiguous nature will help understand one of its subtleties.

## A Challenge for Structuralism?

In the 1960s, the French structuralists (Brémond, Barthes, Genette, among others) incorporated several Formalist concepts into their theories, but *ostranenie* or its translations have somehow failed to catch their attention. This disregard of the concept is probably due to the influence of Roman Jakobson on the French intellectual stage. In the Preface of *Théorie de la littérature*, he is hasty in criticizing the idea of *ostranenie*:

> One would be wrong to identify the discovery, or even the essence of "formalistic" thought in the cliches about what art is supposed to do, which would be to look at things afresh, to deautomatize them so they become surprising ("ostranénie"); while, in fact, the essence needs to be located in the poetic language. In the dynamic relation between the signifier and the signified, as well as between the sign and the concept. [5]

The second part of this assertion is very significant, insofar as it indicates a very precise direction for research as explored by European linguistics and structuralism. That is, it indicates a shift away from Shklovsky and *ostranenie* towards a specifically Jakobsonian-linguistic research agenda.

This shift in research agenda has been noted by other scholars as well. Meir Sternberg, in a text where he revisits *ostranenie* "from the viewpoint of narrative theory and history,"[6] for instance, writes that "Gérard Genette's *Narrative Discourse* [...] and Roland Barthes's *S/Z* [...] never refer to 'ostranenie' and hardly ever to its originator, as if following Jakobson's example."[7] Sternberg is particularly interested in revealing the implicit impact of Shklovsky's theories on structuralist texts:

> [...] Genette's Narrative Discourse [...] proves to be on the whole a zealous rehearsal and ramification of Shklovsky, indeed far more so than certain descendants within Formalism itself. All the essential premises that we have extrapolated, complete with some further Shklovskian aids and hallmarks, now reappear [...] In the modern afterlife of estrangement, Genette's Narrative Discourse is the widest-ranging and, for better or worse, most comparable rever-

sion to [Shklovsky's] *The Theory of Prose*, yet far from the only one. It in turn finds assorted echoes, analogues, variants among contemporary inheritors, even outside its Structuralist persuasion and line of influence.[8]

As for Barthes, Sternberg argues, "in his S/Z, the opposition of the familiar to the defamiliarized reappears in the guise of the 'readerly' (lisible) vs. the 'writerly' (scriptible) text."[9] Sternberg's purpose is very precise and interesting, and the way he insists on emphasizing the complete concealment of *ostranenie* in structuralist texts is certainly very convincing.

Another scholar who alludes to Shklovsky and the concept of *ostranenie* but refrains from calling it by its proper name is Tzvetan Todorov. In his introduction of *Théorie de la littérature*, Todorov merely mentions that "thirty years later, the information theory resuscitates Shklovsky's theses by explaining that the information received by a message decreases as its probability increases."[10] This remark suggests a comparison with Umberto Eco's open work thesis, which states that the poet introduces organized disorder in the linguistic system to "increase its capacity of information." Within this context, Eco stresses that the concept of *ostranenie* denotes "making strange, making different, to be detached from habits."[11] The "effect of strangeness" Eco refers to, however, must not be confounded with the Baroque principle of substituting the complex for the simple. Thus, the incorporation of Formalist concepts in structuralist theories may not have done much for the clarification and proliferation of the term *ostranenie*, but it did show that the concept itself warranted discussion within a structuralist context. On the rare occasions the term was actually used, however, the translation proved to be as precarious an ordeal as it was to fully grasp the complexity of *ostranenie*.

## Terms, Competition, and Ideology

Within the French vocabulary of theory, *ostranenie* had to face the competition of two concepts: Brecht's *Verfremdung* and Freud's *Unheimliche*, which translates as *la distanciation et l'inquiétante étrangeté*, respectively. These two terms contain the idea of a distance from the familiar, but not without ambiguity. In this case, we again witness the effect of refraction produced by the translation, which, for example, can be measured by the subject matter in Film Studies that the two terms have helped to develop. Within Film Studies, a particular film genre seems most suitable for the implementation of the concept. *Das Unheimliche*, translated by *l'inquiétante étrangeté* (literally, worrying strangeness), for instance, suits the genre of fantasy films very satisfactorily; while *ostranenie* seems more appropriate for the specific kind of film where the fantasy effect proceeds less from a transcendent origin (the supernatural) than from a way of making the familiar world look strange and unreal.[12] Although the concept of *ostranenie* appears in some texts about fantasy films, the Freudian reference is used more frequently and extensively. Concerning *la distanciation*, this translation of *die Verfremdung* has led to confusion with the Kantian interpretation of disinterestedness or the idea of a psychic distance in aesthetical experience. The complications of this confusion are addressed in Bourdieu's analysis of pure aesthetics as opposed to popular aesthetics.[13] Instead of interpreting *distanciation* as a formal device that aims to transform the perception of the viewer (this is, for Brecht, the true meaning of *Verfremdung*) in a way that can be compared to the effect of *ostranenie*, Bourdieu considers *distanciation* an intellectual strategy aiming at the absorption of popular art in the intellectual way of experiencing art.[14]

The underlying ideology which determines this position can also explain the suspicion that hangs over *ostranenie* in French Film Studies. In 1970, the well-known French magazine *Cahiers du cinéma* (no. 220-221) published a special issue entitled *Russie années vingt*. In this issue we find two translations of Russian Formalists' texts extracted from *Poetika Kino*: Yuri Tynyanov's "Des fondements du cinéma" (The Fundamentals of Cinema) and Boris Eichenbaum's "Problèmes de la ciné-stylistique" (Problems of Cinema-Stylistics). We should first emphasize the great impact these original translations had at a time when the magazine pursued a theoretical ambition that was abandoned later. At the same time, however, it is clear that the prevailing intellectual atmosphere of criticism surrounding this publication, which saw a transition from neo-Marxism to deconstructionism, led more to an evaluation of the contextual links of these texts with the Soviet cinema than to consider them as useful analytical tools. According to François Albera, *Russie années vingt* was a "rediscovery of the soviet revolutionary cinema [...], which, at this time, was competing with *Cinéthique* for leadership on the 'marxist-leninist theory'."[15] Here, Formalism aroused a suspicion similar to that it had suffered in the context of Socialist Realism. Jean Narboni, in his introduction to the texts, poignantly emphasized:

> Jakobson's reply, with regards to the correct Formalistic method of analyzing the true essence of the work, indicates that the focus should be on the relation signifier/signified because that is all that distinguishes a Formalist 'jamming' from a possible practical materialism.[16]

One notices not only the reference to but the reverence towards Jakobson, as well as the confident manner in which he relates Jakobson's critical position on the correct way to study a work of art, as if in agreement. Narboni continues his argument:

> The influence of Shklovsky's theses on the necessity of "deautomatizing" the perception by devices of "ostranenie," a necessity refuted by Jakobson and abandoned by Shklovsky himself (cf. Interview with Vladimir Pozner, in *Les*

*Lettres françaises*, 17), was considerable in Russia during the 1920s [...]. Within the context of Formalism, however, Shklovsky's theories were criticized of being insufficiently capable of describing the dynamic relation between the signifier and the signified, of focusing too much on the "stylistic effects" level and on the superficial changes, and of lacking a subversive approach to the poetic language.[17]

Clearly, the intellectual atmosphere of criticism during this period did not allow for a favorable reception of Shklovsky's theories, and the reverence towards Jakobson by scholars such as Narboni did not help either. Dismissing the accuracy and importance of Shklovsky's theories was not enough, it seems, it reads as if he needed to be exorcised, removed from the authoritative field of French Film Studies.

## Shklovsky in the French Literary Circle

In contrast, Shklovsky's interview with Vladimir Pozner two years earlier, in *Les Lettres françaises* which was directed by Aragon,[18] showed a much more appreciative acknowledgment of Shklovsky's ideas. The French intellectual field in which it took place consisted of two intellectual circles in which Russian Formalist texts were received more eagerly this time around. In a very recent text, Frédérique Matonti gives a comprehensive account of the reception of such Formalist texts in French structuralism by studying their political reception. She writes, "It seemed as if these two stories, intellectual and political, formed a sort of ring of Moebius where the two faces are indiscernible together [...]."[19] The intellectual reception was represented by the circle of *Tel Quel*, in which Gérard Genette played a mediating role between Philippe Sollers and Tzvetan Todorov, and the political reception was represented by the circle with Louis Aragon at the helm. Before appearing in Todorov's *Théorie de la littérature*,[20] Shklovsky's "The Art as Device" actually first appeared in the magazine *Tel Quel*. The following year, there was a new *Tel Quel* meeting of which Léon Robel gives the following account:

I saw Chklovski [Shklovsky] for the first time in 1967. Not in Moscow, but in Paris. [...] That afternoon, he had an appointment with the *Tel Quel* team in the *Éditions du Seuil*. He asked me to go with him and to act as his interpreter. We joined Sollers, Kristeva and the other "telqueliens" in an office, Vladimir Pozner was there as well [...]. Chklovski started speaking of the book on which he was working, *The Rope of the Bow*. And it was certainly a challenge to follow and rephrase his excitable and fiery monologue concerning "The March of the Horse." It was difficult to make sense of his oblique and rambling way of expressing himself, but I did the best I could. I was exhausted, but the audience asked for more, and it was decided that the interview would continue at home the following day.[21]

That same year, another influential meeting would take place. This time within the political arena, which was centered around Louis Aragon, the director of *Les Lettres françaises* and which involved Pozner and Shklovsky in a one-on-one interview. Aragon, a member of the PCF [French Communist Party] and supporter of the International Communist movement, was very interested in what Shklovsky had to say because, "[...] publishing the formalists or widening their audience [was] part of a strategy of destalinisation."[22]

When it comes to the political reception of Shklovsky, we immediately notice the change of heart towards the appreciation of Shklovsky's theories. Unlike the Structuralists, influenced by Jakobson, this political circle greeted the notion of *ostranenie* with enthusiasm. Antoine Vitez, a major French stage director and Aragon's secretary, for example, underlined that Brecht forgot *ostranenie* in his definition of *Verfremdung*,[23] while Jean-Pierre Faye said that a pole was missing "between Shklovsky and Brecht, between *ostranenie* and the 'V. effekt,' a pole that would be both 'formalist' and 'marxist'."[24]

When one reads the interview between Shklovsky and Pozner, it would be incorrect to suggest, as Narboni did, that Shklovsky somehow abandoned his own notion of the necessity of deautomatizing the perception by devices of *ostranenie*; in fact, Shklovsky reaffirms his justification of *ostranenie*:

> [T]his term of estrangement [written as *étrangement*] was a fitting term. Actually, it was not even a term, it was a feeling. [...] It was a feeling that the connections of the past world were false connections and that the world itself was real, but needed to be rebuilt, and seen afresh. And in order to be seen, it needed to be moved [*déplacé*]. What one said about the picture, the trope, the naming of an object by an unusual word; these only describe a particular case of estrangement.[25]

Shklovsky continues with the idea that there are two methods of thought. A scientific one, consisting of concrete definitions; and an artistic one, consisting of numerous and often contradictory definitions, "like Picasso moving [*déplaçant*] the shapes of the objects as if he was turning them around."[26] The repetition of *déplacer* in this text recalls Freud, especially with regard to Freud's key term "displacement," that is, the move of the psychic accent, during which "indifferent experiences take the place of psychically significant ones."[27] The artist, according to Shklovsky, performs this move in order to rebuild the world, at least, on paper... Furthermore, Shklovsky stresses that "estrangement is not a game, but a way to touch the world."[28] At the end of the interview, Shklovsky justifies his interest inr cinema, proclaiming that cinema offers "a new key to transform reality in art."[29]

Thus, *ostranenie* was a powerful device that could change the way the world was perceived, and was therefore a necessity. Although Shklovsky justified *ostranenie* as a key term, he did admit that he felt that the notion of estrangement underestimated the emotional dimension of art.[30]

## Reception in French Film Studies and Aesthetics

As Shklovsky already mentioned, cinema was the perfect art form in which the devices of *ostranenie* could transform reality. Let us now return to the cinema to see how Shklovsky and the concept of *ostranenie* were perceived, criticized and translated within the context of French Film Studies. In a passage of his substantial book on Eisenstein (*Que viva Eisenstein*, 1981),[31] Barthélemy Amengual expresses his view on the benefit of Shklovsky's concept of *ostranenie* for Film Studies by exploring the way Eisenstein makes use of the concept. As a critical reader of Todorov's *Théorie de la littérature*, Amengual observes:

> [T]he theory of liberation from the perceptive automatism that the writer [Shklovsky] calls the "estrangement" (*ostranenie*), the *singularisation* of what is shown [under] the crucial concern, for Eisenstein, of the angle, the most meaningful point of view, of the rhythmic or visual punch ["striking force"], of the most suggestive and disturbing composition within the frame.[32]

Unlike Narboni, Amengual is not constrained by an underlying ideology; in fact, he is rather open-minded about the so-called Formalist perspective, without being embarrassed by the Formalist label. He is simply concerned with the artistic power of the form. Although Amengual is more appreciative of Shklovsky, the scope of his reference to *ostranenie* is occasional and limited to the parallel he draws between Eisenstein and the Formalists.

More recently, François Albera published two books in which the concept of *ostranenie* is more positively and accurately addressed: *Les formalistes russes et le cinéma* (1996) and *L'Avant-garde au cinéma* (2005). In the first book, in which we find the first complete French translation of *Poetika Kino*, he reminds the reader of the Formalist distinction between the prosaic language and the poetic one: "the latter *distorting* the former, giving to it a new function by making it strange (by keeping it at a distance)."[33] Albera uses the neologism *étrangéifiant* to refer to the phrase "making strange" and *distanciant* to refer to "keeping at a distance." Again, we see that resorting to neologisms is a favorable option. In the second book, Albera enumerates some Formalist devices such as *construction*, *déformation*, *distancement*, *déplacement*[34] to show the range of possible references to the "making strange" element of *ostranenie*. Apart from the interest in and the usefulness of these two books, one can see that the difficulty of determining the translation and hence the meaning of the word *ostranenie* remains a complicated matter in French Film Studies.

We have seen the way translation problems and conflicting interests have made the acknowledgment, understanding, and use of the term *ostranenie*, and thereby the debate about the concept, rather problematic. With regard to the problems of translation, I would like to make a couple of suggestions. The first is that the French translation of *ostranenie* is disappointing because it becomes either conflicted or sophisticated. The problem seems to be that something always gets lost in the translation. We have established that the purpose of art is to make us see things afresh, differently, it goes without saying that the most suitable translation of *ostranenie* will be the one by which we gain the most. That is, the one that comes closest to the essence of *ostranenie* without being burdened by underlying connotations of some sort. *Defamiliarisation*, for example, indicates a loss in the order of what is or sounds familiar, yet this term does not really specify what the result of the process of defamiliarization exactly is. That result is best indicated by the term *estrangement*, if it were not for the old-fashioned connotation it carries, or by *étrangéifier*, if it were not for the sophisticated connotation it has. *Distanciation* or *distancement*, for their part, may be confused with *Verfremdung*. While *Differentiation* is too neutral. And so on and so forth.

One could go in other directions as well. I suggest, for example, studying the possible analogy between *ostranenie* and Arthur Danto's *The Transfiguration of the Commonplace*, awkwardly translated into French as *La transfiguration du banal*. Interestingly enough, the device of displacement is central to Danto's idea of the commonplace.

On the back cover of *The Transfiguration of the Commonplace*, we find an endorsement that perfectly illustrates the subject at hand: "Danto proposes art as a metaphor of the commonplace. Art makes obvious things odd; it paradoxicalizes the ordinary; it defamiliarizes. Danto's book is fun..."[35] This is not the philosopher's vocabulary, of course, but we can be tempted to credit him with it. Surely no formal device applies to the objects that Danto considers, like Duchamp's *Fountain* or Warhol's *Brillo Boxes*. In this case, the familiar object remains familiar, but its *displacement* in the art world gives it a radical new meaning. As we know, Danto rejects the Institutional Theory of Art (an object is a work of art if some institution decides to agree to its exhibiting) because it:

[L]eaves unexplained, even if it can account for why such a work as Duchamp's *Fountain* might have been elevated from a mere thing to an artwork, why that particular urinal should have sustained so impressive a promotion, while other urinals, like it in every obvious respect, should remain in an ontologically degraded category.[36]

Thus, Danto confirms Shklovsky's concept of *ostranenie* when he acknowledges that this transfiguration of the commonplace, triggered by the displacement of an everyday object in the sacred space of a cathedral-like museum hall and defined as an ontological change, makes us aware of the art structures and makes explicit a way of *Weltanschaung*.

Finally, with respect to Danto's Hegelian sensibility, it is commendable to take the propositions of the German philosopher into consideration. Particularly, in regard to resolving the problem about the contradiction between the idea of the pictorial transfiguration, which presupposes that the objects which are pictured have a certain nobleness, and the existence of a painting abounding in simple objects. With regard to the latter, take a look at the following description of a Dutch painting: "velvet, metallic luster, light, horses, servants, old women, peasants blowing smoke from cutty pipes, the glitter of wine in a transparent glass, chaps in dirty jackets playing with old cards."[37] This description "has recreated, in thousands and thousands of effects, the existent and fleeting appearance of nature as something generated afresh by man."[38] Therefore, the solution Hegel proposes combines the renewal of the perception of the commonplace with the accent on the plastic aspect of the things:

> [T]his pure shining and appearing of objects as something produced by the *spirit* which transforms in its utmost being the external and sensuous side of all this material. For instead of real wood and silk, instead of real hair, glass, flesh, and metal, we see only colors; instead of all the dimensions requisite for appearance in nature, we have just a surface, and yet we get the same impression which reality affords.[39]

## Concluding Remark

It seems there are many ways in which the term *ostranenie* can be appropriated and translated. Perhaps the best suggestion is to recommend using the word *ostranenie* itself with an explanation of all the nuances involved; that is, acknowledging the distance vis-à-vis the familiar which is not abandoned but transfigured by a formal device defining the gap as poetic or stylistic. Defining *ostranenie* as a rhetorical figure, Genette writes "between word and meaning, between what the poet has written and what he thought, grows a distance, a space, which, like any space, has a form."[40] A closer look at the terminology used in this case will verify, once again, the precarious nature of *ostranenie*. The French word for distance is *écart*. The verbs *écarter* and *déplacer* are very close in meaning; both are also close to the device of displacement as described here. That is why we have seen both translations used time and again by various scholars writing on the subject, all trying to define a concept that seems to defy definition. What is at work is not the predefined distance we find in rhetoric, in the narrow sense of the scholarly technique of writing, but rather a discovered, invented and personal poetical divergence *dynamically* changing the structure of meaning and creating a new form.

Or better still, a concept as dynamic and ambiguous as *ostranenie* deserves to remain so. Perhaps we need to follow Shklovsky's example and defamiliarize the term yet again by reversing the cunning "choice" he made in spelling *ostranenie* without the extra n. In the interview with Pozner in *Les Lettres françaices*, Shklovsky recalls how he was visited by the collaborators of the Soviet encyclopedia on the eve of the 50-year anniversary of the term. These men were eager to know why he wrote *ostranenie* with a single n, to which Shklovsky replied, "I wrote it like that for just one article. This is how I wrote it; let the word live thus,"[41] dismissing the matter lightly, but knowing full well what his little misspelled "trick" had brought about. The erroneously spelled *ostranenie* survived and was handed down from scholar to scholar, from text to text. It is only fitting then to restore the term to its correct spelling, and thus defamiliarize the now well-known term *ostranenie* by using the word *ostranennie*, with that extra n, as is done in the title of this book.

# Christian Metz and the Russian Formalists: A "Rendez-vous Manqué"?

*Emile Poppe*

When Roland Barthes was asked why he scarcely wrote about the cinema, he admitted that, for him, cinema was a subject that posed serious problems, since the medium was too slick, too slippery.[1] And when Christian Metz was asked why he had not made more analyses of specific films, he replied in the same manner: that he was indeed a little apprehensive of the "amiable and slippery aspects of the film texts." But, "not of the great amount of codes!"[2]

Mastering this "slippery" material was also what the Russian Formalists were hoping to achieve. They proposed to subdivide and articulate the film into minimal units.[3] Drawing from a linguistic background, they were principally interested in the problem of film as a language: in what they called cine-language.[4] In retrospect, the rediscovery of early Russian Formalism by the French Structuralists in the 1960s – thanks to French theorists such as Tzvetan Todorov and Julia Kristeva, who both have an East-European background – can be interpreted as a sort of "rendez-vous manqué" for film semioticians, since the rediscovery for them came too soon. Firstly, one should not forget that, from the 1950s onward, Vladimir Propp was already a central figure in French structuralism, especially in Greimasian semiology. Secondly, the central concerns of French structuralism in those days were in part already formed by the anthropologist Claude Lévi-Strauss, whose close connection to Roman Jakobson is well known; their article on "'Les Chats' de Baudelaire" from 1962 is renowned.[5] Moreover, it must be noted that it was the theoretical work of the professional linguists *not concerned with film* – the work that had a major influence on French structuralism and on Lévi-Strauss – that found its way into film theory. Christian Metz, for instance, discusses at length his debt to Jakobson in "Metaphor/metonymy or the Imaginary Referent," which is a key chapter in *The Imaginary Signifier* (1977). Similarly, Jakobson's celebrated definition of poetic language as the projection of paradigmatic relations onto the semantic axis found a confirmation in Bellour's analysis of classical Hollywood narratives, and it was given a reference to the "textual volume," although Bellour's more obvious source is Metz's "Grande syntagmatique." And last but not least, Jakobson's essay on "Categories of the Russian Verb" proved a fertile impulse for film narratology.[6]

Ironically, the linguists among the Russians Formalists had a far deeper impact on film theory and film semiotics in those days than scholars like Viktor Shklovsky and Boris Eichenbaum, who came from the field of literature and who were more preoccupied with finding a theoretical approach to cinema. They seem to have had hardly any influence at all! Especially the so-called "Prague period" (1920-1939) and the Semiotic period (1939-1949) of Jakobson's work[7] – as well as the work of the Danish linguist/semiotician Louis Hjelmslev – have had an impact on the writings and thinking of Christian Metz. Nevertheless, it is obvious that, in the first part of his oeuvre, before Metz was exploring the psychoanalytical approach to cinema,[8] he was essentially preoccupied with topics which were also central issues in the texts of the Russian Formalists, e.g., cinema as language and the notion of the minimal unit. But where Eichenbaum suggested "[...] that shot-by-shot analyses would enable investigations to identify various kinds of film phrases,"[9] Metz approached these problems in terms of "codes" embedded in a structural network, which determined the categorization and division of the so-called "minimal units." Metz dedicated the entire chapter IX in his *Langage et cinema* to this problem:

> A minimal unit – or a specific type of articulation integrating several units each of which is, in its place, minimal [...] – is never what is characteristic of a language, but always of a code. No minimal unit (for specific systems of articulation) exists in the cinema: such a unit exists only in each cinematic code.[10]

One now wonders why Metz did not make an explicit reference here to what the Russian Formalists proposed on these matters. Remarkably, he does not explicitly acknowledge the Russian Formalists' contribution to the topic. In fact, most of the time he refers to them only in a rather cursory and general way. For instance, in his "Problèmes de dénotation," the text in which he develops his *grande syntagmatique*, Metz does mention several Russian theorists, artists, and directors (Sergei Eisenstein and Vsevolod Pudovkin among them who, at the time, were still seen as part of the Russian Formalists in France), yet in a rather loose and disorderly way:

> Among the authors who have devised tables of montage, or classifications of various kinds – or who have studied separately a specific type of montage – I am indebted notably to Eisenstein, Pudovkin, Kuleshov, Timochenko, Béla Balázs, Rudolf Arnheim, André Bazin, Edgar Morin, Gilbert Cohen-Séat, Jean Mitry, Marcel Martin, Henri Agel, François Chevassu, Anne Souriau....and one or two others perhaps whom I have unintentionally overlooked.[11]

Additionally, in his *Langage et cinéma*, in the chapter where he studies the paradigmatic and syntagmatic axes, Metz refers to Jakobson (and his analysis of the poetical language) and Propp.

> The Russian Formalists, with whose "functionalism" one is well acquainted, claimed that the true meaning of a literary element depends exclusively on its position [...] in relation to all other elements of the text or of a larger pluritextual ensemble (that is to say on its function, in their terminology): its paradigmatic status and its syntagmatic status are thus closely intertwined [...][12]

Despite references to articles by Boris Tomashevsky and Yuri Tynyanov, which were reprinted in Tzvetan Todorov's *Théorie de la littérature*,[13] Metz was clearly more concerned with the work of Propp and Jakobson. Furthermore, when Metz refers to the Russian Formalists, he mostly has Eisenstein in mind. Apparently, the rather "late" rediscovery, in France, of influential writings by Eichenbaum, Tynyanov and Shklovsky was the reason that their names were notably absent in Metz's work. It must be noted, however, that Metz is not the kind of person who fails to give credit where credit is due. When asked by Raymond Bellour whether Metz's *Essais sur la signification au cinéma* could be considered as the first writing on cinematographic semiology, Metz replies:

> [...] it is not the first work in which we find observations on the nature of cinematographic semiology. Several contributions by the Russian Formalists have dealt extensively with the problem of "meaning" in cinema. I am thinking of the collection *Poetika Kino* (1927), with contributions by Shklovsky, Tynyanov, and Eichenbaum, but also of some passages from works by renowned film critics and theorists such as Eisenstein, Arnheim, Balázs, Bazin, Laffay, Mitry, and the, perhaps somewhat less obvious choices, Cohen-Séat, and Morin. These authors (and other names who presently may have slipped my mind) all have posed relevant questions about "meaning."[14]

This may well be Metz's only reference to Shklovsky...Typically, Metz situates his work in a large tradition, not forgetting to pay *hommage* to the work done by writers of earlier generations, while putting his own approach into perspective at the same time.[15] In 1972, Metz specifies that he now wishes to extend his list of names to recognize the importance of the Russian Formalists. Metz does so in a footnote, added to his text "Une étape dans la réflexion sur le cinéma" originally published in 1965:

> I would like to take this opportunity to express an adjustment of appreciation. The writings of Jean Epstein, despite being acutely insightful, now come across as confusing, exalted, and terribly idealized, while the writings of the

Russian Formalists, yet to be discovered back then, have made an important contribution to the study of film [in the meantime], thanks to the interest in these writings by *Cahiers du Cinéma*.[16]

In his conversations with Raymond Bellour, Metz refers once again to the publication in the *Cahiers du Cinéma*. The magazine published a "special" about Formalism, *Russie Années Vingt*, in May / June 1970, with translations of texts by Tynyanov and Eichenbaum from *Poetika Kino*. In additional issues, several texts by Eisenstein were translated as well.

One may wonder how Metz would have responded to Russian Formalists such as Shklovsky, Eichenbaum, Tynyanov, and others had he known about their texts earlier. I tend to assume it may have been similar to Metz's response to the aesthetics of Jean Mitry, who himself can be said to have been closer to the approaches and problems posed by these Russian Formalists, in as far as they focussed on the aesthetic dimension of film. Obviously, Metz is interested in the linguistic aspect of the cinema, and not so much in the aesthetics of film. His main focus of attention, particularly in his psychoanalytic phase, is not film, but the cinema and the *cinematic apparatus*. His distinction between cinema and film is, as we know, crucial in Metz's work. For all these reasons, it is quite understandable that his research had far more affinities with Jakobson's work than with work by Russian Formalists such as Shklovsky, Eichenbaum, or Tynyanov. However, I do not want to dismiss the similarities and overlaps between the work by the Russian Formalists and that by the Structuralists. At least in one domain they had the same concerns.

With the Russian Formalists, the recourse to linguistic notions was part of a cultural strategy: to help break down the division of high culture and popular or folk culture, by developing methods of analysis which could be seen to apply to both with equal success. This agenda may well explain why their writings were "rediscovered" in the 1960s, when, thanks to the pervasive influence of Structuralism, a similar agenda took shape in the fields of study of "mass-cultural artefacts."[17] By the 1960s, this type of research no longer needed to be a strategic target on the scholarly agenda, since it was there now, and it was simply considered a fact for semioticians and structuralists such as Metz, Barthes, Eco, and others. One might therefore say that the rediscovery of the Formalists came too late to be of specific strategic value in the debate on high and popular culture.

In retrospect, making up the balance, one may conclude that, obviously, there *was* a connection between Russian Formalism and French Structuralism. Moreover, theoreticians such as A.J. Greimas, Metz, Lévi-Strauss, and others have undoubtedly seen the structuralist enterprise in the light of Russian Formalism. However, there is an important restriction to be made here. The Structuralists saw themselves working in the footsteps of Propp, Jakobson, and Trubetskoy; it must be stressed that the other members of the group – Eichenbaum, Tynyanov, and Shklovsky – played a far less important role for the structuralists. One reason is that studies by Eichenbaum, Tynyanov, and Shklovsky were not accessible at the right time. Yet another reason, and perhaps a more important one, is that Eichenbaum, Tynyanov, and Shklovsky were principally concerned with *aesthetical* problems. Metz, a semiotician in the Structuralist tradition, can be said to have opted, as these Formalists did, for a theoretical and systematic approach to film in opposition to a *normative* aesthetical approach. Nevertheless, it is quite obvious that Metz and the Russian Formalists worked on different levels. Whereas the mentioned Formalists were more concerned with problems that Metz would situate on the *filmic level* (e.g. the notion of *ostranenie* and the problem of devices), Metz himself worked almost exclusively on the *cinematographic level*, the cinematographic codes, and codification. On that level, a term like "ostranenie," having a rather broad meaning,[18] could not easily have been made operational. Even if Metz would have known the term, it would not have been suitable for his own approach. Yet, from his remarks and annotations on his previous work, we can deduce that he must have regretted not having known the writings of the "literary" branch of the Russian Formalists earlier.

# Part III
# Cognitive and
# Evolutionary-Cognitive
# Approaches to *Ostranenie*

# Perception,
# Cognitive Gaps and
# Cognitive Schemes

# Should I See What I Believe?

## Audiovisual Ostranenie and Evolutionary-Cognitive Film Theory

*Laurent Jullier*

In my contribution to this book, I aim at exploring the potential contribution of evolutionary-cognitive psychology in the study of defamiliarization in cinema. Interdisciplinarity being at the core of the study, an epistemological preamble is necessary before analyzing what cognitive psychology has to say about the question of perception. The findings will then be transposed to the question of perception of the cinematographic spectacle: before being able to know what may be defamiliarizing in a film, one has to wonder whether the whole cinematographic process itself is not defamiliarizing. Three sections will then be devoted to audiovisual *ostranenie*, based on three common distinctions in perception psychology:

- defamiliarizations dealing with the processes of automatic recognition of visual forms (bottom-up);
- defamiliarizations dealing with the routines associated with the exploration of the environment by the whole body;
- defamiliarizations dealing with high-level cognitive processes such as opinions and beliefs (top-down).

More generally, this contribution is based on a *biocultural* approach,[1] i.e., it is neither "universalist" nor "culturalist" but rather explores the interactions between the body – including the "embodied mind" and its perceptivo-cognitive routines – and the cultural products circulating through different periods and in different places.

## Epistemological Background

For a film scholar, resorting to psychological tools amounts to entering a disciplinary field which, like all others, is a place of scientific debate. It is thus important for this article to rely on consensual tools or, in the opposite case, to stress they are debated among specialists. Besides, caution is of the utmost importance when one exports notions from one field of study to another, especially as earlier links between the fields of psychology and cinema are rather uncommon in the history of sciences. Until recently, professional psychologists have indeed paid little attention to cinema, except for Münsterberg[2] and the Franco-Italian staff of the Institut de Filmologie.[3] The advent of Evolutionary-Cognitive Film Studies in the mid-1980s[4] partly changed the situation as professional psychologists (J. Hochberg, N. Frijda...) started to work with involved film scholars (David Bordwell, T. Grodal, Gr. Currie...), and several meetings could take place within the frame of associations (i.e., the Center for Cognitive Studies of the Moving Image) or new journals (i.e., *Media Psychology*, published by Routledge since 1997). In parallel, experiments based on film screenings were made possible by the development of cerebral localization, enabled by the technical progress made in the field of medical imaging.[5]

Yet, reciprocal mistrust is still often at play. For reasons too complex to be explored here,[6] Film Studies often openly rejects the use of psychological tools, while their success cannot be denied. Conversely, psychologists are suspicious of Film Studies for a simple reason: the noblest situation in cinema, namely the screening of a narrative feature film, is based on such a variety and complexity of variables (in the auditorium as well as on the screen) that cinema is not a suitable object offering the opportunity to observe daily life more simply *through reduction*. Indeed, the spectator is almost entirely free in front of a screen.[7] The only two exceptions with regard to this freedom are automatic recognition (of apparent movements on screen, of human figures, of colors, of memorized objects...) and audiovisual anchoring (namely the ventriloquist effect made possible by the con-current use of both screen and loudspeakers). Unsurprisingly enough, the few psychologists resorting to cinema in their research favour these two types of bottom-up psychological processing. Yet interdisciplinary attempts should not be abandoned, especially as the approach is easier from Film Studies to psychology given that most mechanisms at play in daily life can be found in a film sequence.

## The Bases of Perception

To study the process of defamiliarization, one first has to examine how the feeling of the familiarity of things emerges in one's mind. Every day, all over the world, hundreds of millions of people spend a considerable amount of time in front of a screen where they are told stories. But what emerges from this screen is just photons (read as images) and air vibrations (read as sounds): in no way does this screen data form an autonomous whole including the necessary tools to be deciphered. If these audiovisual stories are so successful, it is above all because they are *understood*, and they are understood because they appeal to a perceptivo-cognitive knowledge acquired in real life. This very knowledge transforms physical objects – photons and air vibrations – into a story which will be cognitively constructed and potentially experienced as thrilling, enlightening, amusing, etc., if one accepts being emotionally involved. The main question is then to know how this knowledge is formed before the screening starts.

Psychologists more or less agree on the model separating the individual path from the common path: what we know about the world individually is stored in episodic memory, while what we all know about the world – the knowledge we share as human beings, except if we suffer from a specific deficiency – is stored in semantic memory. This common knowledge itself can be divided into two strata describing our two modes of reading the surrounding world:

- A perceptive, bottom-up reading of the world, in which forms are automatically imposed upon us. Ecological or naturalist psychology defends the *independence thesis*, namely the primacy of the bottom-up reading over the cognitive top-down reading, following J.J. Gibson in the case of visual perception.[8] One of the best-known scholars in this tendency is Z. Pylyshyn; for him "visual perception is best viewed as a separate process, with its own principles and possibly its own internal memory, isolated from the rest of the mind except from certain well-defined and highly circumscribed modes of interaction."[9] J. & B. Anderson hold a comparable position in the field of Film Studies.[10] The most interesting aspect of Pylyshyn's theory, at least for a film scholar, is that among the "own principles of perception" there is a "*visual index* that individuates objects" so "focal attention is directed to objects in the visual field rather than to locations."[11] This may contribute to explaining why, since the very beginnings of cinema, the spectator has been accepting the use of lenses with a focal length different from that of the human eye, and which should normally provoke a defamiliarization effect by modifying spatial relations between objects, or between objects and their environment, while the phenomenon itself is quite unusual and only occurs with extreme distances: either very short ones, provoking trapezoidal distortions of objects near the frame; or very long ones, flattening all objects on the horizon.[12]
- A cognitive, top-down reading of the world, in which we are the first to impose upon the world the forms we are used to. Constructivist psychology defends the *continuity thesis*, namely the fact that perception is permeable to cognition, and thus a top-down reading is preferred, following H.L. von Helmholtz.[13] One of the best-known scholars in this tendency is Irvin Rock.[14] Here, "perceptual processes are applied to the transformation of representations originating in occurrent optical input, [when] cognitive processes are applied to the transformation of representations drawn from the preexisting knowledge base."[15] This theory is much more successful than the first one in Film Studies as it is more compatible with culturalist approaches.

All disciplines dealing with images are full of such oppositions. For instance, in the academic field of aesthetic theories of painting, the difference between the anti-interpretativist, surrogate paradigm (held by A. Danto) and the interpretativist, symbolic paradigm (held by N. Goodman) resembles the difference between the naturalistic approach and the constructivist approach: the surrogate paradigm "claims that seeing a pictorial representation of an object is, with qualifications, like seeing the object itself," while the symbolic paradigm "focuses attention on syntactic and semantic features of pictures."[16] Must we choose between these two tendencies? No. First, the difference between them is not as significant as one may suppose: in fact, the independence thesis "applies only to the perceptual system [because] no one disputes that the preperceptual and postperceptual systems are greatly influenced by cognitive factors."[17] In psychology, numerous attempts have been made to try and reconcile these two trends, if only because both automatic recognition and imposition of figures are part of daily experience.[18] U. Neisser and H. Gardner[19] are important figures of this reconciliation trend, and like Hilary Putnam, they consider that Kant was its pioneer (Kant "built a system where the mind and the world jointly make up the mind and the world").[20]

Another reconciliation figure, less famous but maybe more interesting as far as Film Studies is concerned, is the late neuroscientist Francisco Varela, who supported the theory of *sensorimotor contingency*. Let us take the case of color recognition: the same wavelength can be interpreted differently by different people according to the context and the mental categories accessible to them, some of them cultural and some universal. Knowledge is neither the reflection of a formerly given world nor a simple product of our representations – here the color is in the *relation* between the world and perception. Both the world and the perceiving subject "determine one another" because cognition is linked to "the fact of having a body endowed with various sensorimotor abilities"[21] (the subject being an actor at the same time). Indeed, animals have to move to find food, whereas plants take it directly from the soil in which they grow. The aim of perception is thus first to extract useful information from the environment, useful in terms of actions to be envisaged. Only our surviving ancestors, those who perceived the world in a utilitarian way, transmitted their genes to us, which allows us to speak of *perceptual veridicality*.[22] In this sense, perception does not exactly construct the environment, but it selects information through *expectations* which are acquired (as all pre-school teachers know) by moving around and manipulating objects – what psychologists call enaction, i.e., the idea of experience as an activity of encountering the world. The acquisition of these expectations is based on the distinction between egocentric and exocentric information,[23] and this distinction can be found in cinema with such classical features as shot-reverse shot and point-of-view editing.

The last point is episodic memory, which stores the opinions, beliefs and stereotypes we use. Even if there are actual links between automatic reactions to the world and one's personal opinion on it – these links are the main research object of a branch of psychology called Socio-intuitionism[24] – it is not the object of inquiry of this present study. It is time we leave the privileged field of Cognitive-Evolutionary Psychology to enter that of social psychology, anthropology and sociology.

**Film stills** 1 *A classical shot-reverse shot in* THE MASK *(Chuck Russell, 1994) Left: Tina (Cameron Diaz) 'as seen' by Stanley (Jim Carrey). Right: reverse-shot. The optical point of view is exocentric (we sit at the desk with the main characters, but we are not supposed to see what they perceive), when the ethical point of view is egocentric (the asymmetrical shot-reverse shot provides useful information on the character's thoughts: Stanley's gaze is on Tina alone and lacks a depth of field, as if she was a unique and unreachable goddess; on the contrary, Tina is including herself in her gaze on Stanley, indicating she is seduced and already imagining her life with him, as suggested by the old couple seated in the background.*

## In Front of the Screen: The Reality Effect

Before wondering whether there are particular films or figures which defamiliarize us in cinema, we should wonder whether the defamiliarizing effect does not come from the fact of watching films itself, especially as cinema offers flat images with neat edges and full of cuts, which, on the face of it, does not look like the sensorial experience we have of the world surrounding us. This possibility will be rejected right away:

- we are used to flat images as we do not have the ability to see in relief (we see 2D images in a 3D world, namely we see in 2.5D as cognition specialists say);[25]
- the blurred edges of our visual field constantly run into vertical and horizontal lines restricting it, and the screen – except if very small or situated quite far from the spectator – allows both types of vision (foveal and peripheric) to be called upon;[26]
- we are not bothered by the presence of cuts as we resort to them in real life as well: each time our eyes move to focus on something else, we are practically blind – the nervous message drops to 10% of its value – for two-hundredths of a second.[27] This is our private way to have space and time cut in "shots," and we proceed this way as fast as in a MTV music video: "the eyes typically move *between two and five times per second* in order to bring environmental information into the foveal region of clearest vision."[28]

Moreover, perception itself includes all the possible optical distortions, being both object-related – for instance when you recognize an object you can only see a part of – and aspect-oriented – for instance with ambient lighting, or the angle from which a surface is viewed.[29]

But maybe one should place permanent defamiliarization, if it ever exists, in the category of top-down processes, in the "duality of information," to use J.J. Gibson's words,[30] i.e., the impression of being both in front of the world (I believe in it, I am afraid, I am laughing...exactly as in reality) and in front of an image (I do not believe in it, I know these are just light spots and sounds). This position cannot be held for reasons linked to enaction, which we have already discussed above: in front of a screen, motricity is weak, and as Th. Stoffregen wrote, "viewing of films is partially open-loop (not responsive to perceptual infor-mation), whereas viewing of the depicted events (if we are really in front of them) is wholly closed-loop, or controlled with reference to perceptual information."[31] When we are absorbed by the plot, or simply interested in what unfolds before our eyes, the computational investment ("what is going to happen now?") and the self-management of emotions ("I wish he could come on time!") overflow the sensori-motor reactions to the screen data. "Rather than being drawn into the film (the depiction, as such), viewers are drawn into the story, that is, into the events that took place in front of the camera."[32]

## In Front of the Screen: Perceptive Defamiliarizations

Cinema has two ways of defamiliarizing us: (1) by showing us the world as it is and as we cannot see it because we are enslaved to the limits of our senses (by showing us the world "before we look at it," to quote M. Merleau-Ponty's famous formula on Cézanne's painting); or (2) by showing it in a way that is different from the way we see it daily.

M. Szaloky reminds us that the first option, also called the platonico-phenom-enological option, is favored by such authors as S. Kracauer, S.M. Eisenstein, A. Bazin, C. Metz, or G. Deleuze. "Unnegociated presence... virginal purity... pure state" are all metaphors used by these authors to say that cinema reveals the Real.[33] The problem lies in the fact that their theories are founded on the me-chanical nature of the film medium, which is based more on a belief than on reality. The cinematic apparatus is molded on our body and our perceptivo-cogni-tive dispositions – it does not come out of the blue and is not the product of a mysterious type of "mechanics" independent from the human being either; from Kracauer to Deleuze, nobody relies on Darwin to form an idea of perception as it has evolved in man. Cognitive psychology is all the less inclined to validate this belief in the revelation of a "pure Real" as it intricately links cognition and emo-tion, and even sometimes pleasure and truth, as with a recent experiment carried out by S. Harris.[34]

Let us then examine the second option, for which psychology will provide better heuristic services. To show us the world differently from the way we see it and listen to it every day, cinema can mislead our perceptive routines as cognitive psychologists describe them. To focus on vision only, here are a few examples of these routines, concerning the spatial distribution of objects in their environment:

- most objects in the world do not fly but rely on a dense physical support;
- they tend to exist in a continuous way;
- they are rather rigid, which means that all their parts move together;
- they are rather opaque and partially hide the objects situated behind them;
- a moving object tends to progressively hide and reveal the one in front of which it is moving.

At all times, or at least since Méliès, cinematographic defamiliarization has been challenging the first two routines: flying objects, people or objects suddenly appearing or disappearing or spiriting away are great classics. The second rule also explains why the action match cut without continuity, an editing figure initially prohibited in classical Hollywood cinema, has now eventually become hegemonic in films for the general public, music videos and commercials; it seemingly validates the rule of continuous existence without bothering whether a higher-level cognitive reasoning will later have to correct this reading. Hollywood banned it because of this very submission to bottom-up processes which one was afraid would compete with diegetic absorption.

The third rule was especially challenged by Golden Age Hollywood cartoons and their characters distorting themselves like accordions while running or falling – surrealist painting, at the time, did the same in its own way, for instance with Dali's "melting watches." Even today, at a time when the progress of digital imagery allows the making of photorealist non-rigid bodies, mainstream cinema is reluctant to resort to them beyond the realm of science fiction (Reed Richards's elastic character in FANTASTIC FOUR, 2005). As for denied opacity, it is also confined to fantasy and science fiction (Susan Storm's character in the above-mentioned film). The fifth rule, also called interposition rule, cannot be challenged without denying the distinction between figures and the backgrounds behind them, which explains why it can only be generally found (with the exception of surrealist painting once again) in non-figurative experimental cinema (for instance, in Hans Richter's short films where a geometric figure perceived as being "in foreground" slides "in the background"). Yet some examples can also be found in more popular types of art: the most striking of them may be George Herriman's famous comic strip Krazy Kat (1913-1944), which sometimes transforms a background object – for instance the sun – into a concealing object.

Figurative cinema, and even cinema for the general public, can also play with these routines of spatial distribution, but on a smaller scale – for instance by

**Film still 2** *Zazie dans le métro* (Louis Malle, 1960). *When the police rushes into the café Zazie and her friends have started wrecking, the policemen are moving towards the camera – and indeed the size of their image is growing on the screen – but they do not hide what is situated between them and the camera, even when they are quite close! On the film still, one can see the privates appear bigger than their squadron chief in spite of the fact that he is supposed to be in front of them! The technique of inlaying was then a little basic, so that the spectator immediately perceives the special effect, but the whole is still quite defamiliarizing, so much that even today, at a time when compositing would allow a perfect special effect, this figure remains quite uncommon, even in music videos, which rely less than narrative feature films on the obligation to conform to perceptive routines.*

modifying the two monocular optical indices specific to moving objects, namely (1) variable size (rule: the familiar size of an object changes with the latter moving away or forward) and (2) movement parallax (rule: what is in the foreground appears to be moving faster than what is farther away).

## Defamiliarizations Linked to Enaction

Sometimes the cinematic apparatus solicits the spectator's body entirely, but not so frequently. J.J. Gibson wrote: "when the camera pans, the viewer might perceive her head to turn."[35] But when asserting this, he underestimated the impor-

**Film still 3** *HUMAN NATURE (Michel Gondry, 2001). Lila (Patricia Arquette) is singing while walking in the forest. But neither the trees in the depth of field, nor the branches between the camera and the actress move at the "right" speed. Whereas, since the 1930s, the job of cartoon-makers has consisted in imitating the movement parallax induced by cameras in a situation of lateral tracking (that is why former Walt Disney Studios animator Ub Iwerks designed the first multiplane camera in 1933), Michel Gondry does his utmost to make the background unfold behind the actress at the wrong pace, thus making us feel they are on two moving walkways going at different speeds.*

tance of enaction, the fact that "the act of perception depends upon movement of the perceiver."[36]

How to choose? From one point of view, one must not exaggerate the matter of body movement when seated in front of a screen:

> From visual information alone we have no trouble noticing self motion even when we are being moved passively. [That is why] performance and experience in flight simulators is only marginally improved when body accelerations are imitated by putting the whole simulator on a moving platform.[37]

From another point of view, one has to recognize that the process easily affects the entire body at times, especially when it reproduces some movements driven by bottom-up mechanisms (tracking shot made by a camera equipped with a short-focal-length lens), or even some situations driven by top-down mechanisms (the hero wants to escape as the monster is approaching, but does not manage to do so). The run and gun style may also be quoted: for the last few years it has been "shaking up" spectators by offering images taken by a cameraman running due to imminent danger (THE BLAIR WITCH PROJECT, [REC], CLOVERFIELD).

Yet discovering one's body, either because anti-gravitational muscles are at play or the inner ear transmits feelings of loss of balance (when it was released, CLO-VERFIELD specified, "Please note certain sections of this film may induce motion sickness"), does not necessarily mean being defamiliarized, except maybe for crazed intellectuals not quite used to moving. The sense of defamiliarization is probably stronger not in these run and gun movies, but in the strange sequence of Maya Deren's famous experimental film MESHES OF THE AFTERNOON, in which the actress (Maya Deren herself) is staggering up a narrow staircase and, each time her shoulder hits one of the walls along the stairs, the camera rocks in the same direction, as if the whole house was unstable.

**Film still 4** MESHES OF THE AFTERNOON *(Maya Deren and Alexander Hammid, 1943). A casual postmodern device consists, at least since Steven Spielberg's JURASSIC PARK (1993), of shaking the camera when something big walks or runs near it. It can be seen as a way for computer-generated images to "gain weight." It conforms to our ordinary experience and our "naive physics." In this case, however, the link between Maya Deren's unstable body and the camera tripod creates a "worrying strangeness" (according to the film's Freudian atmosphere), causing "unmotivated" (as far as naive physics is applied) Dutch angles.*

Arts or media, like installations or video games, which include a part of free exploration by the body, are likely to defamiliarize the spectator through motion. What about cinema? When Alva Noë speaks of an art "which provides perceivers

LAURENT JULLIER

an opportunity of self-aware enactment" (what she calls *experiential art*),[38] she refers not only to installations, but also to the work of hyperrealist painter Chuck Close. In front of his work, the viewer can move to "understand" how shapeless pixels (when viewed close-up) form a photorealist face (when seen at a distance). Philippe Parreno and Douglas Gordon's film ZIDANE, A 21ST CENTURY PORTRAIT has a go at it through the close-up of a refilmed display: we are shown pixels, but we are not the ones who decide to take a step forward to see them – the experience is different and less defamiliarizing this time. What is defamiliarizing about this film is simply to see a football player filmed while he is not playing football – but this has to do with artistic innovation more than defamiliarization.o

Let us turn instead to something simpler and the focus of less media attention, namely a gesture made "against nature" by the actor's body. All the flying bodies of kung-fu films made in Hong Kong may be quoted, but there are so many of them – and the cables holding the actors are so "visible" even when they have been erased by cable removers – that they have eventually lost their strangeness. A very simple example taken from DRIFTING CLOUDS (KAUAS PILVET KARKAAVAT, by Aki Kaurismäki, 1996) is much more interesting to explore. At the beginning of the film, Lauri (Kari Väänänen), a tram driver, is so sure he will get a promotion when his boss asks to see him that he buys a huge television set on credit before the meeting. We later see him coming back home and fainting when his wife (Kati Outinen) asks him about the meeting, and we understand that instead of getting a promotion he has been fired. The defamiliarizing element comes from the fact that Kari Väänänen is seen falling flat on his back, without his hands breaking his fall. This transgression of a motor schema deeply buried in early childhood is at first striking even if half a second later its effect is tempered by cognitive reasoning (what you need is just a mattress on the floor and a cameraman not focusing on the actor's feet!).[39]

Yet some cases are worth quoting, where defamiliarization relies on a "subversion" of enaction routines; they are often marked by non-intentionality (awkwardness, indifference or technical limitations sometimes play a role). Most of the time, the films we see do have a biomechanical veridicity: they give a correct depiction of body movement, allowing the famous "mirror neurons" to fire. If "seeing the biological movement of a human hand reach and grasp a target prompts a human observer to represent the agent's motor intention by automatically matching the perceived movement onto her own motor repertoire,"[40] then this is similar in real life and in front of a screen.[41] Meanwhile, some animated cartoon characters or computer-generated creatures (especially if not generated using motion capture or performance capture devices) can perform non-veridical movements, forbidding any automatic matching. The same holds for some amateur films in which the cameraman takes a long time panning (or the editor takes a long time cutting) to show us what a character sees on screen (or what provokes the reaction of a character on screen): it misleads our motor habits (like turning one's head to see what someone else can see and which, from his or her reaction, seems so interesting – a very early habit in one's life as babies turn their head to look at what their own mother is looking at from the age of two or three months). It goes without saying that Dogma films attempt to reproduce this type of "de-layed reaction" (on the part of the cameraman or the editor) to provoke a volun-tary type of defamiliarization.[42]

Our enactive habits also give us a good knowledge of naïve physics, especially concerning the laws of causality. This is the reason why defamiliarization in cine-ma rarely operates at this level, and why "the fictional worlds that have been cre-ated by film directors are mostly natural law abiding" and lack "violations to nat-ural event perception."[43] Yet examples of defamiliarization linked to enaction will be found in exploratory scenographies allowed by the new cameras that accompa-nied the development of postmodern cinema in the last thirty years (Steadicam, Louma, Technocrane, Air Track Cam, Flying Cam). To explore a new space, we move around, turn our head and glance around as we are walking. Locomotion entails rather irregular movements of the head which our perceptivo-cognitive system has integrated and corrects to stabilize the visual scene. This is why chil-dren suffering from motion sickness are advised to watch the unfolding land-scape from the car as this allows a better matching between the sensation of moving and the visual information. But the first time cinema spectators watched scenes shot in Steadicam (for instance in ROCKY or THE SHINING in the late 1970s), defamiliarization was obvious: indeed, the Steadicam is specifically de-signed to limit the irregularities of human locomotion. Its images thus produced an impression of strangeness, before becoming familiar themselves. Nowadays, most films and television series make extensive use of this technique, it having lost its defamiliarizing effect.

Another example of defamiliarizing, then familiar, exploratory scenography is the 360° travelling shot around Trinity in the opening sequence of THE MATRIX. The effect is defamiliarizing because Trinity is frozen in her movement: this forces the spectator to separate the time of exploration (allocentric count) from the time of events (exocentric count), which never happens in reality (events con-tinue to follow their temporal course whatever the speed at which we explore the environment). Here I apply to the category of time the duality allocentric/exo-centric that Alain Berthoz applies to the category of space.[44]

Lastly, our enactive habits, aided by the fact that our eyes are situated in front of our head and that our body is built according to a vertical bilateral symmetry, encourage us to lateralize our visual environment. We make a distinction between what is in front of us and what is behind us, as well as between what is on our left-hand side and what is on our right-hand side. This lies at the core of the 180° rule in the classical Hollywood style, which can also be found on television when cameras broadcasting a football match are all on the same side of the field (or else the goals could not respectively be postulated at the correct place). Once again, ZAZIE DANS LE MÉTRO subverts this system of expectation of respective positions:

**Film stills 5** *After the expected establishing shot, which situates the scenography of the first dinner between Zazie (Catherine Demongeot) and her uncle (Philippe Noiret), on her left-hand side, a right-left pan starting from the uncle eventually centers on Zazie, followed by a cut which brings us back to the uncle for a left-right pan this time. Our initial reaction is, "there is a new guest, or a part of the decor is worth looking at, which explains this pan"...but actually here is Zazie again. She has "moved places," against our expectations at the moment of the establishing shot, which of course creates a defamiliarizing effect (an object cannot be in different places at the same time, at least not on a non-quantic scale).*

## Beliefs and Opinions

To evoke defamiliarization at this "higher" level of human consciousness, where sociology is important as people's *habitus* is at stake, psychology can offer a few interesting tools, among which the *meme* is one. This term has been coined by evolutionary biologist Richard Dawkins: a *meme* is a unit of human cultural transmission analogous to the *gene*, which is a kind of replicator.[45] The most famous example is when we have a song in mind and we hum it without even noticing, thus spreading it all around us, among the people we meet – which can be described using the epidemiologic models of virus propagation. One may imagine cinematographic memes, for instance a famous quote dropped in a conversation, behavior admired in a hero or, more simply, as anthropologist Marcel Mauss had noted in the 1930s, a way of walking seen on the screen and immediately adopted when we walk in the street because we think it is smart.[46] The existence of a "Famous quotes" section on the IMDb site would be, in this respect, comparable to the sneezing provoked by the flu virus of a contaminated person: they are in both cases "inventions" they have "designed" to replicate themselves more efficiently (if one accepts the questionable idea that quotes and viruses have an "intention to reproduce themselves"!). A fine example of epidemiologic study could also be based on the postmodern style, which is particularly fond of allusions, innuendos and quotes from one film to another, for instance the SHREK or the KILL BILL series, which quote dozens of films and are themselves quoted in other films.[47]

As far as *memetics* is concerned, two types of defamiliarization are possible, corresponding to two components of meme replication.

- A type of defamiliarization through internal mutation, on the model of the Darwinian genetic algorithm.[48] For instance, numerous film extracts are "replicated" very rapidly on YouTube™, but with poor quality, sound, and image, which pushes spectators to pay more attention to their narrative qualities (for example) than to their plastic qualities; or they are broadcast without their title or with wrong information on the production date and on the actors, which may induce a strange reading of them.

- A type of defamiliarization through external mutation, due to an imperfect duplication on the part of the imitator.[49] For instance, when Spike Jonze quotes a scene taken from LES PARAPLUIES DE CHERBOURG in his music video for Björk's IT'S OH SO QUIET in 1995, he erases all the metaphors of the scene to keep only the plastic qualities of the visual idea.[50]

Moreover, one may also advance the idea that memes lose their virulence over time, exactly in the same way organisms develop defenses against viruses. For instance, Maya Deren's film MESHES OF THE AFTERNOON includes two effects directly taken from Méliès:

- the instantaneous transformation of an object into another (a key is transformed into a knife);

- the duplication of an actor through multiple expositions (as in Méliès's L'HOMME-ORCHESTRE, in which Méliès films and duplicates himself, or the actress enters a room where she already is).

But the spectator no longer reads these effects in the way he did in Méliès's time: he reads the transformation of the key into a knife as a metaphor ("opening a locked up place is dangerous as one may get hurt"), which is less defamiliarizing than a transmutation; he also reads the multiple exposition as a metaphor for the "possible selves" of the actress or the multiple parts society compels her to play. Conversely, what may have been read as "normal" in Méliès's time may appear defamiliarizing today: thus, the inflating head of L'HOMME À LA TÊTE DE CAOUTCHOUC may have been read as "an inflating head" by contemporaries, while for the twenty-first-century spectator familiar with tracking shots, it is above all a head we move closer to, not an inflating head.

Of course, as can be seen here (since Méliès's films were quite popular while M. Deren's are confined to art theaters and museums), the sensation of being defamiliarized is conditionally linked to *generic knowledge*. What follows is still another example:

- if the unfolding of the film is inverted and people suddenly start walking backwards in a film for the general public (this is what happens in Claude Miller's DITES-LUI QUE JE L'AIME), the spectator will very likely be defamiliarized;

- if the unfolding of the film is inverted and people suddenly start walking backwards in an experimental film (this is what happens in Júlio Bressane's film O MANDARIM), the spectator will very likely find this normal and will not be defamiliarized in the least.

**Film stills 6** *L'HOMME À LA TÊTE DE CAOUTCHOUC (Georges Méliès, 1901). Méliès used multiple exposure and "matte painting" (the term did not exist) in order to insert the tracking shot of his own head. Since the "compositing" (another modern word) is not perfectly locked, the head's image is a little shaky, which now helps to see the so-called "inflating" (exocentric reading of the scene) as a move toward the head (egocentric reading of the scene).*

At last, the possibility of being defamiliarized is linked to *genetic knowledge*, namely the spectator's technical knowledge about filmmaking. Let us take the example of the magic distortion of bodies in fantasy films. Today, it seems difficult to believe that the contemporary spectators of Abel Gance's LA FOLIE DU DOCTEUR TUBE (1916) would have read the optical distortions of the film as visual traces of distorted bodies, the special effects being so obvious (the camera is simply shooting distorting mirrors that can be found in any funfair; besides, the decor itself is distorted – not only the bodies in it). But another more recent example will help us better understand the process: the magic potion that the main characters of Jean-Marie Poiré's LES VISITEURS (1993) drink is here again supposed to distort their bodies. Unlike Gance, Poiré did not simply film basic mirrors, but resorted to a state-of-the-art technology in 1993, namely warping. But warping is a software distorting 2D images, while we are now used to witnessing distortions of 3D images. As a result, a non-intentional type of defamiliarization occurs, as in LA FOLIE DU DOCTEUR TUBE: what we see is not the distortion of bodies, but of images. The same could be said about Chuck Russell's THE MASK (1994).

**Film still 7** *"Old fashioned" image warping in* THE MASK. *Elastic scraps of flesh are now seen as 2D-parts of the image, rendered using some kind of Photoshop™ Smudge Tool, and no longer as parts of Andrew's face in spite of the fact* THE MASK *is only fifteen years old.*

## The Importance of Interpretative Caution

Resorting to psychological tools (but resorting to the tools of reception sociology would yield the same type of results) encourages us to be aware of generalities. When a film introduces defamiliarizing elements, neither their reading nor their effect is easily predictable from a film scholar's point of view for four main reasons:

(1) Both cinema and television are audiovisual media: they provide second-hand perceptions, and it is always possible to attribute the defamiliarization effect to the medium itself. For instance, a shot filmed in slow motion, by modifying the perception we have of human locomotion, can obviously teach us things we ordinarily miss about this type of locomotion (the trembling of chairs or the irregular rhythm of a foot). But it also teaches us much about cinema itself, proving there is no obligation to respect the convention according to which the rhythm of the recordings should be identical with the projection of the fixed images composing the film.

Because of this possibility to reflect on the medium itself, some theoreticians have shown the affinities existing between Shklovsky's defamiliarization and Derrida's *différance*. Yet, for reasons too complex to be explored here,[51] evolutionary psychology and most "Darwinian" disciplines, broadly speaking, radically reject the concept of *différance*,[52] as they would deny the validity – if they had to reflect upon it – of the vision of "automatic and empty perception" developed by Russian

Formalists as opposed to "aesthetic perception" obtained through defamiliarization. Quite similarly, defamiliarization may be attributed to the film's author without necessarily having an impact on our way of perceiving the world. For instance, if the sound transgressions of Godard's films eventually produce a *Verfremdungseffekt*, it is above all because they are perceived as ways of questioning the artistic habits of mainstream cinema.[53]

(2) Both cinema and television are also narrative arts and, as such, are likely to resort to stylistic metaphors; a discursive practice which consists in commenting on historical events.[54] The comment may be defamiliarizing. This is particularly obvious with the constructivist approach used by Dziga Vertov. Here are three examples taken from Vertov's ENTHUSIASM!

- Defamiliarization through Dutch angles (which we do not usually do as we prefer the line passing through the center of our eyes to be parallel to the ground, and which we are not quite used to seeing in cinema): three frames show a church, each one leaning more and more towards the right; a stylistic metaphor for "religion is falling to pieces;"
- Defamiliarization through a rotation around the vision axis (another thing we seldom do, except on a merry-go-round in a funfair): a pope is filmed from below, then through a pan shot around the axis of the lens, he literally turns a somersault; a stylistic metaphor for "let's overturn religion;"
- Defamiliarization through a modification of the speed at which events occur (a thing impossible to impose upon direct perception, and only to be envisaged with our remembrances or anticipations): when workers leave for work, they are filmed in fast motion; a stylistic metaphor for "these workers are eager to go to work."

(3) If defamiliarization is not expressed through a stylistic metaphor, it may be limited to a reflexive (or autotelic) effect. Viktor Shklovsky saw it this way: to him, it had to draw attention to the perception process itself (metaperception) as an aesthetic process that would underline the *artfulness* of the work[55] (an ideal that contemporary art was to realize under various forms since the avant-garde from 1910 onward, especially by "preventing the execution of sensorimotor routines to which objects used in an ordinary way are submitted").[56] Viewed in this way, Shklovsky's conception is a kind of romantic radicalization of aesthetic judgement according to Kant.[57]

Nothing says (and neither does Shklovsky)[58] that defamiliarization will work as the Soviet film-makers of the 1920s, especially Dziga Vertov, hoped it would work, namely as a correcting tool able to change the inegalitarian tsarist vision anchored in the perceptive habits of people. During these years, French writer Marcel Proust used the metaphor of the "optical instrument" to point out this "correcting" effect of art, especially the modifying action of great artists on our vision of the world, likely to open up our eyes once we come back to daily life. But an optical instrument is supposed to follow our main perceptivo-cognitive routines; if it does not do so, it will be unable to defamiliarize us, one way to "explain" the "failure" of Robert Montgomery's LADY IN THE LAKE.

**Film still 8** LADY IN THE LAKE (Robert Montgomery, 1947). This famous film — famous at least in the academic world — provides more unbelievability than defamiliarization. Adrienne Fromsett (Audrey Totter) is supposed to speak to Phillip Marlowe (Robert Montgomery), but she keeps looking at the camera, since the entire movie is supposed to be shot using the "subjective camera" device. Adrienne seems to believe in the "Venus effect,"[59] but we cannot accept such a violation of our perceptivo-cognitive routines.

However, some scholars assert that the search for "optical instruments" is not the only way to achieve defamiliarization. As demonstrated by M. Szaloky, film scholars such as R. Arnheim, B. Balázs and S. Kracauer, who borrowed the estrangement theoretical tool from Shklovsky, used it with regard to the "disinterested perceptual polymorphy of the Kantian beautiful."[60] In those cases, perceptivo-cognitive routines do not apply anymore.

**Film still 9** *THE MAN WITH THE MOVIE CAMERA* (Dziga Vertov, 1929). *We see both the typist and what the typist sees. We can read the image as a simple dissolving view or a double exposure, attributing the defamiliarization effect to the medium itself (1). Or, we can call it a stylistic metaphor of "self-seeing" (or "sense of selfhood"), which according to Charles Taylor is one of the two distinctive characteristics of the modern age[62] (2). Or, we can admit that such a shot underlines the artfulness of* THE MAN WITH THE MOVIE CAMERA, *preventing the execution of the sensorimotor routine which separates egocentric perception (I see the keyboard of my machine when I work on it) from exocentric perception (I see the typist when she works in front of me) (3). What will happen the next time I use a typewriter or the next time I meet a typist at work? Since the cognitive script which aims to differentiate one's self, objects and others in the world is a condition of survival, I cannot expect to forget it in order to simultaneously combine egocentric and exocentric perception (4). At least, from a Darwinian point of view, we may well consider this shot from* THE MAN WITH THE MOVIE CAMERA *in light of the fact it makes us think about our adaptability.*

(4) Nothing suggests either that defamiliarization, if it ever succeeds in the sense supported by Vertov, lasts beyond the time of the screening, and that once we go back to our occupations, we recognize all the surprising things the eye-camera told us about this world when we were sitting in front of the screen in the real world. Of course, Vertov showed the steel workers he filmed in ENTHUSIASM! what their work looked like from the plant's ceiling; but did they continue to see

themselves in this way once the film was over and the Kino-Train left for new adventures? It seems unlikely they did. What is likely to last is a sort of perceptive relativism: one of the most famous examples used by Shklovsky to illustrate the concept of defamiliarization is Kholstomer ["The Horse"], a Tolstoy short story presenting the world through an old castrated and fallen horse, a narratological technique often optically translated by audiovisual media that loves "putting us in somebody else's shoes," for instance through the use of shot/reverse shot. Yet when reading this text, one has to be quite broadminded, like Shklovsky, about the concept of defamiliarization[61] as the anthropomorphism of narration is patent in it (the old horse's social destiny is much like in Kubrick's BARRY LYNDON, 1975), and strictly perceptive differences are very rarely stressed (ethology was founded quite a long time after the writing of this text). According to a psychologist, this short story simply comes close – like shot-reverse shot – to the "decentering" process, a concept developed by Jean Piaget and referring to the capacity to put oneself in someone else's shoes, which appears during the "age of reason."

An instance of a slightly excessive optimistic belief in the virtues of cinematographic defamiliarization can be found reading the already quoted Peter Wuss's essay, "Analyzing the Reality Effect in Dogma films." In a first step, the author confers to Dogma films the power to show the failures of the society in which they take place: "These films do not just present critical observations of human behavior, but rather show a borderline syndrome of the entire society." In a second step, he explains that Dogma films lead to such an achievement because they use multiple defamiliarizing devices, the most obvious of all being a special way to shoot with handheld cameras. Since the cameramen "walked onto the set without final instructions as to what exactly would happen during the scene and attempted to orient themselves to the action as it happened," it leads to an "extraordinary visual form which provokes [on the spectator side] orienting reactions that intensify the impression of authenticity." Not only does Wuss fall into the reflectionist trap[63] by extrapolating from characters to the whole of society, he also postulates that the spectator is an extraordinarily cooperative person reading the defamiliarizing "awkwardness" of cameramen as a proof of authenticity (not artificiality). As we have just seen, this figure may be read in a purely formalist way as a reflexive submission to the specifications of Dogma (which replaces diegetic illusion with the awareness of being faced with a style exercise), or else as a stylistic metaphor illustrating the characters' lack of balance and foresight in a classic way. It is always dangerous to state "the spectator" is safe, except when dealing with the bottom-up level of direct perception. In all other cases, one must not forget the spectator can be a "pervert" (Staiger) or a "poacher" (Jenkins).

## Conclusion

Audiovisual defamiliarization is the type of issue which had better be approached in an interdisciplinary way as it includes bodily, mental, cultural and social dimensions. To know when defamiliarization operates, one first has to know what is familiar, and within the familiar, what is familiar for oneself only, or for a whole body of persons, or for the whole of humanity. Evolutionary-Cognitive Psychology may serve here to understand why such or such figure is perceived as weird or completely unacceptable, in which case we take refuge in a reflexive reading of the image. If there is too much estrangement, we cease to see the "objects" *through* the image, in spite of the fact we know it is made of pixels, preferring to see the image *as* a collection of pixels. If, however, defamiliarization is partly present in or not too "bottom-up" to be "rejected" by our perceptivo-cognitive system, it may challenge our habitus, namely our *acquired* scheme of perception and cognition.

This type of defamiliarization is not confined to modern art or to the avant-garde. One of the branches of Evolutionary-Cognitive Psychology which deals with aesthetics has been underlining it for a long time, as can be seen by reading Ellen Dissanayake, whose famous book *What Is Art For*[64] opens on this very simple statement: *arts* are a cultural phenomenon, while *Art* is a biological priority. Dissanayake aims at going beyond the modern occidental definition of art, which states that the latter should not be useful and should exist for nothing except itself (art for art's sake), and that it should appeal to the disinterested consumption of people of taste; this definition cannot be expected to have anything but a sociologically and historically circumscribed validity as it does not take human evolution into account.[65] On the other hand, one can say art serves many purposes, among which defamiliarization is but one, either through innovation or meta-perception.[66]

Of course, however essential the interdisciplinary approach may be, it will not avoid conflicts. Some of its dimensions are clearly defined and can be attributed to a specific discipline: the issue of style to aesthetics, that of shape perception to psychology, and that of interpretative habits to reception sociology, for instance. But all of this is not always that simple. The concept of defamiliarization lies at the heart of a quarrel between, on the one hand, the culturalists-constructivists (who think our perceptive habits themselves are structured by our social habitus, or even our language, as the theories involved in the Linguistic Turn would have it) and, on the other hand, the universalists-ecologists (who think our perceptive habits are the product of an evolution in which the modern era, even when the appearance of verbal language is included, is quantitatively of little importance). If "I can see only what I believe" (a constructivist vision in which human beings tend to select in their environment what they already know they can find), no defamiliarization will be able to challenge my habitus as, literally, I will not perceive it. If "I believe only what I can see" (an ecologist vision in which human beings tend to dictate the qualities of objects in their environment by their senses), defamiliarization may challenge my habitus, but I will tend to attribute it to the mediation process between objects and myself. Yet these observations share a common point: in both cases, for defamiliarization to have a chance to operate, it will have to be repeated many times.[67]

# On Perception, *Ostranenie*, and Specificity

László Tarnay

In my contribution to this book, I would like to hint at a possible lineage of the concept of *ostranenie* (остранение) in aesthetic and film theory from the Russian Formalists to the present day. My approach is basically conceptual and unorthodox. My particular aim here is to define a golden thread for the conceptual labyrinth that would lead from Shklovsky's idea – both theoretically and historically – to what I take to be a fundamental challenge to the theory of the moving image, namely the arrival of the newest digital technology of simulation. And I hope to be able to unpack the meaning of *ostranenie* without forcing the original concept too much and incurring the wrath of orthodox criticism.

A related but much more ambitious aim would be to show how fruitful the use of *ostranenie* can be if it is subjected to a historically "tainted" conceptual analysis during which a couple of concepts are woven together from various fields such as the history of art, the development of cinematography, the philosophy of aesthetics, cognition and formal analysis (structuralism). The conceptual web that would thus result could prove how the many-sidedness and flexibility of *ostranenie* works and how much it may have contributed to forming the theory of arts and culture in the last hundred years or so. The accomplishment of this task, however, requires the format of a book.

Focusing on the particular challenge that moving images pose to film theory, we understand that moving images are consistently charting never experienced fantasy worlds of an entirely different substance than our everyday reality. We as viewers whole-heartedly indulge and immerse ourselves in them and point to film theory to explain our indulgence and immersion. In this paper I hope to be able to show that *ostranenie* is a useful tool to come up with such an explanation. My key insight in defining the required golden thread is that the fantasy worlds the moving images simulate for us are no less "realistic" than the world that surrounds us, with the very important condition that realism here constitutes the realist functioning of the senses: what we take to be real depends first and foremost on the nature of our perceptual system. Realism is a question of its automatism. Art – and this is Shklovsky's major insight – lies in deautomatizing our perceptual system. My qualification is that the best way for art to deautomatize perception is to mobilize a special part of our cognitive apparatus adapted to identify individuals, events and objects as a unique and singular phenomenon. I call it "specificity recognition," and I will argue that what Shklovsky prescribes is diametrically opposed to the simulation, and hence realist, effect of digitally produced moving images. What is needed is a special, built-in capacity of our perceptual and cognitive system by means of which the automatism simulation can be sidetracked or blocked. However, more often than not, it is more complex than that. Toward the end, I will propose a four-tier model to account for the various ways in which deautomatized perception can be triggered in viewers. I would like to state that *ostranenie* harbors the core idea of the model.

## Perception and the Task of Film Theory[1]

One of the most comprehensive, if not the biggest, challenge that film theory has to answer to these days is posed by the new digital technology in film production. It started with the change in the material substance of the film "vehicle." After video had partly replaced, but mainly co-existed with celluloid, the classical print, digital production and primary post-production introduced a whole gamut of new technical possibilities from a "perfectly clear" imagery to digitally synthesized figures, from shocking sound effects to variously animated scenes, from "unnatural" colors to extreme close-ups. And not only that; with the latest developments of the camera, the reduction of its size, it has become possible to visualize for the human eye never-previously-experienced scenes like tunnels of rodents, food processing in the intestines, or even sub-atomic physical processes which are not even "visual" in their nature.[2]

It is true that contemporary film theory has already met this challenge to a certain extent when it traced the continuity between ontological realism in film theory (Bazin and Kracauer) and "new age" digitalism. It was ecological film theory, and Joseph D. Anderson and Barbara Anderson in particular, who advocated a realist standpoint vis-à-vis the digital image. They argue that it is not the way motion pictures are produced – analog or digital – but the way they are perceived. As Anderson puts it, movies function "as a programmed surrogate world" in the sense that they interact directly with the perceptual system of the viewers *and* make use of the *same* cognitive system that is employed in everyday life for understanding the natural world.[3]

Their basic claim is that the two acts of perception (of reality and digitally produced images) are the same for our cognitive system. This means that the perceptual similarity or sameness between the "real" thing and its digital image is inherent in our cognition: it is implied in how our perceptual system works and not in how things are out in the world. For there – and we know it by deduction – every single thing, image or object, is dissimilar or specific, to use the term in the title of my contribution to this book. This specificity is, however, perceptually and cognitively lost for us when we turn to mechanically or digitally reproduced images, and we do not regret it that much because we get an enormous compensation: the visual and emotional sense of immersion in an imaginative world experienced as if it were – many times the only – reality. But do we as film viewers ever ponder on what is being lost here, the specificity of individuals, events and objects? A reflection on the specificity of images in the context of *ostranenie* and Benjamin's idea of mechanical reproduction may help to regain a part of this perceptual and cognitive "loss" in mechanically and digitally reproduced images. In calling attention to specificity, my contention is that it is an inherent property of aesthetic perception and stands in diametrical contrast to what has been said to be mass culture.

To buttress my thesis, I will first elaborate on some points found in a seminal article by Walter Benjamin, who is the principal source for anyone reflecting on the consequences of mechanical reproduction. Media theorists often describe the invention and the use of "new" visual technology, like the microscope, magnifying glasses, or the camera, as prosthetic devices which in most cases improve normal human perception. Making use of them, we see better or even see things which otherwise would have remained invisible to us. The human perceptual system and the artificial aid collaborate to produce a heightened visual effect. Consequently, it seems fairly unproblematic to extend the prosthetic case to cover the most recent digital technology. We can say in a slightly modified manner that the new digital technique creates images or visualizes things just as the human perceptual system perceives visual stimuli in the eye and creates images in the mind. In this paper I build upon this parallel between digital technology and the human visual system as the basis of the major perceptual shift that digitalized motion pictures caused, both culturally and aesthetically. The major propagators of this shift were Paul Virillo and Vilém Flusser.[4] They argue that the introduction of the camera and other "new" technology more than a hundred years ago created a new regime of perception, despite the fact that the physiology of the human eye has remained the same. Against an ecologically committed theorist like Joseph D. Anderson, who claims that viewers watch movies with the same perceptual apparatus we have evolved with, philosophers of the new media highlight the cultural determinants of vision and the role of prosthetic devices in shaping human perception. I think that the ecological and cultural conceptions of vision do not necessarily exclude each other, but I cannot argue that issue now. Here I would only like to recall that people quickly become habitualized to a new technology after the "novelty" period has worn off. Having become habitualized, it is a very small step for viewers to "immerse" in the "surrogate" world that the new technology makes accessible to them. Even if we accept that the new technology has indeed *changed* the viewers' mode of perception, they soon take the new regime for granted. When the young generation goes to see fantasy films like the HARRY POTTER series, they do not question the "reality" of what they see: culturally speaking, they are born into the new regime of vision. The immediacy of the medium has had its effect. Film theorists would put it slightly differently. Making use of Richard Wollheim's famous distinction between *seeing through* and *seeing in*, they would argue that by seeing the scene through, film viewers would not be aware or primarily conscious of the fact that images appear in the surface of the screen.[5] To put it in semiotic terms, seeing the surrogate world directly through the image amounts to closing the distance between the image and its model; the two are no longer distinguishable for the viewers. As a consequence, the perceptual process becomes automatic and impermeable to consciousness. And it is all the more so, if the image is indistinguishable not only from its model, but also from other copies of the same image, a commonplace in an age of mechanical reproduction.[6] It is as if any two *acts* of perceiving a copy of an image were indistinguishable from each other, hence they appear to be the same. It means that similarity between image and model applies not only to the higher level of copies of the same image but to the meta-level of acts of perception. Let us call it *perceptual sameness*: it derives from the way copies are reproduced, and it means that because of the lack of perceptual distance between the individual copies, the viewer does not distinguish between the "original" image and the image object; they are the same. Images thus become *simulacra*, which have lost the "original" relationship with their referents. They are images which *float* in a space of pure similarity, a space in between the signifier and the signified.

Now it is an aesthetically crucial consequence that an image which is "indistinguishable" from its model cannot be perceptually relevant to the perceiver since it masks all differences – if there are any – between perceiving it and perceiving its model. It means that there is virtually nothing in the image that would attract the viewer's attention to its status *as* an image vis-à-vis its model.[7] In other words, the secondary consciousness of the medium cannot be perceptually anchored. Similarly, if something is automatic and non-conscious, it cannot be aesthetically relevant either. It is at this point that *ostranenie* reveals all its relevance to contemporary aesthetics. Undoubtedly, the term can be understood in many ways, some of which I will elaborate on in the subsequent paragraphs. Without denying its inherent historicity and relativity, in my view the concept of *ostranenie* rises above history. In its *applications* in formal analysis of particular technologies, trends or individual pieces, *ostranenie* is subject to history and can therefore be relative. Any concrete perceptual act may become automatic and hence may have to be defamiliarized. The concept itself, apart from its particular content, is rather like a norm aloof of history. Like the principles of evolution, it specifies a guideline for aesthetics (or its history), which says that the formal character of art is very closely tied to the *type of perception* to which it lends itself.

Walter Benjamin's seminal article about the reproducibility of the photographic image popularized the idea of the *aura* as a "unique phenomenon of a distance" between the perceiver and the perceived object. He claims that every natural and art object is tied to its *hic et nunc*, its position in space, in which it is historically rooted and to which it owes its uniqueness and singularity. As such it exists in a "splendid isolation," at a distance from the perceiver, which at the same time safeguards its aura. As soon as it is detached from its *hic et nunc* and is appropriated, its distance evaporates, and its aura is lost. Benjamin seems to imply that an object of art loses its artfulness and becomes an object of distraction for mass audiences. Although for him reproducibility is a form of appropriation and is not very beneficent to the aura, I will try to show that artfulness is not dependent on reproducibility, an assertion that is also firmly grounded in Shklovsky's idea of defamiliarizing perception.[8] As I already hinted, the capacity of recognizing unique physical substances in contrast to categorical perception relies on a specific part of our cognitive apparatus. I therefore borrow the term "specificity" as a common denominator not only in reference to the core concept of *ostranenie*, but also in reference to Benjamin's aura, Sontag's photographic distance, and Sobchack's view on "the film's body," in the sense that in each case the recipient is to recognize the specificity – the uniqueness and singularity – of the experienced object. Finally, my methodological thought in tracing the lineage of *ostranenie* is shaped by Shklovsky's idea of defamiliarization as deautomatized perception. In the process of tracing its lineage, I will focus on the relation between the formal elements of *ostranenie* and not so much on its historicity by primarily following Benjamin's line of thought.

Before I begin my discussion, let me briefly revisit the elements of the original concept of *ostranenie*, especially those which were echoed, rephrased or modified in subsequent theoretical thought. *Ostranenie* is fundamentally two-sided, as it resides on the one hand in *the form of the artwork itself*, but it is also expected to produce a corresponding *effect during the act of reception*. This latter effect is generally called – by the Formalists – "defamiliarization." The way they formulate defamiliarized perception, the core element of *ostranenie*, allows for two different interpretations. It can either be taken as (i) object definition (literariness) or as (ii) a conceptual tool. I would like to address the first one. The Formalists' main aim was to define literariness, or the proper object of literary theory, which they identified mainly in different forms of language (prose, poetry, rhythm, etc.). Yet they were ready to embrace other media like film and extend their definition so as to include moving images. They generalized the idea that the defamiliarization of perception fosters or enhances the capacity of seeing new conceptual relations among or linking otherwise different objects, and they opposed it to nineteenth-century associativism, which emphasized the underlying or reflexive associative chains, innate or marked out by past experience. Accordingly, they contrasted perceiving with knowing, the latter standing roughly for automatized knowledge. Automatized or habitualized perception is not only opposed to defamiliarized perception but is very closely related, if not reduced, to knowledge. "The purpose of art is to impart the sensation of things as they are perceived and not as they are known."[9] It is knowledge as categorical perception which can become habitual.

From the formalist argument it even follows that the specificity of an object cannot be known but only perceived; if it were to become part of our overall conceptual scheme, it would lead to the habituation of perception which needs to be defamiliarized or distanced once again. Furthermore, knowledge of an object is a way of appropriating it, that is, reducing the distance between the subject and the object.

Athough Russian Formalists refrained from using *ostranenie* as a methodological tool, Shklovsky insisted that it should be applied to the history of art in order to describe it as a series of formal changes: according to their historical poetics, it is not so much the images that change from period to period but rather the poets' technique to create a style which challenges the *principle of economy and energy* that "delivers the greatest amount of thought in the fewest words."[10]

The history of art is then defined as a history of changes in style. And changes are effected by the poets precisely because old forms have become automatized. Defamiliarization is needed to play down the effect of automatization. It is in this sense that *ostranenie* applies to the history of art.[11]

## Knowledge as Closeness vs. Specificity as Distance

Although there are two basic layers of *ostranenie*, a perceptionist and an analytic-historic one to be precise, the former is the fundamental one. Apart from how one would translate the term (defamiliarization, distanciation, etc.), to say that "[t]he technique of art is to make objects 'unfamiliar', to make forms difficult, to increase the difficulty and length of perception because the process of perception is an aesthetic end in itself and must be prolonged"[12] is to claim that "the artfulness of an object" resides in creating or preserving a distance from the object itself. Yet it is not easy to understand what the prolongation of perception really constitutes. Does it mean that the perceiver should not strive for easily accessible knowledge but remain in uncertainty or "half-truth" about the object perceived? If it is, Shklovsky would be found to echo the idea of English Romanticism. Take the famous dictum "Beauty is truth, truth beauty" which summarizes Keats's idea of literariness or artfulness described in detail in his letters. There he compares what he takes to be the highest form of poetry, that of Shakespeare, to the meaning of ancient myths: both are doomed to remain forever dim and inscrutable. He values Dante, Shakespeare and other eminent authors because they did not want to squeeze "the truth, the whole truth and nothing but the truth" from reality. They keep a distance. For them, prolonged perception constitutes the foundation of poetry as well as a failure to know. *Ode on a Grecian Urn* is an apotheosis of that failure, as is Samuel Taylor Coleridge's *Kubla Khan*.[13] Obviously, the examples could be multiplied. What matters here is the basically Kantian coupling of aesthetic feeling and ethical judgment,[14] which also lies at the core of Benjamin's aura. By refraining from absolute knowledge, the poet demonstrates respect for the object perceived. In renouncing possession of it, his humbleness shows. But this is not the whole story. By reversing the poles of the equation, beauty and truth, Keats echoes the Kantian idea of recompense that is gained in and by means of the ethical stance taken toward the world. This may be the point where things show their real nature, especially when they are not "pressed" to do so, when they are kept at a remove from knowledgeable man. As I understand, it is by means of such a distance in or during perception that, following Shklovsky, the "stony character of the stone" is given to the subject (perceiver). I would add that what is actually given to us is the object's specificity, but let me explain. Maybe it would be better if we define knowledge as procedural knowledge, the knowledge of *how*. Such knowledge is always functional. Knowing the stone in this sense means you are able to throw it, kill birds with it, hammer a nail with it, build or pave roads with it, etc. Thus, it is exactly how we functionally categorize things, so we have chairs to sit on, tables to write on, or stones to throw. But the question is this: does the "real" character of the stone show itself during such appropriations?

Let me summarize. I have been trying to weave together three different threads. The first is Shklovsky's idea that perception should be prolonged so that objects get removed from the automatism of perception when they fall under various already known categories. The second idea – crucial for Deleuze – is that deautomatizing perception is tantamount to constituting a challenge to the intellect which "normally" can only classify. The third and final element in this line of thought is the core element of the Romantic Sublime itself by constituting a challenge to the system of human perception. In this case, either the familiarizing and appropriating automatism blocks the new perception, or the perception of the new leaves the object for the viewer at a distance and in a penumbra of half-truths to such a degree that – as Shklovsky says – the object "itself" does not matter.[15] Can we really say that prolonged perception, perception *per se*, is a perception without an object? Do we really not perceive anything? My suggestion here is – as I indicated earlier – that by rejecting categorical perception, that is, by not being able to place the object within already known categories and thereby prolonging the perceptional process, our cognitive system resorts to "specificity recognition," thus the perceiver comes into contact with the object itself, i.e. with the object in its specificity.

Seen in this light, perhaps it does not seem too far-fetched to say that Benjamin's aura preserves the core element of the Sublime of Romanticism. And maybe it would be worth comparing his concept and *ostranenie* in terms of the formal characteristics of the Romantic Sublime. He also uses nature as an example of being distant *and* having an aura.

We define the aura of the latter as the unique phenomenon of a distance, however close it may be. If, while resting on a summer afternoon, you follow with your eyes a mountain range on the horizon or a branch which casts its shadow over you, you experience the aura of those mountains, of that branch. Namely, the desire of contemporary masses to bring things "closer" spatially and humanly, which is just as ardent as their bent toward overcoming the uniqueness of every reality by accepting its reproduction.[16]

Certainly, for Benjamin distance and closeness are spatial attributes, while *ostranenie* seems to be an attribute of perceived objects or thought-objects. It is a distance between perceptions that "delivers the greatest amount of thought in the fewest words."[17] Here Shklovsky quotes Spencer about the working of the principle of economy which he accepts, as long as its domain is "practical" language; however, he refuses to extend it to the language of poetry. A possible – and maybe the only – explanation is that for Shklovsky the purpose (*raison d'être*) of practical language is still knowledge, whereas poetry is for the "senses," that is, it is deeply perceptual in its nature. (Note the recurrent reference to rhythm, the most musical aspect, in poetry.) The contrast is once again between the appropriating of knowledge and the defamiliarization of perception.[18] Thus, it would be difficult to argue that bringing things "'closer' spatially and humanly" is essentially different from appropriating or knowing them. Listen to what Benjamin says about the epistemic potential of the new media:

> Every day the urge grows stronger to get hold of an object at very close range by way of its likeness, its reproduction. Unmistakably, reproduction as offered by picture magazines and newsreels differs from the image seen by the unarmed eye. Uniqueness and permanence are as closely linked in the latter as are transitoriness and reproducibility in the former. To pry an object from its shell, to destroy its aura, is the mark of a perception whose "sense of the universal equality of things" has increased to such a degree that it extracts it even from a unique object by means of reproduction.[19]

Clearly, uniqueness or specificity of an object of art is resistant to the "sense of the universal equality of things" that the photographic image is saturated with according to Benjamin. The fact that Benjamin calls this knowledge "perception" brings him even closer to Shklovsky, for whom such a sense would be nothing but automatized perception.

## Recasting Ostranenie in Cognitive Poetics

Benjamin is very skeptical – to say the least – with regard to the fact that films can ever have an aura. At the same time, he seems to be desperate to find some aspect of the photographic image that would indicate it has a special quality that other art forms lack. Thus, in the second half of his paper, he hits on two elements, the close-up, especially of the face, and slow motion, which can render the film image unique and singular in his view. It is beyond the scope of this paper to delve into the entire argument Benjamin constructs in favor of the film image despite its loss of aura because of its reproducible character. Instead, I would like to restrict his argument to an analogy of the senses: touch and vision. By emphasizing tactile visuality as opposed to optical visuality (the classical paradigm), he paves the way for a multi-modal conception of film viewing that film phenomenologists after Merleau-Ponty have developed in its entirety. With regard to the close-up and slow motion, Benjamin argues that films do not simply give a sharper and more detailed view but reveal completely "new structural formations of the subject," qualities and sensations which the viewer never experienced.[20] That is to say, close-up and slowness in films prove to be the best means to *defamiliarize perception*. Writing half a century later, Vivian Sobchack suggests that the film experience constitutes an encounter with the Other: the film itself makes visible the Other's intraceptive world, the enclosed innermost territory of one's phenomenological life, which can never be shared in everyday communication. On the basis of a multi-modal theory (or phenomenology) of perception, cinematic visuality appears to be a unique and singular experience, despite the way moving images are produced, projected and reproduced. (Note however that in Sobchack's approach the distance between the perceiving subject and the perceived object or the Other – which, in Benjamin's view, the film dissolves by penetrating into the "flesh" of the world – is re-established.) Thus, starting with the multi-modality of film perception (haptic visuality for one), it can be argued that films can be credited with a kind of specificity that is close to the way the Formalists thought about literariness and defamiliarized perception. The range of defamiliarized perception extends significantly if tactile, and possibly other, forms of perception are considered for analysis.

Setting Benjamin's argument about the loss of aura aside, it remains to be seen how the experiential situation of viewing relates to the Formalists' doctrine concerning the economy principle of mental effort. When Shklovsky refers to the "stoniness of the stone," he is attacking the doctrine that art constitutes "thinking in images." He replaces this doctrine with the idea that art constitutes the arranging of images in a particular manner so that the artfulness of an object, and not the object itself, could be experienced: "The purpose of art is to impart the sensation of things as they are perceived and not as they are known." But what does "artfulness" really mean for Benjamin? To avoid begging the question – art is experiencing the artfulness of things – he turns to the perceptual process itself and states that "the process of perception is an aesthetic end in itself." But why insist on the purpose of making objects "unfamiliar"? Most likely, Benjamin brings up this particular purpose because unfamiliar objects deautomatize perception *and* dissolve its transparency. The subject becomes conscious of her perceptual processes. However, art should not aim at creating new concepts, something the imaginists wanted to do; rather, it should find the way to prolong the process and to increase its difficulty.

If the purpose of art is to enhance perception, the object of perception must be quite "complicated." But what does complicated mean here? We cannot simply answer that it refers to triggering a "long and difficult" process. In Tarnay/Pólya we argued for an independent cognitive mechanism, which from a very early evolutionary stage was responsible for recognizing individual objects, in the animal world mostly individual conspecifics.[21] We called this capacity "specificity recognition" and contrasted it with "categorical perception." The latter is a very general, all-purpose cognitive mechanism by means of which individual objects are assigned to their respective categories. We use this capacity every time we want to know what things are like, to identify them, or we use procedural knowledge. In contrast, we need the other capacity, specificity recognition, in our social and family life.[22] Our argument becomes relevant to the present discussion when we move onto the field of aesthetics and extend the argument about specificity to cover individual works of art or, more precisely, aesthetic pleasure, or in the terminology of the present paper, aesthetic perception. In short, Pólya and I stated that as spectators of art we make use of the very same capacity, *specificity recognition*, when we perceive and process individual works. The underlying idea is that to recognize an individual as such requires a much more fine-grained sense organ or sensitive apparatus than with categorical perception. While categorical recognition can be coarse-grained, as for example in *Gestalt* perception, individual recognition can easily go wrong if the "pattern" is not identified finely enough.[23]

Aesthetic perception, in our view, capitalizes on the inherent hyper-sensitivity of the sense organs which is a result of evolution, although it lost most of its function when social evolution foregrounded visuality. Although our system for visual recognition is very limited in individuating singularities,[24] it displays an extremely fine differentiating capacity. While natural languages have some 80 terms for shades of color ad maximum, the human eye can distinguish up to 1600 different shades if necessary.[25] Although we possess a very finely tuned visual system, experiencing art can be more than challenging for an "untrained" eye just because the "hyper-sensitive" range of our visual system is not used in everyday life.

Seen in light of the difference of *categorical* perception versus *specificity* perception, there are still two ways to unpack the meaning of the conception of *ostranenie*, but this time the equivocation stems from the definition of a "property" like stoniness. Is it something unique or uniquely perceived, or something that other objects, other stones, can have as well? Does it singularize its object, or does it align it with other objects? Accordingly, we have the following two options:

**A)** *Defamiliarization* or *ostranenie* is the artistic technique of forcing the audience to *see common things in an unfamiliar or strange way*, in order to enhance perception of the familiar. It is a didactic tool in the history of twentieth-century art, including Dada, constructivism, Postmodernism, Brechtian epic theater or even science fiction.

The list of art movements and trends is by no means exhaustive. The core concept originates with the Surrealists and is rooted in their dictum – once stated by Lautrèamont – about the juxtaposition of otherwise different, incongruent or even incoherent properties. The concept can be traced back and forth within the history of film theory as well as in literary theory. Let me illustrate with one example how defamiliarization might work in this sense. Take visitation, a very common topic in Renaissance painting. We can even say that the topic itself became so canonical that it automatized perception. Painters strove to give an individual taint to a familiar topic. Although it is not easy to define where defamiliarization begins, surely one typical way to defamiliarize the concept of visitation perceptually is Tintoretto's solution exhibited in the Scuola San Rocco in Venice. Tintoretto presents a decrepit house for the setting of Mary's visitation by the angel Gabriel. Poverty contrasts with the spirituality of angelic conversation. Thus, Tintoretto achieves a highly unique and singular – defamiliarized – representation of a familiarized topic.

It is especially cognitive film theory which foregrounds the processing of film images regarding classical Hollywood and mainstream popular movies, as well as avant-garde and experimental films.[26] Drawing upon the findings of cognitive semantics and cognitive pragmatics, cognitive film scholars investigate both the bottom-up and top-down cognitive processes that film viewing may trigger in the viewer. Naturally, what is preserved from the original concept is the idea of defamiliarization, yet reinterpreted in cognitive terms. Already inherent in Shklovsky's original concept of defamiliarization was the idea that poetry is meant to play down the effect of the principle of mental effort or economy. The latter principle signifies that when trying to understand a given "message," people aim at retrieving the maximum informational content with the least possible effort. Thus, the principle of economy presents ideas in a way that they can be apprehended with the least possible mental effort or to deliver the greatest amount of thought in the fewest words.[27] This is almost exactly the same principle that Sperber and Wilson introduced as the guiding principle of understanding language: to achieve the greatest possible contextual effect, to make it possible for the subject to apprehend the greatest number of contextual inferences and/or to increase the epistemic value of her beliefs with the least possible effort.[28] The only – and not insignificant – difference is that the Formalists considered the principle the very thing that genuine art like poetry should oppose, whereas relevance theorists argued for a general application of the principle. They claimed that the principle accounts for all kinds of language use, including metaphoric, ironic and poetic speech. The principle of relevance appears to be a general human capacity that works equally well when the recipient of art is confronted with disparate or seemingly incoherent elements and has to make the most of their juxtaposition. The recipient is still guided by the principle of squeezing out the maximum amount of information with the least effort, even if it is the *Ulysses* she is trying to understand. To put it more formally, according to Sperber and Wilson's relevance theory, to understand the meaning of a proposition or, let us add, an image means to draw the highest number of contextual implications made available to the recipient by the given proposition or image with the least possible mental effort.[29] Automatization and deautomatization are subject to the same laws of cognition. The difference lies not in the types of processes they evoke, but rather in the time of processing. Deautomatization may be compared to a deviation route. To arrive at a destination through deviations does not mean that the traffic rules are different. Hence automatized and deautomatized routes also differ in their respective history: deautomatized routes are never, or almost never, trodden paths which may or may not take longer than a normal path.

The other meaning of *ostranenie* is diametrically opposed to the first in that it indeed marks out a qualitatively different route of processing.

**B)** *Ostranenie* is a mechanism by means of which the *specificity* of the world is perceived: "it exists to make one feel things, to make the stone stony."[30] In this sense, it contrasts with knowing things, which always implies appropriation by means of concepts or categories when the new is being reduced to the already known. While the latter is automatized knowledge, *ostranenie* is the idea that the meaning of the unique and the singular is not constituted even by an exhaustive list of shareable properties.

In Tarnay and Pólya (2005) we proposed a four-tier model of aesthetic pleasure.[31] The four levels are:
1. categorical
2. aspect change
3. specificity recognition
4. modulation

The first meaning of *ostranenie* can be explained by our first level, where thing and event perception occurs. Agreeing with Ramachandran and Hirstein[32] that recognizing camouflaged objects was a crucial ability in human evolution and that it triggered a strong positive emotional reflex, I would say that recognizing the elements of the scene of the visitation in Tintoretto's painting is of the same kind. If the viewer hesitates in recognizing the figures against the background, as may be the case with a William Turner painting, I would say that the viewer's perception is being "prolonged" which is a first step toward "artfulness of perception," as Shklovsky would have it. The importance of the object recedes into the background, and the importance of the process of perceiving the object takes over. It belongs to our second level of aspect seeing. It may be argued that the first two levels, category perception and aspect change, can partly overlap, especially in cases of defamiliarization in Shklovsky's sense of the word. If the result of defamiliarization is such that the previous automatized category is still – at least partly – applicable to the new image/object, the viewer may find herself switching between the "old" and "new" categories when contemplating the "defamiliarizing" picture. Thus, the viewer of Tintoretto's visitation may want to compare Tintoretto's unusual setting with the canonical setting of the same scene in a church or a Renaissance city structure. Not unsurprisingly, Tintoretto himself painted a visitation of this kind. However, "defamiliarizing" cases differ from genuine examples of aspect change in that they imply the use of memory, since the two aspects are not directly perceivable in the *same* image as they are in, say, the duck/rabbit picture. That is, the viewer switches between a *seen* aspect and a *remembered* one. Another clear example of the second level of perceiving aspects is Andrea Mantegna's picture of St. Sebastian, in which viewing *shifts* take place between two different aspects (identifications): a mass of brick beneath the marble column, or a grotesque head being chased away by the horsemen of the Apocalypse in the cloud. Similarly, perception seems to be forever locked between two competing categorical perceptions like "head" and "landscape" in the painting by Joos de Momper.[33] The logic behind our model is very simple. We think that aesthetic pleasure derives basically either from categorical perception, when we recognize members of already known categories, or from recognizing the singularity and uniqueness of a given object. In addition, there can also be some "extra" pleasure generated if the object is constantly shifting categories like the famous duck/rabbit drawing, or if its specificity is changing. Thus, by analogy with the first two levels of categorical perception, we define the third level as specificity perception (of texture). The fourth level, which we call "modulation," is the level where perception is shifting between two forms of specificity recognition.[34] Recalling the touch/vision analogy in Benjamin, I claim that specificity of an object is located mostly in its *texture*, for it is especially the graininess of the picture which requires a very highly tuned perceptual apparatus. The latter stands in neat contrast to what Shklovsky calls "algebraic method of thought" with which "we apprehend objects only as shapes with imprecise extensions; we do not see them in their entirety but rather recognize them by their main characteristics.[...] The process of 'algebrization,' the over-automatization of an object, permits the greatest economy of perceptive effort."[35]

A very telling example of textural specificity can be found in Antonioni's BLOW-UP. It has become almost a commonplace to refer to the parallel between the photographic process of blowing up and revealing secrecy. The crucial point in the film's narrative comes when Thomas begins to retrace the direction in which Jane is looking in the picture shot in the park. While his suspicion of mystery is aroused by the woman's eerie gaze, his hunch becomes overwhelming when he first scrutinizes and then magnifies the crucial section of the fence in the original photo. By magnifying the photograph, he alters the textual quality of the image that enables him to see what he failed to notice before, but that does not mean he is able to solve the mystery. It displays two important properties. First, the series of snapshots trigger a shifting categorical or figure perception in the viewer (Thomas and the audience); from seeing the figures in the foreground to seeing the killer's face and his gun in the background. As the latter becomes more and more perceivable, the "original" picture turns less and less clear-cut. Finally, the face stands out, together with the gun, after which the dead body "emerges" within the grains of the magnified photo. All this seems to be a fairly straightforward categorical identification on a par with the famous picture of a Dalmatian dog used in psychology to demonstrate Gestalt or figure/ground perception. The image is an example of "Emergence." The Dalmatian in this well-known image is not recognized by first identifying its parts, but rather as a whole and all at once (as an emergence of parts). The whole cognitive procedure can be assigned to the second level of our model of aesthetic pleasure. But this is not the whole story. The photo must have the property of infinite magnifiability inherent in its material substance. It is by this property that the close-up reveals its specificity – to repeat Benjamin – "[t]he enlargement of a snapshot does not simply render more precise what in any case was visible, though unclear: it reveals entirely new structural formations of the subject."[36] The surface visibility of the image is then determined by the underlying granular structure of the image. It is this granular texture that constitutes the specificity of the image like the inner structure of the iris constitutes one's individuality. In effect, BLOWUP thematizes the making visible of the photograph and realigns it with Post-impressionistic pointillist painting. It belongs to the third – specificity – level of our model of aesthetic pleasure.

Making the underlying granular structure of the image visible is nothing but a way of defamiliarizing or deautomatizing the "original" image: by changing the figure/ground relation in the image, it is not simply that another object is being focused on – something similar to the zooming effect – but that the new figure/ground relation becomes extremely difficult to perceive. There is hardly anything else that defamiliarizes perception to such a degree than the micro-texture of a physical substance.[37] It corroborates Shklovsky's diachronic idea that there is no form outside history, first because it is always a given historical context in which a formal feature defamiliarizes habitualized perception, and second because a defamiliarizing form may later become habitualized. Granular texture was once a "natural" attribute of documentary films, so much so that people "saw through" it without being conscious of it.[38]

## Conclusion and Beyond

In conclusion, it seems that it is not the reproducibility of art objects in itself that leads to the automatization of perception. It is the ambition to appropriate the image by reducing it "economically" to the already known. What art as "defamiliarization" and experimental films do, in contrast, is that they constitute a challenge for higher-order cognition by presenting a manifold of experience that cannot be subsumed under any known or a priori categories and thereby cannot be individuated consistently as determinable objects of experience. This theme highlights an important aspect of human perception. It was Gilles Deleuze who developed a philosophy of moving images, foregrounding the role of the sensible in creative thinking. One of his key terms is "deterritorializing," by which he means that a given set of concepts should be defamiliarized, that is, subverted.[39] Capitalizing on Bergson's reflection on creative evolution, Deleuze assigns the role of deterritorializing to the senses and the sensible.[40] For him the radically new, a radically new experience, can only come through the senses and not through some rearrangement of the already known. For Deleuze it is only the sensible that can challenge thought: "The sensible is opposed to the model of recognition since it is not a component of a remembered, imagined, or conceived object [...]."[41] It escapes or challenges all knowledge innate or based on previous experience. Furthermore, it is the sensory challenge, that is the perceptually new, that gives "new" fuel to thought.[42] Ostranenie is an important landmark in conceptualizing this challenge. When Shklovsky talks about defamiliarization as the prolongation of perception and opposes it to associativism and the use of images, he in fact foregrounds the sensible as the source of poetry and art. Its legacy is preserved in the cognitive approaches to art and film, which focus on the so-called bottom-up processes in the brain like specificity recognition. But it is also upheld in aesthetic theories which, following Benjamin, argue for the uniqueness and singularity of the art object as a form of distance in the digital age.

# Estrangement and the Representation of Life in Art

*Barend van Heusden*

Viktor Shklovsky considered estrangement, or "ostranennie," to be the basic function of art. He was right, but for the wrong reasons. In his work on the subject, he mingled three theoretical perspectives: a theory of perception, a theory of semiosis, and a theory of abstraction. On the basis of an analysis of his discourse, I will argue that the concept of estrangement can and should be reassessed in contemporary art theory; that is to say, in the context of a theory of art as a specific instance of human semiotic cognition, realized in a variety of media, and focused on imaginative self-consciousness.

In "Art as Technique,"[1] the famous essay he wrote in 1917, Viktor Shklovsky argues that perception "as it becomes habitual, becomes automatic."[2] Thus, he says, for instance, that "all of our habits retreat into the area of the unconsciously automatic."[3] This process of habituation accounts for the fact that in ordinary speech, we often leave phrases unfinished and words half expressed.

The process Shklovsky points at here seems to be a very basic cognitive one, namely that of habit formation. This process is certainly not restricted to perception; it pertains to behavior as such. Habits are not genetically programmed (in which case we would speak about "instincts" or "responses") but are learned, as in the case of language use. We learn how to walk and talk, and in the long run we forget about it and perform these activities more or less unconsciously. Habituation is a general characteristic of human action, it is a way of saving energy. By relying on habits, we save the energy with which we deal with what is strange or different and therefore potentially more dangerous. From this perspective, habituation is certainly to be cherished. The more we can rely on habits, the better.[4] Why spend energy on dealing with what is a little different, but not different enough to jeopardize our habits? Why bother about, for instance, "the stoniness of stones," when we can rely on our habits to make sense of the world?

Shklovsky, however, takes us one step further. Perception, he states, not only becomes automatic. In the process, he says, things are replaced by symbols: "In this process, ideally realized in algebra, things are replaced by symbols."[5] I suggest that we try to disentangle the intricate argument that underlies this statement. How do we get from the first step in the argument, which was about the habituation or automatization of perception, to this second one, which is about the replacement of the thing by a symbol? Should we assume that a habit of perception is the same thing as a symbol? This seems to be highly improbable, as it is unclear what the notion of the symbolic would add to that of a habit of perception; unless, of course, one term is just a synonym for the other. In that case, however, the semiotic is reduced to the habitual. But a habit is not automatically a symbol. A habit (of perception or otherwise) is not "about" the object perceived, nor is intentionality required for successful perception. We find habits everywhere in the world of the living. Many animal species rely on habits of perception and action without being able to use signs. However, in Shklovsky's argument about the defamiliarization in art, the *symbolic nature* of habitual perception plays an important role.

Where does the sign come from if it is not simply the result of habit formation? Apparently, perception becomes semiotic when the cognitive process involved is not only a process of perceiving, but also a process of signifying (or signification). Objects, in semiosis, are not only perceived but are also signified, which means that they are recognized as an instance or "token" of a more stable representation or "type." The stable representation can be a perceptual image or schema, or it can be a concept or a logical structure. The difference between the stable representation (the "type") and the occurrence (the "token") turns perception into *semiotic* perception, and human cognition into *semiotic* cognition, that is, into a process of signification or semiosis.

The semiotic process is therefore a process of dealing with the difference between more or less stable types (the signs) on one side and ever-changing tokens (the occurrences or "reality") on the other. As humans we have only a limited number of semiotic strategies at our disposal: from simple negation of the difference, via the imaginative transformation of the available schemata, to the use of abstract concepts and structures. The "algebra" Shklovsky refers to in the quotation above refers to these stable types or signs.[6]

Insight into the nature of semiotic cognition allows us to understand the point Shklovsky is trying to make in "Art as Technique." The habit formation of which he speaks is at work in the process of signification as well. Instead of dealing with the difference a situation or object confronts us with, we tend to ignore it, relying upon the available schemata. We tend to assimilate, not accommodate to a changing world.

In the process of signification, ignoring differences is hazardous. Shklovsky points out the dangers of such a fundamentally "lazy" attitude. He also stresses the fact that by discarding signification, which is not, of course, restricted to perception, we are in danger of losing our humanity: "And so life is reckoned as nothing. Habitualization devours works, clothes, furniture, one's wife, and the fear of war. If the whole complex lives of many people go on unconsciously, then such lives are as if they had never been."[7] Instead of dealing with difference and change, and questioning the worth of our semiotic habits (our schemata, concepts, etc.) in each new situation, we rely upon them almost unconsciously, and reality recedes into the background. "By this 'algebraic'[8] method of thought we apprehend objects only as shapes with imprecise extensions; we do not see them in their entirety but rather recognize them by their main characteristics. We see the object as though it were enveloped in a sack. We know what it is by its configuration, but we see only its silhouette."[9] This is a crucial point: humanity is tightly connected, not to perception as such, but to semiotic perception, and to the semiotic in general. Our elaborate semiotic capacities distinguish us from other living organisms and allow us to deal with the world in a very specific way, using our imagination and our faculties of abstraction. What is at stake here is the semiotic process, rather than perception as such.

The argument has become a complex one, as Shklovsky's criticism can be understood as aiming at three different flaws at least: simple habit formation in perception (the most unlikely variant), the general abstraction process which is inherent in the use of signs (as derived from the "algebra" quotes), and the one-sidedness of a semiotic process that is reduced to the assimilation of that which differs from the available schemata. I strongly suspect that the latter is what Shklovsky's argument is really about, but due to a lack of a refined theory of perception, cognition, and semiosis, this isn't self-evident.

We can now turn to Shklovsky's argument about art. The passage from "Art as Technique" about what art must achieve is deservedly famous:

> Art exists that one may recover the sensation of life; it exists to make one feel things, to make the stone *stony*. The purpose of art is to impart the sensation of things as they are perceived and not as they are known. The technique of art is to make objects unfamiliar, to make forms difficult, to increase the difficulty and length of perception because the process of perception is an aesthetic end in itself and must be prolonged. *Art is a way of experiencing the artfulness of an object; the object is not important.*[10]

We have argued that unfamiliarity is inherent in the semiotic process. A certain degree of unfamiliarity assures us that the reality we live in does not coincide with our representations of it. Thanks to the ubiquitous difference, we are able to distinguish occurrences ("reality") from our representations (signs). Semiotic cognition means, therefore: dealing with difference. The greater the difference, the harder the semiotic work. It is therefore semiosis itself that forces the unfamiliar upon us. But if that is correct, then what do we need art for? The unfamiliar is part and parcel of our semiotic life, and why would we need more unfamiliarity than we get already?

There is a remark by Shklovsky which could be of help here. When he says that art may *recover* the sense of life, "the sensation of things as they are perceived and not as they are known," he recognizes in art the power to represent through *recreation*. From the perspective developed in this paper, if art recreates a sense of life, this is because it represents the semiotic process itself: it represents our dealing with the unfamiliar, with difference, with what exceeds the sign. What is represented in and with art is the experience (or feeling – the somatic)[11] which is inherent in the semiotic process. "Ostranennie" or estrangement is not so much a characteristic of art but of human (semiotic) life. Art cannot turn the stone stony, but it can represent the stone as "making a difference." It thus represents life.

The questions that remain to be answered now are: Why would we represent the semiotic process, and how is this done? To answer the first question, we have to take a step back. As I argued above, cognition becomes semiotic once a stable pattern is matched against an unstable occurrence. But what could "an occurrence" be? More specifically, how can we ever know about an occurrence if we recognize it in terms of stable patterns? How does the instability of the occurrence escape these patterns, how does difference arise? Apparently, what is experienced as an occurrence is represented as a "fuzzy set," as an always changing new combination of known elements. It must consist of elements from the stable patterns but organized in such a way that they do not fit any of the patterns available. Semiotic cognition thus implies the matching of stable with unstable patterns, although these patterns are all constituted by the same elements. The stable patterns serve to interpret, give form to, or simply "recognize" the unstable patterns or occurrences.

The analysis of the structure of the semiotic process allows us to understand Shklovsky's analysis of the "estranging" techniques, or "devices" in literature and film, such as the striking use of language in poetry, the unfamiliar perspective and the tension between fable and suzjet in narrative, or montage in film. In art, the semiotic "fuzziness" of reality and the subsequent process of signification, be it in perception or in thinking, is "recovered." It is imitated in a specific medium or combination of media (movement, sound, images, language). Signs that are more or less conflicting are superposed on each other, the result being a multi-layered structure which generates an interpretation process. Thus, life is represented mimetically in art through the recreating of the fuzziness of reality, and by forcing the reader or spectator to deal with that fuzziness. There is something ironic about the fact that what makes the stone "stony" is not so much its alleged stoniness (whatever that may be), but the way in which it is *represented* in a complex semiotic structure. But precisely because of this, Shklovsky could add that "Art is a way of experiencing the artfulness of an object; *the object is not important*."[12] Shklovsky seems to acknowledge that the stone (the object) is not so important; art is really all about semiosis. It is about the knight's move of human semiosis: never straight, but jumping over a void of meaning.

There remains one last question to be answered, which is: Why? Why would we want to represent our semiotic life? The answer is simple: insofar as the semiotic process is itself an unfamiliar occurrence, it triggers a process of signification. The reflexive semiotic process that ensues is again an attempt to relate an unstable occurrence to a stable form, that is to an image, a concept, or theory of life. Semiotic self-consciousness develops along the same lines as semiotic consciousness, that is, from self-images via self-imagination and self-conceptualization to self-analysis. If we want to reflect upon our semiotic life, this life has to be given a form, and it is the process of imaginative self-representation, both personal and collective, that we have been calling "art" at least since the eighteenth century, but which has been with us since times immemorial. The imaginative or mimetic representation of human life entails the imitative recreating of semiosis, that is, of a process of relating stable and unstable patterns, signs and occurrences.[13] In order to do so, what we have identified as "art" incorporates the unfamiliarity of reality in its own form. Depending on the historical context and circumstances, the unfamiliarity is more or less strong, more or less prominent. The stronger this unfamiliarity is experienced in a culture, the stronger it will appear in its mimetic reflection, that is, in the arts. Instead of revealing to us something which is absent from our lives, art shows us what is at the heart of it. Foregrounding difference, it mimetically represents the sensation of life. By doing so, it definitely contributes to the "somatic homeostatic regulation of our sense of reality."[14]

We can now round up the argument. Art does indeed represent the sensation of life, but it does not recover it, as it was never lost. Instead of representing life in terms of concepts and theories, it represents it mimetically by recreating the unfamiliar and confronting the recipient with an unstable reality. It does so not because life has become a sign, but because life, in its unfamiliarity, asks for signification. This process of signification always starts with attempts to give life a more or less stable yet at the same time faithful representation. These faithful representations of life are exactly what art provides us with. Once they are in place, life can be dealt with also in more abstract terms, it can be conceptualized and analyzed.

In art, devices such as narration and montage, are employed to strengthen, mimetically, the strangeness, the difference of the experience that is conveyed. This is, ultimately, what the concept of "estrangement" refers to: the ways in which a work of art confronts its public, through a mimetic representation of the semiotic process, with life as it is, or could be experienced.

That Shklovsky himself stressed the unfamiliar in art hardly comes as a surprise, considering the circumstances in which he wrote. Around 1917, times in Russia were turbulent. Life was very "estranging" indeed: habits of thought and action were of little use during this period of revolution and modern warfare. As he writes himself:

We Russians didn't know how to write about today. Art, no longer coupling with life, from its continuous marriage with relatives – old poetic images – shrank, expired. Myth expired... The application and simultaneously the coexistence of all artistic epochs in the soul of the passéist most fully resembles a cemetery where the dead are no longer enemies. And life was left to chronicles and cinema.[15]

Life for Shklovsky was not automatized at all. But many representations were: old art and new entertainment joined forces in dealing with life by obfuscating it, creating a smokescreen of worn-out language and easy-to-digest images. The cruelty of war as Shklovsky experienced it was there, and it was real.[16] People experienced it, but they didn't see it represented. Therefore, art once again had to do what it had always done (and will always do), it had to represent life as well as it could.

When Shklovsky urged literature to make us feel life as it is, he was actually reminding literature and the arts, among which cinema figured prominently, of their one and only task: to be art. Not surprisingly, in the review on Mayakovsky's "A Cloud in Trousers" quoted above, he also remarks that Formalism and Futurism are allies. But in contrast to what he seems to think, Futurism was not the result of Formalism; rather, Formalism provided the theoretical parallel to Futurist art. Art has never had the task to render the world "unfamiliar." It's task has always been to represent the representation process, not the world, but human life as faithfully as possible. When and where life is unfamiliar, art will represent it as such. In times of great stability, the unfamiliar may be limited to variations on a well-known theme or even to the uniqueness of a single work or performance. The stress on renewal in perception is not only a characteristic of Romanticism[17] but also, in general, of periods of cultural change and renewal (or "renaissance"). From that perspective, Shklovsky didn't necessarily rely upon the Romantics, he may have simply taken an analogous path in a different era. Today, at the beginning of the 21st century, we see once again a turn toward perception, away from a hyper-linguistic and self-referential postmodernism.

Shklovsky seems to have had it right when he stressed that art is a representation of life. He appears to be wrong, however, when he attributed the unfamiliar to art, instead of discovering it in life itself. His theory of art reflects his own experience, as has happened so often in the history of aesthetics, precisely because art does represent personal and collective experience: Just tell me what you think art should be, and I'll tell you what your life is like!

Thus, Shklovsky was right about art, but for the wrong reasons. The three perspectives he brings together in "Art as Technique": a theory of perception (habit formation in perception), a theory of semiosis (the object as symbol), and a theory of abstraction (the "algebrization") are related, but have to be distinguished if we want to get a clear picture of the artistic process. Perception is not the same as semiosis, and semiosis is not the same as abstraction. The concept of estrangement ("ostranennie") can and should be reassessed within a more sophisticated and complex theory of human semiotic cognition and of art as a specific instance of semiosis, realized in a variety of media and characterized by imaginative self-consciousness. The concept would refer to the experience generated by the mimetic representation of the estrangement which is inherent in all human semiotic cognition, and which is the result of the difference between sign and occurrence that functions as a continuous catalyst of the semiotic process. Estrangement is basic to art because it is basic to (human) life.

Reflecting upon the fruitfulness of the concept of "ostranennie" for contemporary criticism, we have to be very aware of the consequences of the foregoing critical analysis of the concept. For Shklovsky, and in this respect he really was a revolutionary thinker, the estrangement is caused by the *formal structure* of the work of art. For him, the form is a substantial reality, and it was precisely this reality of the artistic *structure* – the artistic techniques or devices – which gave the new scientific study of literature of Formalism its stable ground. For Shklovsky, as we have seen, these devices were directly related to the perceptual experience they generated in the public of a work of art. In a later phase, which has become known as Structuralism (with capital "S"!) and which originated in the work of Jakobson and Tynjanov, the "locus" of structure moved, so to say, from the form to the meaning. In an early stage, Jakobson repudiated Shklovsky's crude "formalism," replacing it by an apparently more sophisticated theory of linguistic meaning. The "estrangement" of the form became a "tension" or "deviation" on the level of meaning. This tension (or "*écart*" as it was coined in French) demanded interpretation, and literary studies moved from a phenomenological to a hermeneutic structuralism. The transition was made possible by the replacement of the *analysis* of the structure of the literary form (causing the experience of estrangement) to the *interpretation* of the meaning of the literary, or artistic deviation. In a third phase, research focused on the *grammar* of artistic texts. Estrangement was now understood in terms of the relation between the deep and surface levels of this grammar – such as, for instance, between *fabula* and *suyzhet* in narrative texts. Neo-formalism in film studies belongs here. In a fourth phase, the seeds of which had been present already in the work on the "aesthetic object" by the Prague structuralist Jan Mukařovský, and for which the philosophical movements of deconstruction and pragmatism prepared the ground, the structure of the text was replaced by the structure of interpretation, that is, by the structure of a cognitive process. Pioneers of this development of reader-response research were Wolfgang Iser in Germany and Norman Holland in the United States. In film studies, Gestalt-psychologist Rudolf Arnheim paved the way. Estrangement was now no longer an aspect of the literary form nor of literary meaning or grammar; instead, it had become a dimension of the human cognitive process. It is in this fourth, cognitive perspective that my own analysis of the concept of estrangement has its roots. The estrangement that characterizes human semiotic life, and which may be mimetically represented through a work of art, is a dimension of the cognitive process performed by a reader, viewer, listener, or spectator. And it is precisely there – and not in a supposedly stable form or meaning – that it must be studied. Thus, in the course of roughly one century, the study of the arts has moved from a study of artistic forms, via the study of artistic meaning, to the study of artistic cognition. If we want to keep the concept of "ostranenie" alive, we will have to take this changed context of research into account and treat estrangement, accordingly, as a concept that refers to a crucial dimension of human semiotic cognition.

# The Perception of Reality as Deformed Realism

*Miklós Kiss*

"Our eyes may move like a camera, but our attention jumps like editing."
– Jarmo Valkola[1]

Viktor Shklovsky stated that "[t]he purpose of art is to impart the sensation of things as they are perceived and not as they are known."[2] Although this assertion's influence on cognitive studies is comparable to Hugo Münsterberg's deservedly acclaimed study, it says less about the purpose of art than about the purpose of Shklovsky.[3] In the following, I would like to re-evaluate Shklovsky's highly progressive intuition on the cognitive distinction of "perceiving" as a *bottom-up* and "knowing" as a *top-down* logic.[4] The opposition will highlight the discrepancy between the *reality* of perception and comprehension, and the *realism* of representation. My aim is to point out the consequences of Shklovsky's cognitive hunch, which led him towards introducing his theory on the method of *ostranenie*.

Let us start with Mark Seddon's laconic statement: "The real world in which we live is continuous in time and in space. The world of the film is not."[5] No matter how true this is in theory, the statement formulates an insignificant difference in practice if we take recipient practice as a highlighted viewpoint. We must add the supplement that the "reality" surrounding us is a physically chronological continuity, but its reception does not conform to this order; rather, it is closer to the representational practice of film. The reception of reality appears in our mind as edited, taken out of chronology; thus, it resembles film-like material. The process of seeing guarantees this non-linear functioning: the omissions of the quick, "jumping" saccadic eye movement;[6] the fovea's focused and detailed field against the periphery's diminishing information areas; or the processing of visual data, which is primarily stored rather than filtered during the eye's visual decoding;[7] all prove that even the slightest physiological features of the eye cannot perfectly detect the chronology of physical reality. Accordingly, following Seddon, the eye functions much more like a "biological camera."[8] It is not fully clear, even for natural science, how our neural workings, constrained by the limited functioning of the eye, are capable of creating a feeling of reality with linear continuity. However, it can be assumed that the narration-technique bluff of the *Classical Narration*[9] imitates and, in addition, helps to restore the feeling of a linear physical reality. In whatever way it works, one thing is sure: one of its most apparent, if not the most prominent principle is *narrative linearity* as the facade of this temporal manipulation. Thus, this film-language method can be considered as the "most gracious fraud" of Hollywood, upholding the norms of a classic mode of narration.

But does the narrative deformation through "'the laying bare of the device,' whereby art, having eliminated the usual lifelike facade" indicate any kind of estrangement;[10] more precisely, does it induce any processes of cognitive deautomatization against these norms?

## Narrative Deformation ≠ Cognitive Deautomatization

In his early sketches on the psychology of the filmic perception, David Bordwell claimed, "A filmmaker who presents story events out of chronological order thus risks forcing the spectator to choose between reconstructing story order and losing track of current action."[11] Insofar as the recipient agrees to take part and *constructs* rather than *re-constructs* a possible fabula of the plot, the viewer might create the foundation of a new pattern as well, or might execute the affirmation of a still evolving pattern including a non-linear formal schema.[12] According to Bordwell, the dynamics of changes in narration-technique patterns can be imagined gradually, step by step: in comparison to the previous ones, deviant narrative schemata can be firmly fitted into the well-known patterns and can become determinative over time, thereby creating a complex narrative template schema, a norm. With this narrative schemata theory that prefers transition, we can smooth away the subjectively selected threshold moments of film historical canon since "Problems and solutions do not respect borders."[13] Bordwell, based on his own theory, describes Jean-Luc Godard as a brave innovator who, instead of the step by step "traditional" method of changing patterns through schemata versions, aimed at changing almost all narrative patterns at the same time. The most apparent of all these is the narrative pattern that signifies an absolute tumbling of the patterns: it challenges fossilized schemes of linear narrative, of linear temporality.

The temporality of the narration can be taken as a separate narrative template schema, where patterns of the different sets of time-handling knowledge are being formed during the film-watching activity of the recipient. Warren Buckland also refers to Godard, or more precisely to the structure of one of the escape scenes of PIERROT LE FOU (1965).[14] He compares the treatment of time and space, influencing the temporality of the narration, with the narrative montage of the escape scene in which Pierrot and Marianne must flee from Frank (Marianne's lover). The scene mixes shots within the runaway sequence "according" to the distracted situation:

*The order of the syuzhet:* (1) Marianne is about to leave the apartment, (2) Marianne is driving a red car while Pierrot gets in, (3) Marianne and Pierrot

MIKLÓS KISS

are stepping out of the bathroom, Frank is lying unconscious in the bathtub, (4) the red car drives faster and faster, (5) Pierrot and Marianne are looking down from the top of the apartment, (6) two men are running towards the apartment, (7) Pierrot and Marianne are still on the roof, (8) Pierrot and Marianne are climbing down the gutter from the roof, (9) a shortened repetition of sequence (2), (10) the red car is speeding towards a barrier indicating height, (11) Marianne gets into the red car and heads off, (12) the car reaches the barrier, (13) the Statue of Liberty "waves friendly" at them, (14) the red car drives to a petrol station (see the stills from PIERROT LE FOU on page 168-169).

Unfolding a cognitive approach from a semiotic foundation, Buckland describes the film mode of structuring as a carrier of three possible meanings: he enumerates [a] grammatical and comprehensible, [b] ungrammatical but comprehensible (meaning can be deduced from the context, for example), or [c] ungrammatical and incomprehensible units.[15] The hectic montage of Godard disobeying time and space relations is deviant compared to the classic film language which is in keeping with the principle of linearity, but remains comprehensible with the help of the context (the scene as the emotional representation of escape). According to this, "[t]he sequence from PIERROT LE FOU is an ungrammatical but acceptable filmic sequence," a clear-cut example of type [b].[16] It is true, however, that it innovates its editing technique: it utilizes a montage based on the showing of variations of shots that defy space and time continuation, but it does not eliminate the fundamental narrative function and working of the montage. Buckland, referring to the similar activity ascribed to the recipient, (re)arranges the non-linear shots of the syuzhet into a linear, chronological order. He supposes that "these features include spatio-temporal coordinates, together with the cause-effect narrative logic linking the events."[17]

*After the (re)ordering of the non-linear shots of the above syuzhet (in the more chronologically and causally structured order of a potential fabula) the scene unfolds as follows:* (1) Marianne is about to leave the apartment, (3) Marianne and Pierrot are stepping out of the bathroom, Frank is lying unconscious in the bathtub, (5) Pierrot and Marianne are looking down from the top of the apartment, (6) two men are running towards the apartment, (7) Pierrot and Marianne are still on the roof, (8) Pierrot and Marianne are climbing down the gutter from the roof, (11) Marianne gets into the red car and heads off, (2) Marianne is driving a red car while Pierrot gets in, (9) the shortened repetition of sequence (2), (10) the red car is speeding towards a barrier indicating height, (12) the car reaches the barrier, (4) the red car drives faster and faster, (13) the Statue of Liberty "waves friendly" at them, (14) the red car drives to a petrol station.

Stills from Jean-Luc Godard's *PIERROT LE FOU*, 1965.

I believe that ordering the ungrammatical non-linearity of the syuzhet into a linear chain does not enhance the facilitation of the episode's comprehensibility, since the scene did not take a discontinuing form for the solving of a mystery: it is not the denouement of a narrative speculation that provides meaning. Analyzing this same scene in accordance with Buckland, Bordwell states, "The sequence invites us to rearrange the shots into 'correct' chronology."[18] The confutation of the relevance of this approach is done by its wording: it is worth noting the use of the expression "rearrange" which presupposes a previous, correct order and opposes the recipient's constructive (vs. reconstructive) interpretative process that was deduced convincingly by Bordwell himself.[19] Buckland's claim, "I shall attempt to reconstruct this sequence by putting its shots (back) into a grammatical sequence," faces the same problem; that is, it induces a notion of previousness, implementing some vague hierarchy among the different stages of comprehension.[20]

Sequences like the image of the Statue of Liberty, which do not fit into the plot of the narrative course, reinforce my assumption against this rearranging effort. The connotation of freedom of the statue will reduce the narrative emphasis of the plot's time and space, similar to the color psychology of the car, or the excitement of escaping from the roof. The statue animates such, mostly film-related, connotations that belong to the conventional (meaning film historical) pattern of escape (with regard to the reflections on tradition by Godard, this is an almost commonplace palpability). As long as we look thoroughly at the viewpoints of creating comprehensibility, the scene as it is probably offers a more realistic picture of the nature of escape than the Bordwellian or Bucklandian linear ordering of the supposed process of the chronological construction, because it stresses the psychology of the excitement of escape in its essential non-linearity. The real excitement accompanying an escape, the real feeling of panic is probably closer to the hectic, non-linear Godard representation than to the classic, continuity-based linear form.[21] In this scene – and in many other instances – Godard creates a more realistic and comprehensible story with a non-linear plot construction than with a linear experience of the reality-imitating classic mode of narration. Through the representation of the real recipient experience, Godard's non-linear approach exposes the reality-imitation technique of the classic Hollywood film language, hiding behind sequential linearity and temporal chronology. The space-time continuity of the classic norms' realism is subordinated to the psychological, cognitive processes' reality. It turns back the fraud of the classical narration style: realism cannot be represented through the imitation of reality but through the showing of reality itself. Physical reality might be linear and chronological, but the perceptual experience of this reality is non-linear, achronological.

## Conclusion

I see the realistic effect of the hectic montage of PIERROT LE FOU in its non-linearity, in direct opposition to the method of placing the events in a chronological order, which was recommended by Bordwell's or Buckland's narrative analysis. We are not watching cubist paintings as narrative puzzles. The heart of the matter is not to solve some riddle, to understand what is represented, but what matters is the alteration of sensation. As Shklovsky poignantly remarked:

> An image is not a permanent referent for those mutable complexities of life which are revealed through it; its purpose is not to make us perceive meaning, but to create a special perception of the object – *it creates a "vision" of the object instead of serving as a means for knowing it.*[22]

Here I would like to emphasize again that physical reality might be linear and chronological, but the experience of this reality is non-linear, achronological. This train of thought – remaining with Godard in connection with his À BOUT DE SOUFFLE (BREATHLESS, 1960) – is continued by András Bálint Kovács, who believes that with the help of its scene-entangling functioning, the non-linear Godardian montage emphasizes "primarily not the narrative meaning of the events, but their unexpectedness and hectic emotional content [...], it does not describe a narration, but conveys the narration's emotional content through the fracturing of space and time."[23] Mobilized against classic narrative norms, *ostranenie* at best deautomatizes the film-viewing practice; that is, it raises awareness[24] and actually reduces the level of immersion through the self-conscious effect of the non-linear narrative. Despite bringing about a deautomatized viewing perception, its efforts are just not able to alienate, to distance from the psychological, cognitive-physiological functioning of the real experience. The deautomatization that works against *habitualization*[25] by means of narrative deformation only threatens the realism of the classical norms of representation. To be more precise, it threatens the viewers' routines of understanding as maintained by the Classical Narration. However, on a cognitive level it has no influence on the real, fundamentally non-linear processes of perception and understanding. It cannot alter our biologically determined, essentially non-linear, perceptive and comprehensive operations.[26] The aesthetically motivated Godard, deforming the routines of realism, dismantles and even supersedes the need of the reconstructible, indirect, *top-down* logic of the narrative norms. He creates a provocative sequence of shots, without relying on any previous narrative knowledge, so that it works on a physiological rather than an inferential level. Bordwell, however, proposes an *inferential* model of narration:

Instead of treating the narrative as a message to be decoded, I take it to be a representation that offers the occasion for inferential elaboration. [...] I suggest that given a representation, the spectator processes it perceptually and elaborates it on the bases of schemas she or he has to hand.[27]

Godard's hectic montage, which works viscerally, supersedes this schemata-based inferential logic. Additionally, on a cognitive level, the shuffling of shots exactly mirrors the real, non-linear process of perceiving and understanding.[28]

Chrono-logic does not require chronology. Challenging everyday perception and challenging realism are sometimes not against reality at all. Moreover, the ensuing provocation of this challenge exactly mirrors the ways of our cognitive interplay between perception and comprehension. Richard Shusterman's highly inspiring *somatic theory*, which integrates John Dewey's pragmatic aesthetical philosophy and the ecological approach of cognitive theory, brings the biocultural interaction between aesthetical and biological functioning to deeper, even organic levels of our being human.[29] The theory implies that it is high time to leave the objective rational (inferential) proposal of (neo-)formalism for what it is and turn to the analysis of the "strange," not as a detached form but as a complex aesthetic experience: an experience which takes both cognitive, physiological and even psychoanalytical consequences into consideration.

Godard's neo-cubist montage, aptly commented on by Pier Paolo Pasolini as a "poetic restoration of reality,"[30] not only visualizes this complexity but at the same time enforces us to revisit our tenacious theories.

# Part IV
# Discussions

# On *Ostranenie*, Différance, and the Uncanny

# *Conversation* with András Bálint Kovács

## Laurent Jullier

Let me begin by introducing my fellow colleague and interviewee, András Bálint Kovács, Professor at the Institute of Art & Communication, ELTE (Budapest), where he holds the Chair of the Department of Film Studies. He was born in 1959 in Budapest, Hungary. Because of his work on defamiliarization, he was invited to contribute to this book. On the one hand, he frequently uses modern items (films, directors and essays) as objects of research. His book *Screening Modernism: European Art Cinema 1950-1980*, published by Chicago University Press in 2008 (Limina Award, 2009) is well known, and so are his writings about Tarkovsky and Gilles Deleuze.[1] On the other hand, he is a fellow of the Society for Cognitive Studies of the Moving Image (SCSMI), where he studies the narrative universals.[2] His ongoing research deals with the psychology of causal thinking while understanding cinematic narrative. In academic Film Studies, this kind of combination is unusual. When choosing modern artworks and authors as objects of research, scholars usually prefer aesthetic, deconstructionist, historical or cultural tools to analyze them, since Modernism is the main purveyor of *non-familiar things* in the field of culture and art. Cognitive Film Studies are supposed to provide tools to explain how the audience perceives *familiar things* on the screen. András Bálint Kovács is well aware of this paradoxical combination, since he has been, and still is, involved in epistemological debates (see his article on the book *Imposture Intellectuelles*).[3] This is a good opportunity to ask him some questions about this paradox in Film Studies (points 1 and 4), and about two mechanisms involved in the defamiliarizing process: narrative causation (point 2) and veridicality of knowledge (point 3).

## Defamiliarization and Film Studies: Historical Context

**LJ:** The project text of *The Key Debates. Mutations and Appropriations in European Film Studies* reminds us that "In the field of European Film and Film Studies, the weight of an 'American' paradigm and all the institutional forces behind it is strongly felt." Nevertheless, the question of cinematic *ostranenie* was, in the beginning, a typically *European* one. I am thinking of Walter Benjamin and Belá Balázs writing about the close-up and constructive editing; I am thinking of the *cinéma dada* and René Clair looking for new ways to show ancient artworks.[4]

After these pioneering times, there is a first move towards more essentialist preoccupations. I am thinking of Siegfried Kracauer and André Bazin (followed in France by Jean Cocteau and Amédée Ayfre), and their ambition to subscribe to the camera the power of revealing the Real and showing the audience the world "before we look at it."[5] The idea of defamiliarization is still there, but reverted (the cinematic apparatus produces defamiliarization only when – and because – it tells the truth about the world). A second move, especially when one considers French scholars, consists in subscribing the defamiliar, or defiant, to the artist, in order to concentrate on other problems – narration (narratology), ideology (marxist approach), gaze and identity (psychoanalytic approach), etc. On the contrary, it seems that the "American paradigm" is once again including the question of defamiliarization in a somewhat essentialist way in Stanley Cavell's *Projection of the World*, and the same goes for the field of Analytic Film Theory (Kendall Walton, Noël Carroll, Richard Allen). Do you think this evolution has taken shape strictly due to contingencies and "historical accidents," or is it more logical to assume that it evolved due to a deep divergence of view between Europe and America regarding the cinema and the ways of comprehending and studying cinema?

**ABK:** Let me first say that I can see no "deep divergence" between Europe and America. The basics of film theory were born in Europe in the first half of the twentieth century, and it stands to reason that no American theorist can be imagined without those points of departure.

Up until the mid-1980s "European" film theory was dominated by French and British film theory both based on Marxist ideology critique, semiotics and psychoanalysis, to different extents of course. The critical analysis of film from a structural and ideological point of view was at the center of this theory, which was primarily concerned with finding "the meaning." Now, let me put this in a very provocative way: asking "what a film means" is not a theoretical question. One can embrace as many theories and philosophical, scientific, or psychological theses as one pleases, finding "the meaning" in an individual film, or in a group of films, always remains the film critic's work. To me, this kind of theorizing comes across as an extremely erudite way of talking about movies addressed to an erudite and theoretically demanding audience at a time when philosophers, writers, artists, even scientists regularly went to the movies not merely to have fun, but with the conviction that cinema was a form of art in its own right. They believed that they could learn as much about the world from cinema as they could from books and theater. This kind of erudite film criticism remains very important and instructive, but we should stop believing that it is a theory in its own right. A theoretical question is not about what something means, but about how something is possible.

Meanwhile, another paradigm started to emerge. From the late 1980s cognitive science appeared in the writings of some literary and film theorists, and this new scientific paradigm, it seems, firstly conquered American literary and film theories. That is not to say that it was exclusively American in nature. If we look at the membership of the Society for Cognitive Studies of the Moving Image, which was founded in the United States, we find many Europeans (from Denmark, Great Britain, the Netherlands, Germany, Hungary and other countries, too). All things considered, right now I can see no other productive theoretical paradigm than the cognitive one: post-structuralist paradigms, having lost their credibility regarding their potential to become all-embracing general explanatory theories, are nothing more than auxiliary tools for interpretation.

Now, defamiliarization can be an interesting area of research in cognitive theory since it can be viewed as a psychological effect a film exercises over the viewer: the circumstances, conditions and process of which can be researched or analyzed by a cognitively slanted aesthetic-analytical approach as done by Carroll or Allen. Again, this is not an American paradigm. I believe it to be the most unified and virulent theoretical paradigm that presently exists in film theory. I say this accepting that other vast areas of film studies like different disciplines of interpretation, such as cultural studies, political, psychoanalytical or feminist criticism, still provide interesting insights for understanding the meaning of films.

## Defamiliarization and Narration

LJ: You mentioned that defamiliarization is an interesting area of research in cognitive theory, particularly with regard to film and narration. One can easily assume that a lack of causality in a film narrative automatically means defamiliarization, since inferring causality is a built-in mechanism that helps human beings comprehend the world around them, but things are not so simple. In "Things that come after another,"[6] you used David Lynch's MULHOLLAND DRIVE (2001) to point out that "a narrative can be understood by similarity and variation even when causal connections are hopelessly blurred." You go on by introducing:

[T]he category of narrative situation to suggest that all narratives consist of such narrative fragments (situations) that suggest to the viewer different possible causal or non-causal continuations, and if a certain logic (causality, similarity or varied repetition) of the changes within the sequences of the situation can be grasped, the viewer can understand it even if causality is blurred or non-existent in it.[7]

Does this interpretation imply that narrative defamiliarization is quite unobtainable, even in the most modernist and deconstructed experimental films, since the spectator is always able to find some "narrative coherence" even in the absence of a "certain logic"? This would mean that the only way to provoke estrangement is to modify representation (because modifying narration in this case would be pointless).

**ABK:** I don't think that narrative defamiliarization is impossible on the basis that the viewers always find some coherence in a film. Defamiliarization simply means the usage of such poetic narrative devices that thwart the audience's automatic associative processes and provoke the audience to find other ways of making sense of the work of art. Narrative defamiliarization occurs all the time when events in a narrative sequence are such that most viewers cannot link them to one another causally or in any other way. If, for example, a character shifts identity from one scene to another, this is unfamiliar to us, and we consider the event sequence as not linked causally. If, on the contrary, a rule is set in the film according to which characters often change their identities, the event sequence becomes familiar very easily, and we can now see the causal connections (this is how fantastic films work). Modernist defamiliarization of narratives occurs when event sequences do not elicit causality, and the film does not set rules by which the audience could easily construct causal or other cohesive connections. But most of this kind of defamiliarization inevitably becomes familiar after a while, which is one reason why modernism ended. Defamiliarization is only a temporary effect that just vanishes after a certain time in relation to a specific artistic solution. Incoherence is obviously one way of initiating defamiliarization, but if no new associative rules are proposed by the work of art, it simply becomes uninteresting. It stands to reason that rules unavoidably become familiar or automatic after a while. Some defamiliarization techniques remained effective, however, and we could explain this by their self-reflexivity. The main effect in self-reflectivity is that it disrupts narrative illusionism when, for instance, the author addresses the audience directly. This device is always disturbing because it provokes a radical change of attitude in the viewer. No matter how many times I watch À BOUT DE SOUFFLE, it always strikes me when, at the beginning, Jean-Paul Belmondo starts talking to the camera. Defamiliarization always has an effect of estrangement, but not all estrangement is self-reflective.

What has all this to do with people's tendency to find coherence in narratives? In the case of defamiliarized narratives, one could predict that to a certain extent the viewers continue to construct causal connections even when the sequences are unfamiliar to them. In the early 1970s a Hungarian filmmaker, Gábor Bódy, performed an experiment that specifically tackled this problem. He created a film entitled HUNT FOR LITTLE FOXES by randomly piecing together shots he found in the garbage can of an editing room at the Hungarian television. He screened the film to an audience and asked the audience to comment on the film's meaning. Almost all of the members of the audience found some meaning in the film, which is to say that they found at least some connections in the randomly edited sequences, and some of them were causal. Bódy emphasized that this process of finding meaning has a time limit. If random shots follow each other long enough, and there is no structure in the sequence, we just stop looking for a sense. This is an empirical question and thus deserves to be investigated. So if we see a narrative situation (someone is doing something somewhere) that provokes us to extend it in time and space in our minds, followed by another narrative situation, we automatically try to connect the two by various means: causation, similarity, repetition, as unfamiliar as the given connection may seem. When we find a rule that works, after a while the sense of unfamiliarity disappears, and we have a sense of understanding even if causal connections between the situations are blurred.

**LJ:** If the disturbance of narrative codes and traditions occurs at specific points in time, then the question would be: should defamiliarization (as Shklovsky explained it in 1917 in "Art as Technique") be considered "deeply modernist" since in most cases the defamiliarizing effect is short-lived, because new rules of comprehension nullify the estranging effect? Clearly, defamiliarization, in this sense, only "culturally *authorizes*" basic perceptual and cognitive schemes to be used by the spectator. The Nouvelle Vague jump-cut, for instance, would only have been effective for a couple of years before losing its defamiliarizing powers. Is it not also a matter of *film genre*? A jump-cut is no longer disturbing in an independent art film or a MTV music video, it seems, but would it not be disturbing if used in a *Harry Potter* movie? The sociocultural "training" is an important factor here: once introduced into a new "world" (in Howard Becker's sociological meaning of the term "world"), you learn to enjoy some new figures or you simply learn not to find them strange anymore.

**ABK:** I agree, and it is also a matter of style. We cannot evaluate artistic devices ("priom," in Russian Formalist terminology) separately from their contexts. This was one of the fatal misconceptions of early film semiology. A new solution may appear and may disturb artistic reception in a certain context. It becomes familiar after a while in that particular context, while unfamiliar in another context. Jump cuts are no surprise, as you say, in music videos or commercials, nor are they in art films, or contemporary action films, and they also infiltrated into recent television series, like 24 or THE WIRE. Nonetheless, they remain unfamiliar in most romantic comedies and children's films, like HARRY POTTER (although I haven't seen the last one yet). A jump cut is a sort of "error" in editing (cf. the French term *faux raccord* explicitly refers to that), and pure convention determines whether the error is tolerated or not. Nothing prevents "shocking" effects from becoming familiar and even boring after a while, independent of the context in which they occur. We could call this "socio-cultural training," but bear in mind that this is also a perceptual or cognitive training. We just learn how certain visual effects affect us and what they mean. We learn how to differentiate between two visual effects, the way a child learns how to differentiate between shapes of objects.

## Defamiliarization and Knowledge

**LJ:** Let us move towards the question of the "veridicality" of the knowledge one can acquire through defamiliarization. In my essay, I claim that evolutionary psychology and most "Darwinian" disciplines, broadly speaking, radically reject the concept of Derrida's "différance" because these disciplines primarily consider the "useful part" of the knowledge (the *know-how*, for instance: how can I find food, safety, heat, partners...). Richard Allen and Murray Smith, following the same line of thought, assert that not only "Darwinian" disciplines, but also analytical philosophy do not share the Derridean "epistemic atheism." So, what does this atheism entail? According to Allen and Smith:

> [T]he presence of an object in the mind's eye is guaranteed only by the presence of something – the material signifier – that is by definition absent. Thus, for Derrida, any knowledge claim, founded by definition upon the presence of the object in the mind's eye, must make reference to its own impossibility in the very act of being made.[8]

That is why defamiliarization would be a "better way" to get to know something: it escapes the failure of the absence/presence dilemma because the material signifier is not intended to be there in the first place. The fallacy of its presence (i.e., at the movies the so-called "illusion of reality") is therefore avoided. To my mind, the Derridean argument is stronger in literature than in the cinema, because a wide range of cinematic "information" about the world is not encoded in words but in kinesthetic schemes for instance. I do not understand why estrangement *per se* – at least at the movies – would necessarily allow me to learn better or truer things about my environment.

**ABK:** I agree. Defamiliarization or estrangement do not *per se* allow getting in touch with truth or reality. This is the modernist ideology about these techniques. This is by the way one of the main differences between modernism and postmodernism: in postmodernistic thinking, reality does not exist behind the image, there are only more images behind the image. It is no big news that someone inspired by evolutionary theory and analytic philosophy does not share Derridian deconstruction.

*Différance* is Derrida's clever neologism to express his opinion about meaning, namely that meaning always escapes us, because we can grasp it only through what it is not. The meaningful element, the present, can only be defined "by means of this very relation to what it is not: what it absolutely is not, not even a past or a future as a modified present."[9] What happens when we accept this idea? Do we get any closer to the reality of what we want to talk about? I don't think so. Something can be defined against an infinite number of "others," and what we get is still the idea that the identity of the thing we want to know more about escapes us all the time. If I have to choose between poststructuralist ideas about identity, I would rather choose Deleuze's *répétition*, which also stretches the knowledge of identity in time, but the concept of *répétition* explains at least something of the difference about what something is against what something is not. Do we know more about what a pipe is when we read from Magritte's painting: *Ceci n'est pas une pipe?* No. What we do understand from this is that it is hard to know what something is at any rate. And that what we can see is only a part of the "real" identity. And maybe we never grow to learn it. But we have no other choice but to look for it in a series of appearances, each of which provides an aspect of the "Whole," as Deleuze says, which is open and never ends.

So we always have to deal with partial aspects of reality. Nobody needs to be warned that watching a movie is something else than watching reality. What sometimes needs warning about is that what we see is only a partial appearance of a reality that can never be grasped in its entirety. If there is any "truth" in defamiliarization or estrangement, it is this general truism about the partiality of all representation of reality. And this is in harmony with the cognitive approach to perception. According to the cognitive approach, perception is a constructive process by which we always compare external stimuli with complex patterns we have in our minds. With the help of this comparison, we always complete or augment what we physically see in order to construct an entire image with our mind's eye. This process always changes the image as we move forward; we add more details, change the shape and so on, and we change the pattern, too, even though we can never physically see the whole object at any time.

To put it really bluntly, the reason why cognitivist researchers cannot make use of the concept of *différance* is, I think, that this kind of philosophy, rather than trying to find a way of accomplishing the really difficult task of explaining human understanding, explains to us why we cannot ever accomplish this task. I think it is a more productive standpoint to suppose that things can be made intelligible, can be understood, even if this understanding is partially our own construction, and necessarily partial as it is, understanding escapes us all the time, and identity cannot be grasped even for a moment, and meaning is never where we look for it.

## Defamiliarization and Film Studies: Interdisciplinary Perspectives

**LJ:** You probably know Gender Studies and Cultural Studies are reluctant to use any part of the cognitive-evolutionary paradigm. One might even say they totally reject it, even though some cognitivists demonstrated that a "biocultural" approach could indeed be useful to describe cultural problems related to gendered behaviour.[10] One might also say that there is no debate at all. French researcher Dan Sperber describes the problem in terms of a meeting he once attended, between psychologists and anthropologists, trying to work on the same object. After a while, Sperber writes:

> [T]he disappointment is strong on both sides. The anthropologists fail to see the relevance of experimental evidence... They object to what they see as the artificiality of experiments collected outside of an ethnographic context. Moreover, they find the psychologists' view of culture, exemplified by the fact that they are talking about Western and Asian cultures in general, far too crude. The psychologists feel that the anthropologists are just blind to the importance of experimental evidence, that they criticise experimental methodology without understanding it... In the end, the thesis itself is not given any discussion. [11]

Dan Sperber labels the miscomprehension as a language problem (as does Bruno Latour):

> The two communities, psychologists and anthropologists, have different vocabularies, presuppositions, priorities, criteria, references. In general, different disciplines have different sub-cultures, and the difference is made worse, not attenuated, by the existence of superficial similarities, for instance identical words used with quite different meanings ("culture" and "mode of thought" in the present example).[12]

In our case, *ostranenie* is a typical interdisciplinary object. It is the perfect example of an object whose studying needs both cognitive and cultural approaches, but I do not see such a collaboration happening any time soon, I'm afraid. More than a language problem, it is a *political* problem, don't you agree? Perhaps culturalists are "just blind to the importance of experimental evidence." They seem to associate cognitivism with a *conservative* point of view on account of the built-in automatic schemes of perception. They may perceive cognicians as behaviorists, helping the industry of low entertainment to sell more of its non-defamilarizing products... If my reading is correct, the "disappointment on both sides" (as Sperber puts it) is going to last.

**ABK:** I'm afraid so, too. There are several problems here, and none of them are easy to resolve. The first problem is that there are many trends in cognitive science, and there are many conceptions about how our biological construction is related to our minds and to our culture. Some hardline cognitivists think that at the end of the day, all our mental products are reducible to material, physical or chemical processes. Those are called "physicalists." On the other hand, most culturalists adopt a Cartesian dualist approach, according to which our mental phenomena are located in an independent realm with its own rules and logic, none of which can be explained by material processes. The two extremes will never be able to enter into a dialogue. There are so many mental phenomena that cannot be explained by known biological or neuronal processes, so dualist explanations will always survive, or for a very long time anyway. There are different ways in contemporary cognitive theory to try to find the theoretical framework of fitting higher-level mental processes to lower-level biological or neuronal processes. "Embodiment" is one of the very fashionable terms.[13] Thermodynamics and "phase transition" are also often-heard catchwords.[14] What we can say for sure is that we do not know. But we cannot say that we will never know, or that this is a sheer mystery, impossible to know.

Take the example of the *conscious will*. This is one of the central topics of philosophy, law, aesthetics, and all kinds of culturalist arguments. A psychologist, David Wegner dedicated his career to the research of the real meaning of conscious will. In his writings[15] he argues that conscious will is in fact an illusion and explains how this works. He refers to tons of experiments and cases which prove that most of the time when we think that we do what we will, in fact it is the other way around: we will what we do, and then we explain it. In none of those cases is something that can be called "conscious will" the cause of our actions. All his examples and experiments are highly compelling. Why will this never convince a dualist culturalist? That is probably because, regardless of whether the idea that our own "conscious will" determines our actions is true or not, Wegner fails to give an alternative. He cannot say what it is that causes our actions if it is not our "conscious will." With his scientific methods he can go as far as gathering phenomena that refute the idea of the causal power of "conscious will" and support the conception that "will" is the feeling which assures us that we are the authors of what we are doing, but by no means can this feeling be conceived of as the causal source of our acts. But what is the causal source of our acts? Because there is a huge knowledge gap here, there is enough room for radical culturalists, theologians, biologists, and physicalists to impose their own seemingly coherent theories about such an intricate issue like the "conscious will," theories which are at the same time impossible to justify or refute. So, as long as we do not know enough about how our brain works, many mutually exclusive theories and beliefs will continue to survive.

The other problem is that even if we know enough or very much about something, politics and religious convictions will always enter into the debate. When there are moral or political consequences at stake, rational arguments can prevail only to a certain degree. Especially theories about the causes of human acts become the subject of different theories that are closely linked with certain ideologies. The main problem here is that the culturalist approach is almost necessarily "blind" to experimental evidence, because they think that the essential part of human actions – its meaning in a specific context – cannot be an object of an experiment. Meaning comes out of the complexity of "real life," and no experimental situation can reach to those levels of complexity. Even someone like Freud did not think that his psychoanalytical theory needed experimental justification. He thought that a great amount of empirical data interpreted the way he did sufficiently underpinned his theory. Culturalists believe that the mere interpretation of empirical facts is a good methodology for creating theories, because (1) this kind of interpretation is based on the complexity of real life, (2) real-life facts cannot be repeated for experiment's sake, (3) culture and society are essentially historical, so cultural and social facts are basically ruled by historical contingencies, (4) if there are any non-historical rules in culture or society, they are nonetheless independent of the biological or psychological nature of humans, (5) interpretation is based on intentions and values rather than natural causes. Political use of the culturalist approach comes much easier than the political use of the cognitivist approach. Yet many culturalists condemn cognitivists for political reasons just because they refrain from supporting political ideas based on mere interpretation.

The third problem is that the culturalist approach focuses on individual differences in cultures, whereas the cognitivist approach looks for the mechanisms and general conditions of knowledge and cognition common to human nature. They mutually ignore each other's field of interest. But in reality there is no real contradiction between the two approaches if we do not push them to the extreme. As Torben Grodal said in his Embodied Visions, "Even if many of the fundamental aspects of culture work within innate specifications and boundaries, the possibilities of making culturally specific products are, nevertheless, unlimited."[16] Which is to say that both approaches can very well survive next to each other if they are willing to accept the specificity of one other's field of interest and are willing to respect one another's justifiable results, even if as a consequence they will be required to change some of their own ideas. The differences of cultural products can best be explained by historical contingencies, and cultural and historical traditions. But there are undeniable regularities across even the most distant cultures, there are recurrent patterns in human behavior at all levels, from history to personal behavior, which may be traced back to the psychological and neuronal construction of the human being. People and cultures follow patterns. Some of these patterns are historical or based in tradition, some are biological or psychological. There is a merit in studying all of them.

# *Conversation* with Laura Mulvey

*Annie van den Oever*

New questions in Film Studies seem to have acquired urgency recently. We have seen some major changes in Film Studies, such as a focus on the spectator and the viewing experience, and cinema's special appeal to historical audiences. Moreover, the current rapid transitions in digital and optical techniques and viewing practices have also called for attention. These current research interests in Film Studies are explored by Laura Mulvey, Professor of Film and Media Studies at Birkbeck College, University of London, who, in her latest book *Death 24x a Second. Stillness and the Moving Image* (2006), addresses the role new technologies play in the viewing experience and re-evaluates the nature of the filmic medium. By investigating the ramifications of these new technologies, Laura Mulvey is able to explore some aspects of spectatorship and the film's materiality that have been transformed by the new developments, particularly the way the viewer experiences the unfolding of time, space, and movement. She also looks at the arrival of the cinema and the ways it affected the, as yet, "inexperienced" moviegoer. In doing so, she reconsidered some interesting aspects of the early movie going experience and the unexpected confrontations with the *uncanny* it elicited in particular that are relevant to this present discussion on *ostranenie*. As Laura Mulvey has explained, one may see the introduction of the cinema into culture as an abrupt one, and as a decisive point in its history. She agrees with film historians that the cinema and its prehistory "are too deeply imbricated, ideologically and technologically, for an abrupt 'birth of the cinema' to be conceptually valid," as she wrote. But she does not agree with them that this is all that there is to it. In her last book, she argued that "from the perspective of the uncanny, the arrival of celluloid moving pictures constitutes a decisive moment."[1] Early cinema "baffled" its audience by reproducing "the illusion of life itself," as she analyzed, but "the image of life was necessarily haunted by deception."[2] Laura Mulvey's approach creates some fundamentally new insights into the nature of these early viewing experiences, highly relevant for our rereading of Shklovsky's "Art as Technique." It is in the light of this that I invited Laura Mulvey to elaborate on some of the issues concerning *ostranenie* and film at the end of this book.

**AvdO:** Within the context of our debate on *ostranenie* ("making strange"), it might be a good idea to start our conversation with a reflection on early cinema's "alienating" qualities and their specific appeal to early audiences, or to what André

Gaudreault recently referred to as "early cinema's alien quality, a properly irre-ducible alien quality which traditional film historians have always tried to paper over."[3]

As you know, the alien, uncanny or "barbaric" powers of the cinema, as Virgi-nia Woolf called them, were the very powers which impressed the early cinema's audiences. The "alienating" powers of the cinema and the new optical techniques "making things strange" seem to have been *center stage* at this specific moment in time. In retrospect, it is very hard for us to understand these early, and slightly destabilizing, viewing experiences. It seems to me that, due to a cascade of re-search on early cinema (by Aumont, Gunning, Gaudreault, Tsivian, Christie, Kessler, and many others) as well as separate reflections on the experience of the "alien" or "alienating" powers (or techniques) of the cinema (e.g., Casetti's, Sob-chack's and your own work, to name but a few), the impact on art and on culture at large of what mostly *was* a truly alienating viewing experience has indeed been tremendous, particularly between about 1900 to 1920. So now let me pose my first question.

When we look back on this specific period in time with the extensive knowl-edge we have of it now, would you say that we need to reconsider some major reflections of those days *as we understand them now*? Do we need to historicize the key texts once again? Of course I think of Shklovsky's "Art as Technique" here, which was written in 1916, while the issues raised in the crucial paragraphs on perception were already presented by Shklovsky to his Futurist friends as early as 1913.[4] And of course, with regard to your own work, I also think of Freud's reflec-tion on the uncanny, *Das Unheimliche*, from 1919.[5] In *Death 24x a Second* you write that "there is a coincidence of chronology in the 1890s between Freud's ambition to find ways of analyzing the irrational and the arrival of the cinema" and that "Freud's great contribution to modernity was to recognize that the irrational was intrinsic to human reason, 'housed' in the unconscious."[6]

Within this specific context, it seems beneficial to re-read Freud on the uncan-ny as a reflection that in part may have been initiated by the alienating impact early cinema as a new medium had on audiences, that is, as a reflection on the *uncanny* experience of being face to face with something that was inexplicable, leaving the audience baffled by what they saw on the screen. As with the automa-ton, Olympia, in the grotesque story "Sandman" by E.Th.A. Hoffmann, to which Freud also refers in his Uncanny essay (the example is well-known in German aesthetics), one is not sure about the ontological status of the seen. It seems that the intellectual uncertainty it triggers has a strong impact on the imagination. Is it in fact possible to perceive the "automaton" – half machine, half animated being – as an emblem for the new medium, that miraculous machine which produces still images of "humans" and makes them come to life? Did Hoffmann (and Jentsch, who also brought up the example in an early reflection on the aesthetic exploitation of uncertainty in 1906)[7] in fact provide a well-known example for

ANNIE VAN DEN OEVER

Freud to reflect on the uncanny experiences triggered by that new automaton, the "cinema machine"? In short, would you say that Freud's text, read within its specific historical context, might be appreciated as a rather brilliant reflection on the *destabilizing* powers of the new optical medium and its sudden and strong impact on the imagination?

**LM:** Thank you for inviting me to participate in this "conversation" and giving me the opportunity to return to Freud's essay "The Uncanny" from a perspective that differs from the chapter "Uncertainty" in *Death* 24. Perhaps predictably, however, I did find some, if only incidental, pointers towards this conversation when I reread that chapter. I would like to distinguish a couple of points here in your very rich and suggestive commentary above. I think perhaps they relate to each other, but it might be worthwhile beginning by taking them separately.

To my mind, the first issue raised in your question about the "new medium's work" in its early days, its allegorical relation to the automaton and then to the fusion between the animate and inanimate created by the cinematic illusion, goes straight to the heart of the paradox of cinema. From this perspective, as you point out, defamiliarization of the everyday, inherent in its translation onto the screen, works on two levels: the still frames that, when animated by a projector, mimic human perception and, then, the filmic rendition of time as flow, capturing the passing of time in the present and recording it for the future (to mention the most obvious). The first has to do with cinematic mechanics, the transition from material, inanimate, filmstrip to illusion of movement on the screen. The second has more to do with the fascination of the images watched either due to their content or, more to the point here, to their visualization of passing time. The automaton that is "brought to life" (wound up, as it were) by the projector "materializes" into an image on the screen and performs beautifully, usually concealing its inanimate nature. The raw mutation of one into the other might or might not raise questions in people's minds about its actual mechanics, but a certain uncanniness would probably have been particular to early film because the effect was, literally speaking, unfamiliar. But that strange animation of the inanimate, although familiarized by the everyday and by fiction, is carried across time from then until now and is central to the cinema's potential for defamiliarizing the everyday. On the other hand, it might have been a means of engaging with the modern that I will return to later.

You begin by suggesting that, alongside the important, recent research into the history of early cinema itself, the theoretical essays by Shklovsky "Art and Technique" and Freud "The Uncanny" could benefit from being restored to, or read alongside, that expansion of cinema as a key element in their historical and cultural context. Both essays are clearly addressing questions of perception, albeit from very different perspectives. Freud was attempting to restore the rigor of psychoanalytic theory in the face of Ernst Jentsch's speculations on the "uncanny" phenomenon, while also making a few, both rigorous and quite speculative, observations of his own. Shklovsky, of course, was concerned with stimulating a "strangeness" effect through techniques of writing for radical aesthetic purposes. I am interested in the way that the cinema might be seen (perhaps retrospectively) to offer a "threshold" between the two: the term "uncanny" arguably describes (attempts to name) a psychic mechanism that the device of estrangement exploits (or taps into). Both involve disorientation of a norm and thus an enforced pause. I will return to these points more specifically towards the end of our conversation.

You have pointed out that although neither essay mentions the cinema, it would have been hard, at that moment in history, to avoid consciousness of it altogether. While there is copious evidence of Shklovsky's interest in cinema, he does seem to have been concerned in this essay with actual procedures of writing and the practice of poetics. I doubt that Freud had the cinema in mind. By the time he wrote "The Uncanny" in 1919, cinema was no longer "early" and had become very widely diffused. His lack of interest, even antipathy, to it has been traced very convincingly by Stephen Heath who points out that even in 1925, Freud preferred to use the "magic writing-pad" as an analogy for understanding the psyche. Heath comments that contemporaneously:

> Virginia Woolf writes an essay celebrating cinema's capacity to give the 'dream architecture of one's sleep', to depict deep fantasies no matter 'how far fetched or insubstantial', to offer a reality of the mind in defiance of conscious syntax and propositions of identity 'some secret language that we feel and see but never speak'.[8]

However, it seems to me that, in spite of Freud's own indifference, your question stands. Freud was put off by the cinema's literalness and the anxiety he felt about translating the "abstractions" of psychoanalytic theory into "figurations." A more rewarding approach may lie not so much in the images projected onto the screen, but rather in the cinema's mechanism, perhaps its "technique" as such that I mentioned earlier. From this point of view, the cinema's illusion might well touch the kind of imponderables that make the human mind "boggle," that reveal its vulnerability and reach towards the unconscious. With the hindsight generated by recent work on early film, it might be possible to consider ways in which the cinema concentrated these kinds of effects and brought them to the surface of experience in a new way. But I will also speculate (perhaps recklessly) that the cinema did visibly, for its early spectators (and then, even post-narrative, continue to), fuse incompatibles (alongside reality and illusion, for instance, stillness/movement and "then"/"now") into a special kind of paradox particular to its formal, technological structure.

In a sense, the uncanny, distanciation and cinema bring together three quite contrasting phenomena. First, an involuntary shudder caused by something that

ANNIE VAN DEN OEVER

touches a repressed anxiety or reaches back into primal, animistic beliefs supposedly, Freud points out, "surmounted" by civilization. Second, a "technique" devised specifically to jolt the reader out of habit and into sudden consciousness of its dulling effects on the human perception. Finally, a new means of generating an illusion of living reality, unreal in its obvious displacement from its original time and place, but utterly convincing to perception. Your questions suggest not necessarily that the phenomena are linked in some way, but that they might share, even if only coincidentally, some appeal to the human mind's vulnerability to "estrangement" and also, it should be emphasized, its pleasure in these jolts or surprises. The three phenomena lead into the debates on the attractions of early cinema and Tom Gunning's original formulation that popular entertainment (particularly early cinema) could incorporate "uncanny" or "estranging" effects that the avant-garde would continue to try to reproduce through a conscious deployment of "techniques" of defamiliarization.

First of all, I would like to think about ways in which it might be possible to bring the ideas of "uncanniness" and "estrangement" into some kind of shared framework. My first point relates to space and has a closer relevance to the kind of disorientations someone might experience in life rather than in art or poetry. The second relates more to time and brings the two concepts rather closer together.

Freud's discussion of the uncanny revolves (from multiple perspectives) around the human mind's response to certain kinds of shocks that are, by and large, sudden and unpredictable. In this sense, the uncanny is posited on a distortion of normal, continuous, and significantly habitual experience into something strange and frightening. Leaving aside Freud's concern to identify the (unconscious) sources of the uncanny effect, he reiterates the immediacy of a particular experience, as a shift in perception involving loss of ego control. In a short and perhaps quite minor discussion, he brings up three examples of topographical disorientation. In the first, he cites an experience of his own in an Italian town: wandering, he found himself in what was unmistakably a red-light district and describes how, in his efforts to get away, he found himself back three times in the same location and experienced the "uncanny" effect. His ego, disorientated by anxiety and embarrassment had failed to operate normally. He then mentions two generalized experiences: of being lost in a mist and returning, willy nilly, to the same familiar spot repeatedly and, in the dark, searching for a light switch, bumping unexpectedly and repeatedly into a familiar piece of furniture. All of these leave the subject with a sense of mental as well as spatial disorientation. There are, it seems to me, two points of particular interest here.

Freud is describing an experience of estrangement, a defamiliarized sensation. Habit is no longer of use in these situations, and any dependence on automatic bodily movement, guided by pre-existing spatial orientation or established instinct, dissolves into a physical and raw feeling of uncertainty. There might be resonances here with Shklovsky's concept of estrangement: for the poetic effect to have the necessary impact, the reader should be disorientated, taken away from normal or habitual aesthetic expectations, and left in a state of vulnerability comparable to that of the disorientated ego, stripped of defenses as it were.

The second point relates to time. Freud's concept of the uncanny and Shklovsky's of distanciation are located within a particularly heightened experience of the present, accompanied by a falling away, or dissolution, of a normal sense of passing time within which the self/ego feels at home. Habit depends on the invisible progression of moment to moment that carries everyday actions smoothly forward. Both the uncanny and estrangement plunge the subject into a relation to and sensation of time. (Incidentally, Proust occasionally evokes a similar sensation of time detached from its usual flow; this happens when something – an emotion, perception, or quite simply drunkenness, for instance, in the Rivebelle episode[9] in Volume 2 – breaks the hold of Habit, liberating the mind into a non-sequential experience of time in its immediacy.)

**AvdO:** While on the subject of time, Vladimir Nabokov opens his writer's memoir *Speak, Memory* with a reference to the movies and their impact on his imagination in terms of a changed consciousness of time. His words indeed strengthen your argument. He describes the deeply alienating experience of watching his mother in a home movie that was made a few weeks before his birth, noticing that at that specific moment in time nobody "mourned his absence." When watching the movie in Petersburg in 1903, he, a four-year-old "chronofobiac," suddenly felt plunged into "the pure element of time." While firmly and explicitly *rejecting* a connection between the strong appeal of the movies on his immature imagination and Freud's Ur scene and castration complex, Nabokov reflects on the problem of time:

> I felt myself plunged abruptly into a radiant and mobile medium that was none other than the pure element of time. One shared it – just as exited bathers share shining seawater – with creatures that were not oneself but that were joined to one by time's common flow, an environment quite different from the spatial world, which not only man but apes and butterflies can perceive.[10]

The denunciation of Freud is a running gag in Nabokov's novels, as you well know. Instead of exploring the workings or symbols of the "fundamentally medieval" (in Nabokov's words), primitive world of the Freudian subconscious, Nabokov, as an author, seems almost exclusively interested in exploring and describing the poetic effects of such moments of alienation or disruption on his imagination, which he, contrary to Freud, wishes to see not as basically primitive ("shabby" or "vulgar") but as supreme: "the supreme delight of the immortal and the immature."[11] In retrospect, "probing my childhood," Nabokov labels this disruptive early viewing experience as an awakening moment:

> I see the awakening of consciousness as a series of spaced flashes, with the intervals between them gradually diminishing until bright blocks of perception are formed, affording memory a slippery hold.[12]

Interestingly, he describes both the awakening of consciousness and the formation of memory, and many other things besides, in terms of the cinema and cinematographic techniques (a series of spaced flashes, the intervals or ellipses between them, bright blocks of perception), which once again points at the huge cultural impact these early viewing experiences have had on him and his generation, as Yuri Tsivian already stated in his *Early Cinema in Russia and its Cultural Reception*.

**LM:** This is certainly a very vivid example – one that I hadn't come across before. And beyond the temporality memory (a past "then" returning to a later "now"), Nabokov's moment of "awakening consciousness" seems to me also to evoke an extended present, both in the act of memory retrieval and in the memory itself, both, as you point out, "cinematic." This takes me back to "dehabitualized" time, as experienced in estrangement. The immediate "strangeness" of the moment prolongs time beyond the sense of an extended linear flow, carving out a space of sensation outside it, in an overwhelming "now." For Shklovsky this experience was aesthetic and an effect of "art as technique," that is, the defamiliarization essential to poetic language:

> The purpose of art is to impart the sensation of things as they are perceived and not as they are known. The technique of art is to make objects 'unfamiliar' to make forms difficult, to increase the difficulty and the length of perception because the process of perception is an aesthetic end in itself and must be prolonged.[13]

The "sensation" in which "perception must be prolonged," essential for the defamiliarized aesthetic, has a parallel in the sensation of the uncanny, its immediacy in which the subject experiences the present as prolonged until, that is, the ego's habitual defense is reasserted. Although one (Shklovsky) might have been concerned with an agenda for a radical poetics and the other (Freud) with analyzing the human mind, one with exploiting disorientation, the other with explaining it, the experience of time might offer a point of linkage.

Perhaps Freud, in spite of some freer speculations, tended to overstate his case in "The Uncanny" essay, partly to counter Jentsch and the idea that uncanniness might be precipitated by the new, strange and unfamiliar, partly to insist on the primary presence and influence of the unconscious. It seems to me that a rather more flexible approach is needed in order to consider the psychic implications of uncanniness, one in which the unconscious is a constituent element but different "levels" of repression and response may be incorporated into the effect. This would perhaps enable a "rapprochement" between Freud's 1919 insistence on the unconscious sources of uncanniness and the estrangement produced as an effect of art or writing. I hope the following point might be relevant.

My friend and colleague, Ian Christie, recently pointed out to me that the new translation of Freud's 1936 letter to Roman Rolland "A disturbance of memory on the Acropolis"[14] uses the term "estrangement" in such a way as to invite discussion in this context. Freud describes his "disturbed" experience: in a sudden change of plan while traveling during the Summer of 1904, he and his younger brother went unexpectedly to Athens. On the Acropolis, instead of the happiness that this moment, longed for since childhood, should have brought him, Freud experienced a sense of unreality, "what I am seeing here is not real." He goes on to analyze these kinds of moments generally as "estrangements," as "sensations'" in which "a piece of reality or a piece of one's own self has become strange," and he compares them to experiences such as déjà vu, illusions or false-recognitions or depersonalizations.

Freud discusses this kind of estrangement from two perspectives: first, the mechanism as such and, second, its source in memories or painful experiences that might have precipitated this particular sensation at that particular moment in time. From the point of view of my argument, this analysis interestingly reiterates the topographical with the temporal, as the strangeness of place disrupts time into an elongated "sensation" reminiscent, I think, of Shklovsky's evocation of the prolonged moment of perception. But Freud's "estrangement" has other implications that will take me back more specifically to questions of cinema. For him, this sensation is caused by a failure of the ego's defenses. That is, between the total irrational force of repression and the normal rational and habitual workings of recognition, judgment and so on are "a whole series of modes of behavior on the part of the ego that are clearly pathological in character." Here he acknowledges a more nuanced working of the psyche's pathology than he was prepared to accept in the "Uncanny" essay; there he allows little space between repression and the rational in which the kind of uncanniness suggested by Jentsch, or indeed the uncanniness of the cinema, might make itself felt. This uncanniness might hover in between the unconscious and the rational, located precisely neither in one nor in the other.

Freud describes the estrangement he felt on the Acropolis as a "double consciousness" in that it involved a strong denial of an obvious reality. To push the point beyond his argument, as the process of denial creates a break with the ego's habitual forms of perception, the raw, unmediated sensation of "now-ness" stumbles into an excess of reality, untranslatable and "strange." In the first instance, there is nothing more to this than the psychic mechanism, a feeling of strangeness. On the other hand, for Freud, needless to say, this psychic mechanism was a symptom of something deeper, and the purely psychological effect might enable the subject to engage with his or her own history and psychic dilemmas and so, in the process, bring "forgotten" but "familiar" material to consciousness. Freud's analysis of the content aspect of his moment of estrangement does indeed lead back to his memories of childhood, his family and, most of all, to his father. From this perspective, the experience leads directly into the "politics" of his psychic structure, opening up a new perspective on his own history but also on a wider history, bringing new understanding with it. First of all, there is the paternal/filial relation, guilt at dissatisfaction with home, family and its limitations, and then, awareness of his family's place within the class and racial structure of its surrounding society. It might not be too far fetched, I hope, to see Freud's experience of estrangement and its analysis as throwing some light on the aspirations of Shklovsky's radical poetics: changed perception, triggered by the sensation of estrangement, might lead, past the mechanism as such, to new ways of perceiving the world. (Ultimately, this would lead towards Brecht and his adaptation of Shklovsky's term for overtly political purposes.)

Although the material that I am discussing here (on the Acropolis) dates from 1936, much later than the "Uncanny" essay with which we started our "conversation," I have tried to "read backwards" from the later to the earlier, to engage with a more nuanced consideration of the uncanny than the 1919 essay allows at first sight. Thus, Freud suggests that the experience of estrangement involves a "double consciousness" that contains both a denial of an obvious reality and the presence of a lost, past feeling from which the present sensation emanates. Both these phenomena might lead into our discussion of the cinema.

But it might also be interesting to note, in passing, that Freud does acknowledge a literary uncanny towards the end of the 1919 essay. While he continues to dismiss the strange events of fairy stories, he makes a remark that seems to point towards "an aesthetic uncanny" or the possibility of an "estrangement device" constructed by a writer:

> In the main we adopt an unvaryingly passive attitude to our real experience and are subject to the influence of our physical environment. But the story teller has a *peculiarly* directive power over us; by means of the moods he can put us into, he is able to guide the current of our emotions, to dam it up in one direction and make it flow in another...[15]

He seems here to have shifted his attention away from character and what uncanny events happen in fiction, towards the mechanics of writing and the writer's ability, as a storyteller, to conjure up certain feelings... "art as technique" perhaps?

It might be particularly telling for this discussion that he mentions our "passive attitude" to real experience. It is tempting to see this "passivity" in terms of habit and the self's unthinking integration into daily space and time that the estrangement device is intended to shatter. However, on a personal note, I have always felt a rather uncanny shudder when Freud says: "We should hardly call it uncanny when Pygmalion's beautiful statue comes to life."[16] Although I will return to the question of the animate/inanimate later on, this comment might remind us that, for Freud, the category "beautiful" and the category "uncanny" seem to be incompatible.

**AvdO:** I fully agree that Freud's comment is quite surprising. Basically, I am not at all convinced that the category of the beautiful forms the heart of the matter. To my mind, beauty is a perceptual category, used for "what pleases the eye," that is often viewed in terms of the senses, of colors, proportions, symmetries, regularities, and so on. The category of the uncanny, however, inevitably points towards some sort of conceptual or cognitive problem (to what Jentsch calls "intellectual uncertainty"). A statue being beautiful is one thing, it coming to life and starting to move about is quite another.

The story of E.Th.A. Hoffmann that Freud and Jentsch reflect on in their discussion of the uncanny is part of the grotesque tradition in German aesthetics. The fundamental problem in this story on the beautiful "automaton" Olympia coming to life is, no doubt, the category problem Hoffmann created (which Freud seems to understate): is she a woman or a robot, animate or inanimate, dead or alive? As Wolfgang Kayser convincingly argued in his standard work on the grotesque, The Grotesque in Literature and Art, the "uncanny" ("das Unheimliche," in Kayser's words)[17] was exactly what Hoffmann was playing on while keeping his readers in uncertainty about the ontological status of Olympia. Hoffmann was deliberately aiming for this type of effect, as was Edgar Allen Poe, who followed Hoffmann's example. The aesthetics of the grotesque point in the direction of a use of techniques which purposefully yet secretly disturb fundamental biological and ontological categories when representing beings (humans). Therefore, we may respond strongly when we are face to face with the grotesque: "Die Kategorien unserer Weltorientierung versagen," as Kayser put it.[18] The categories of the understanding fail. I always felt that Kayser is very close to Kant here, who stated that when face to face with the sublime, the categories of the understanding momentarily give way to a free interaction between Reason and the Imagination. Kayser, however, stresses the particularly uncanny feeling of "Verfremdung" triggered by the grotesque.

As for Freud, perhaps he toned down the uncanny effect Pygmalion's statue had on him, for the sake of argument. Or perhaps he just quietly enjoyed the statue's beauty without giving much thought to whether he was in front of a statue or an animate being. It may also be that, due to habitualization, the experience was not very deep or immediate at all, since he had seen statues like Pygmalion's before and read stories like Hoffmann's many a time.

The trope of a sculpture so lifelike it seems about to move is a commonplace with writers on works of art from Antiquity to the present day. The well-known rhetorical figure seems part of a discourse strategy to help sculptors stun and stupefy their viewers in a *well-organized moment of "monstration,"* as André Gaudreault labeled such moments in relation to early cinema: moments of demonstration and celebration of new techniques devised to make viewers marvel at the novelties, to stun and stupefy them.

Interestingly, this type of stupor and distinct feelings of the uncanny are also described as part of the experience viewers had when seeing the Pietà by Michelangelo for the first time. This is very hard to understand, in retrospect, since the statue is beautiful to us in the first place. It is well-proportioned, made of a pearly-white marble, and its depiction of a grieving Mary is of course full of tragedy. Michelangelo succeeded in coming closer to real life than any sculptor before him had been able to, using new techniques to represent the body in an anatomically correct manner, a typical Renaissance discovery. The problem for Renaissance viewers was, as David Summers describes, that they could not distinguish the statue from a real human being and were confused and deceived by the resemblance.[19] Once again, a category confusion is at the basis of this disturbing experience: the categories of "real" and "mediated" were being confused by viewers who did not yet know the new techniques Michelangelo used to represent the body. It might also be interesting to note that Michelangelo worked for the Pope and was paid by the Pope and may well have been looking for a good moment of monstration to "stun and stupefy," as it were. Monstration is part of Catholic tradition, as a friend of mine, the art historian Eric de Bruyn, pointed out to me only recently. It is a well-known element in Catholic liturgy and part of a practice of adoration I have never seen described within the context of monstration in early cinema so far. In Catholic Mass, a golden, so-called "monstrance" containing the "blessed sacrament" is displayed by the priest for veneration during the mass's climatic moment of "consecration" (admiration). In terms of the liturgy, this is the pivotal moment of transubstantiation or transfiguration of the common bread and wine into the blood and body of Christ. Strikingly, Arthur Danto labeled Andy Warhol's presentation of close-ups of Marilyn Monroe and Jackie Kennedy (enormously enlarged, highly stylized, ornament-like, decorative) exhibited in museums all over the world as "transfigurations of the commonplace."[20] The point I am trying to make here is that it is not so much the category of beauty that is fundamental to this "practice of admiration" (or to these other experiences described here), but rather the uncanny, which you described as a distinct experience of something outside the common. Would you agree that the elevated as well as the abyssal may be part of the experience? And that it is not triggered by the techniques to establish beauty but rather by techniques which confuse animate and inanimate, the living and the dead?

One of the problems for Freud, as well as for us, trying to understand the impact of early cinema, is to explain why the uncanny seems so at home in this context. It seems that, particularly in the field of the pictorial and the visual, an uncanny effect is easily triggered. As the pictorial tradition of the grotesque has elaborately shown in its long history, a relatively small formal change already manages to trigger a radical and unexpected twist in meaning. For example, a close-up, distorting the natural scale and proportions, poses a disturbing category problem that may well induce a sudden uncanny shudder. In fact, a novelty like the gigantic eye in GRANDMA'S READING GLASS (1900) was thrilling to its early audiences for this very reason: an eye the size of an elephant is not an eye but a monster, the same way a gigantic spider is not a spider but a monster. The same could be said for the enormous ear, shown as a maximum close-up in black and white in Eisenstein's OLD AND NEW (1928). The close-up of the ear is sinister and crater-like, and according to Shklovsky, a perfect example of one of the "grotesques" found in Eisenstein's work.[21] When suddenly and "aggressively" put in front of an audience, such a close-up, as Sergei Eisenstein understood perfectly well, would undoubtedly have been perceived as deeply uncanny and an attraction in itself. Eisenstein, his mentor Meyerhold, Shklovsky and Eichenbaum: they were all familiar with this type of distortion and with the tradition of the grotesque in theater, art, and literature. For them, this tradition may well have functioned as an historical model for understanding the "deformations" early cinema and the avant-gardes provided to them. I have always felt that Boris Eichenbaum was quite right when he reminds us in Poetika Kino that "deformations," as in the grotesque, are the basis of "photogenicity" (Delluc) in the cinema and that defamiliarization is really at the heart of it: because film is a lens-based art and optical technology is basic to it, films easily provide deformed and distorted images of the world. According to Eichenbaum, "Art lives on that which removes itself from the everyday," and as he explains further, "If art does make use of the everyday, it uses it [...] in an explicitly deformed state (as in the grotesque)."[22] We must keep reminding ourselves that only a slight technical deformation, caused by a new technology or new artistic technique (like Michelangelo's), may turn a normal human being into something uncanny and that historical audiences indeed may well have responded accordingly. A real problem for Film and Media Studies, it seems to me, is trying to understand these ongoing confrontations with the uncanny, because in the end these instances all seem to lose the power to defamiliarize due to habitualization, a process which makes the history of film (and the media, and art) so very hard to understand in retrospect.

LM: I think your points about changing responses to the Pietà remind us very clearly of the contingent nature of aesthetic perception, which is also relevant to changing attitudes to the cinema. And included in those must be the shift from the early sense of something "alien" with which you started this discussion to its incorporation into a habitual mode of perception, smoothed on its way, it has been argued, by narrative. In his essay [in Rethinking Media], Tom Gunning makes the very thought-provoking suggestion that the move from one mode of perception to the other may be reversed. He begins by tracing the simple shift from (in his terms) wonder and astonishment to their subordination to habit and the incorporation of the strange into second nature. He then argues that Shklovsky's concept of defamiliarization through art could enable habituated perception to once again recover its strangeness. Furthermore, he points out that the uncanny is constantly "crouching ready to spring" in the threshold space of these transitions, bringing with it Freud's sense of those "primitive beliefs" that civilization seemed to have, or should have, surmounted. Uncertainty about the seemingly magical functioning of the cinema, its illusion of life easily collapsing into a bewildering consciousness of the living dead and the human machine, would make it a particularly appropriate technology for triggering these kinds of sensations. But here the cinema's uncanniness seems to be caught in the underworlds of ghostliness and the automata. It might be interesting to reconfigure the question in terms of the cinema's modernity and its ability to offer a means of negotiation between residual uncanninesses and their transcendence, or rather their incorporation into new forms of perception that accompany the modern world.

**AvdO:** Interestingly, Shklovsky connects "making strange" with "techniques" and the technical in art in his "Art as Technique." In my view, he thus opens up a conceptual space for a radically new reflection on the crucial connection between the technical deformations and distortions, caused by the optical technology of the apparatus, and the *artistic* techniques, invented and used by artists of all disciplines (from Michelangelo to Giacometti, Tolstoy to Mayakovsky, Meliès to Eisenstein): all techniques may have a disruptive impact on perception, and as such all techniques are equal, as he states. Eisenstein would repeat these very words in the 1920s. As early as 1913, Shklovsky understood the disruptive perceptual experience to be fundamental to art, and not specifically to art associated with the avant-garde or avant-garde techniques (such as collage techniques), as many have come to think in later decades.

Rereading Shklovsky on art as a technique from our current perspective, one may suddenly become aware of subtle hints and traces that might well refer to early confrontations with the new "cinema machine," and although Shklovsky does not refer to the cinema per se in "Art as Technique," his manifest certainly gives the impression he was indeed influenced by the impact of the new medium. The world "made strange" by the new optical techniques and a sense of destabilization may well have been center stage in those early days.

Whereas Shklovsky and *Opoyaz* laid out a new research agenda for the study of art "as technique," basically from 1913 onwards, Freud became *the* author to elaborate on the impact of disruptive experiences on the imagination. The avant-garde movements, in the meantime, seem to have understood the destabilizing powers of all sorts of optical, formal, and visual techniques quite early on. So when the cinema (still very young as an institution) started to reject, repress, and domesticate these very powers to create a stable story-telling system, the avant-garde movements were the first to reinforce those destabilizing powers yet again. There is indeed an interesting simultaneity between all these developments.

Now let us suppose that there was a "shared historical experience"[23] at the basis of all these discursive reflections and explorations of the disruptive perceptual experience. Moreover, let us suppose that the early cinema experience was at the heart of the shared experience of the modern. That is, the experience not just of a film but of the whole "cinema machine" (as you call it), which "alienated" its early audiences from the world they were familiar with by (optically, perceptually) "making it strange" all of a sudden. The "uncanny" experience of a world "made strange" by the new mass medium may have been a very important factor in the shaping of the way people "experienced" the modern. Because it was *shared* experience enjoyed on a massive scale, the new medium most likely deepened its cultural impact far more quickly and effectively than any other medium could. The *shared* experience may even have functioned as a model for the new experience of the new century as opposed to the old century, now *past*, in other words: now *lost*. In that case, understandably, "it" (the new experience, the new medium) may have resonated, culturally, in many different ways, in many different discourses, in many different fields – and in the end, contributions to the discourse may well have come from authors who even tried to stay away from the new and the modern... Of course, I am not thinking of Shklovsky here, nor of the avant-garde movements, but of Freud.

**LM:** It would probably be logical, at this point, to consider whether the medium's devices used across the long tradition of avant-garde film (as Gunning emphasized in his original "Attractions" article) to "defamilarize" and "estrange" are in any way uncanny, or whether they enable this kind of perceptual transition. I would be tempted, in the first instance, to echo Freud's dismissive 1919 voice and put them on the side of the too rational, too obviously exposing the mechanisms of film and thus failing to cause the spectator to shudder. However, in many of its aesthetic strands, avant-garde aesthetics bring the spectator face to face with the way that, unlike other art forms, film is an emanation of a machine, ultimately beyond the human, however closely it might be guided by human intention.

As Vertov constantly reiterated, the kino eye is detached from and unlike the human eye. MAN WITH A MOVIE CAMERA, from this perspective, pushes our argument beyond the uncanny into a "materialist" celebration of the machine.

While the film makes use of cinema's implicitly uncanny mechanisms to introduce the "shock" of the modern, the sensation it provokes may no longer be one of the uncanny but of a more modernist estrangement, as though, in the process of learning modernity, the archaic shudder gives way to a more questioning curiosity. For instance, as still frames give rise to an illusion of movement (illustrated in the editing room sequence), so images of machines shift from stillness to movement and, even more so, shop window automata come "to life" alongside the city and its working day. This is a liberating rather than a mystifying phenomenon. The film conjures up a new and modern world, in which the time has come to "surmount" any primitive feelings of uncanniness that might have been lurking in the cinema and its surrounding machines. Just as Freud considered religion simply as a "respectable" version of primitive superstition, Vertov shows that there need be nothing "mind boggling" in the magic of cinema... Here, I am (obviously, to those who know it) thinking of Annette Michelson's article about MAN WITH A MOVIE CAMERA, "From Magician to Epistemologist,"[24] in which she traces and celebrates the brilliant way in which Vertov carries his audience from residual amazement to jubilant understanding.

However, Vertov's film draws attention to and dwells on those paradoxes of cinema that I mentioned at the beginning of our conversation: those that go beyond the workings of the mechanism to the very special relation it has to time and its passing. The mechanism's fusion of movement and stillness entrances the audience, showing that the perceptual threshold of "estrangement" brings pleasure and might well be a means of incorporating new sensations within new configurations. However, MAN WITH A MOVIE CAMERA introduces, and reflects on, the paradox of the "then" of registration and "now" of illusion, once again finding its own way of visualizing this dimension of cinematic engagement with time. At the end of the film, as we see its original audience watching MAN WITH A MOVIE CAMERA, the cuts between the point of view of the 1928 audience and the screen image are supplemented by shots of the screen in which the point of view of future audiences is implicitly inserted. This fusion of temporalities could be understood as uncanny: the sequence addresses the spectator directly, "now" from the "then" of a ghostly past, as just one historical moment en route to audiences of the future. I find that the way this sequence conveys the physical sensation of time as being "beyond" my grasp (bringing with it the characteristic shudder that marks the momentary retreat of ego and reason) is not diminished, but rather mutates. The sequence generates a reflection on time itself and a sense of "physical exhilaration" at the way in which cinema mediates between past and future, between the living Moscow audience then and me at the moment of watching now, as well as vividly illustrating the importance of film's mechanisms for an aesthetics of modernity. The sense of being directly addressed (that Gunning evokes in "The Cinema of Attraction(s)") tends to draw the spectator's attention to the presence of time in film, especially when the address comes from beyond the grave. From this perspective, the substance of the address is more or less irrelevant; it is the sensation, or rather the mechanism, of psychic disorientation that counts (as in Freud's initial feelings on the Acropolis). But ultimately the disorientation leads to questioning, to the pleasure in mutation and a vertiginous sense of a new phase of understanding.

I would like to return to the question of changing perceptions of cinema throughout its history, in keeping with your earlier comments on the Pietà. To my mind, the experience of film time varies according to varying modes of audience experience as well as according to variations in the cinematic mode of address. I would like to suggest that, at the present moment in time, consciousness of the cinema's history and its specific relation to temporality comes to the surface along the lines that Gunning evokes as a "renewable" defamiliarization. However, this sensation contrasts with that of early audiences.

For instance, Mitchell and Kenyon (British showmen/entrepreneurs active at the very beginning of the twentieth century) filmed working-class people in the cities of northern England, coming out of factories, in the streets, and then invited them, with placards and handbills, to view the results later that day in the fairground. In this instance, uncanny animation of the film-strip through the machine into movement might be overtaken by the uncanny recognition of the newly animated self on the screen, heightened by the closeness in time between the moment of being filmed and the moment when people saw themselves projected on the screen within, and extracted from, the continuum of the everyday. But this experience might also offer a way of thinking between a disorientating uncanniness and an exhilarating sensation of modernity. Although it's difficult to speculate, it might, in fact, be possible to imagine that this encounter with oneself on screen, animated by a machine, transforming an ordinary gesture into an extraordinary enlargement, embalming the very immediate past into a chunk of impossibly repeated time, would have been an experience in which uncanniness mutated out of the deception of artifice into curiosity and engagement with the paradoxes of cinema. The photograph's preservation of a frozen moment would have been a familiar phenomenon at the time, but the strangeness engendered by cinematic "animation" and the extension of a single moment into the impossible flow of preserved time complicates and considerably adds strangeness to the photograph's fusion of "now" and "then."

The immediacy and the direct address essential to these films recall the "exhibitionist cinema" that Tom Gunning describes in "The Cinema of Attraction(s)," and it is, perhaps, this raw sense of "being there" that carries another kind of uncanniness, the sensation derived from witnessing not only the past but that chunk of extended time past, across one hundred years until now. Then, it was the closeness of one moment experienced in life (registration) to the next (the witnessed projection) that created an estrangement from a habitual sense of passing time, a jolt in a continuum. Now, on the contrary, the actual distance in time between then and now introduces a new dimension to the animate/inanimate fusion, and the sensation of uncanniness is intertwined with the preservation of these informal, casual beings animated on the screen long after their death. From this perspective, the way that the cinema is increasingly inhabited by ghosts, literally due to the passing of time, returns it to the uncanny and has perhaps reduced the exhilaration of the modern. These points relate to my arguments in *Death 24...* When I first started working on the ideas for the book, I was struck by the way that a shift in aesthetic sensibility can introduce, retrospectively and, as Gunning points out, reversibly, a new sense of amazement at an old technology. Suddenly, one sees the cinema as it had always been... but with its familiar features estranged into a reconfigured profile, its patterns shifting their well-known contours into a new relief.

**AvdO:** If we return for a moment to our first questions and to the start of the cinema: would you say that the "automaton," central in Jentsch's and Freud's reflections on the uncanny, comes close to being a metaphor for the new "cinema machine"? Does early cinema not "work" on its viewers the way the "automaton" (Olympia) works on the reader of Hoffmann's story? Does the "automaton," the way it (she) *moves and seems animate*, not create an "intellectual uncertainty" in the viewers about its (her) true ontological status? In effect, does it not push them outside their stable relations to tradition (representational) and the symbolic? Could it be that the new medium (early cinema) created such a strong impact on the imagination precisely because it challenged intellectual certainties? Of course, I am well aware I touch upon your own reflections on pre- and early cinema in *Death 24 x a Second*. Could you share some of those reflections with us, particularly those regarding Freud and the automaton?

**LM:** Freud covered a number of different approaches to the uncanny in his essay. Beyond the examples of spatial disorientation that I mentioned before, he was ultimately interested in the presence of an unconscious fear behind a sensation of uncanniness. As I tried to suggest in *Death 24...*, he was concerned to attribute the uncanny sensation to something old and familiar that "returns," and thus to distance himself from the new "technological" uncanny that had caught Jentsch's attention. For Freud, unlike Jentsch, the actual confusion of the animate and the inanimate encapsulated by Olympia (the automaton with which Nathaniel falls in love in Hoffmann's "The Sandman") was of little interest. He attempted to displace the automaton, to make her irrelevant to the argument, and analyze instead Nathaniel's castration complex. For Freud, castration was deeply rooted in the archaic nature of the unconscious, and perhaps, this perspective also enabled him to insist on the primary, structuring theories of psychoanalysis and avoid the newfangled – whether it might be theoretical or technical.

I suggested in *Death 24...* that Freud overreacted by dismissing Olympia so easily in his 1919 "Uncanny" essay... But this may have been anachronistic on my part: it was in 1927, in his essay on "Fetishism," that Freud associated castration anxiety with the over-valuation of a reassuring substitute, a fetish object, that could disavow the female body's missing penis. It is here that one might be able to find a key role for the automaton in the slippage between the "Uncanny" essay and "Fetishism." In the light of Freud's later theory, Nathaniel might be seen to "fetishize" the automaton Olympia, the artificially beautiful, mechanically perfect woman who, without a messy "inside" or frightening "wound," provides a fascinating substitute for the real female body and its lack. From this perspective, the Olympia of "The Uncanny" might be reconfigured, retrospectively in the light of "Fetishism," not to dismiss the centrality of castration but to include disavowal in Nathaniel's fetishistic over-valuation of the automaton. The mechanical female can then be included in an analysis of the story, no longer irrelevant but an essential displacement and substitute for the fear initiated by "the sandman's threat to Nathaniel's eyes, on which Freud based his analysis in the 'Uncanny,'" The mechanical woman fends off the fear triggered by the female body. In quite an interesting way, the uncanniness of the automaton, which triggers the shudder of strangeness, can then be traced to its source in his castration complex in the case of Nathaniel. From this perspective, neither Nathaniel in the story nor Freud in his analysis of it realizes the essential connection between the two. One might follow this argument further: if the machine's presence erupts into the spectator's consciousness, if the mechanism of projection makes itself felt, the sense of "breakdown" threatens the illusion on which so much narrative cinema depends. For this kind of cinema, there is a possible analogy between the anxiety provoked by castration and the anxiety provoked by the threat of mechanical failure. Both share a fetishistic investment in illusion.

I would like to end by returning to a point you raised at the beginning of our discussion. You cited André Gaudreault's question: what happened to the "properly irreducible alien" quality of early cinema? Following on from my reflections above about "The Sandman" and the fictional character Nathaniel's castration anxiety as the unconscious "source" for his inability to acknowledge that Olympia is an automaton, I have been thinking about my 1975 article ["Visual Pleasure and Narrative Cinema"][25] in which I make an association between the erotic spectacle of women and castration anxiety. There might be a way in which, as the cinema evolved into an industry and a more sophisticated means of storytelling than those early films had been able to manage, consciousness of the mechanism (as a source of uncanniness and amazement) became displaced onto the excess of spectacle personified by the female star. In "VP and NC" I saw her as disruptive to conventions of narrative, asserting the instantaneous aspect of voyeuristic pleasure that threatened to assert the "now-ness" of the spectacle over the integrity of fictional time. From this perspective, the alien nature of the film mechanism (perhaps alongside narrativity) retreated into the unconscious and found a "home" in the "alien nature" of female sexuality, which threatened to emerge as an excess of spectacle, only to slip back, as the story's fictional time reasserted itself, into the over-riding demands of male narrative control. The eruption of the female star as spectacle, needless to say, cannot be understood as smooth and well balanced within a given film/story but as a startling presence at certain privileged moments, often, I argued in 1975, rationalized as disruptive performance became actual "show girl" performance. Here, as I said in the 1975 article and developed in the later collection of essays *Fetishism and Curiosity*,[26] the beautiful woman's surface distracts from her unpleasant, hidden body just as the surface of the screen covers over the unsightly process of projection. The beautiful automaton might then be seen as a figuration of both.

I am very grateful, Annie, to you for sending me Eric Naiman's essay "Shklovsky's Dog and Mulvey's Pleasure: The Secret Life of Defamiliarization"[27] which I had never come across before now and I read, by chance, soon after reading Scott Bukatman's essay "Spectacle, Attractions and Visual Pleasure"[28] in *The Cinema of Attractions Reloaded*. Both point out that I must have been familiar with Shklovsky's argument and the concept of "estrangement." Although I am pretty sure that I had not read the actual article "Art and Technique," the recent revival of interest in Russian Formalism, during the 1960s and early 1970s (and particularly due to Peter Wollen's close involvement with both the aesthetic theory and the Soviet avant-garde in general), the articles and reprints in *Screen* would have meant that I must have been influenced by the idea, probably loosely connected with Brechtian aesthetics, similarly going through a revival at the time. It is interesting to look back at the 1975 article reconfigured in these terms which draw attention to the way that the argument about Hollywood cinema was closely connected to my political intuition that any feminist engagement with film would have to be through avant-garde aesthetics.

# Notes

## Introduction

1. Lee T. Lemon, and Marion J. Reis, *Russian Formalist Criticism. Four Essays* (Lincoln: University of Nebraska Press, 1965), 3. In retrospect, these early post-war re-readings of Russian Formalism may be said to have been part of setting a research agenda for the new post-war field of General Literature or *Literaturwissenschaft*.

2. For information on Shklovsky's lecture as a freshman in 1913, see Richard Sheldon in his "Introduction" to *A Sentimental Journey* (New York: Cornell University Press), 1970. Shklovsky's *Theory of Prose*, from 1919, is often mistaken as the text in which *ostranenie* was introduced for the first time – but it was not. It was preceded by several other texts presenting the concept, or principle, if you will.

3. Yuri Tsivian, *Early Cinema in Russia and its Cultural Reception*, trans. A. Bodger, and ed. R. Taylor (London & New York: Routledge, 1994), 12.

4. *Ibid.* 217.

5. See Svetlana Boym, "Poetics and Politics of Estrangement: Victor Shklovsky and Hannah Arendt," *Poetics Today* 26, 4 (winter 2005).

6. See Dominique Chateau in this book.

7. An earlier and interesting attempt to rethink the avant-gardes from the perspective of a *new* vision on (artistic) *technique* (mainly painterly or pictorial techniques) was undertaken by the late Dietrich Scheunemann and a team of researchers at the University of Edinburgh. His book and the "new perspectives" he presented explicitly go against the assumptions regarding artistic technique held by the highly valued Peter Bürger, an authority in the field of avant-garde studies from the 1970s onwards. It was Scheunemann's attempt to enrich the field with new insights by criticizing Bürger's indeed slightly elevated and idealist attitude towards artists and their artistic techniques. Cinema and media studies, however, do not play a crucial role in this book. See: *European Avant-Garde: New Perspectives*, ed. Dietrich Scheunemann (Amsterdam & Atlanta: Rodopi), 2000.

8. Marshall McLuhan, *Understanding Media. The Extensions of Man*, (London & New York: Routledge, 2008), 6.

9. A new and extended edition of *Poetika Kino* (Poetics of Film) was presented in a German translation in 2005. This interesting volume contains many earlier and later writings on the cinema by the Russian Formalists, apart from the texts published in Russia in 1927 under the title *Poètika Kino*. A considerable amount is written by Shklovsky. Wolfgang Beilenhoff, ed. *Poetika Kino. Theorie und Praxis des Films im russischen Formalismus*, trans. Wolfgang Beilenhoff (Frankfurt am Main: Suhrkamp), 2005.

10. See Yuri Tsivian in this book.

11. Meir Sternberg, "Telling in Time (III): Chronology, Estrangement, and Stories of Literary History," *Poetics Today* 27, 1 (2006): 125, 168-178. Sternberg devoted several long

articles and a special issue of *Poetics Today* to the problem of *Ostranenie*. See also Chateau in this book.

## The Gesture of Revolution or Misquoting as Device

1. An earlier version of this contribution was published in *October*. See: "Turning Objects, Toppled Pictures: Give and Take Between Vertov's Films and Constructivist Art," *October* 121 (summer 2007): 92-110.
2. Aleksey N. Tolstoy, "Vozmozhnosti kino," [The Potential of the Cinema] *Kinonedelya* [Cinema Weekly], published in installments in numbers 1, 2, 3, 8: № 1, c. 2; № 2, c. 2-3; № 3, c. 2-3; № 8, c. 3 (1924).
3. Tolstoy, *Kinonedelya*, 2, 4.
4. Ibid.
5. Ibid.
6. Ibid., 3.
7. Ibid.
8. The qualification "primal" seems to have come from Tolstoy, although the idea of the superficial and profound gestures is, of course, not his. It is considered to go back to Lessing's *Hamburg Dramaturgy*. There, Lessing teaches Hamburg actors that there are ordinary gestures (*Geste* or *Gebaerde*), but also a special sort of gestures (*Gestus*), which were once the secret of the actors of the ancient theatre. Lessing's *Gestus* is the gesture touching the very essence of human existence. See Daniel Albright, *Untwisting the Serpent: Modernism in Music, Literature and the Other Arts* (Chicago: University of Chicago Press, 2000), 108-110.
9. Ibid.
10. Ibid.
11. Ibid., 4.
12. Viktor Shklovsky, *O teorii prozy* [Theory of Prose] (Moscow: Krug, 1983), 73.
13. Ibid., 74-75.
14. Isaak Levitan, *Pis'ma. Dokumenty. Vospominaniya* [Letters, Documents, Reminiscences] (Moscow: 1956), 132.
15. Ibid., 213.
16. Here is how Kandinsky saw art of the end of the nineteenth century in the early twentieth century: "Ladies fainted and men felt sick in front of a Repin painting, so vivid was the blood which flowed and clotted in his *Ivan the Terrible and His Son Ivan*. "'What have I got to do with art,' Repin seems to be saying, 'I just need the blood to flow and smell bloody.' The only subtler material for art was 'mood,' the song of sadness and inconsolable longing. This was the art which, like the great Russian literature, reflected the despair of closed doors. Both in Chekhov's works and in Levitan's landscapes, the inescapably dreadful atmosphere of a viscous, boundless, suffocating cloud lived and multiplied. In such works art fulfils only half of its mission." (Vasily Kandinsky, "Kuda idet 'novoye iskusstvo'?" [Where is the 'new art' heading?] in *Selected Writings on the Theory of Art 1901-1914* [Izbranye trudy po teorii iskusstva] (Moscow, 2001), 1: 90.
17. Vasily Kandinsky, "Stupeni. Tekst khudozhnika," [Steps. An Artist's Text] in *Selected Writings on the Theory of Art* (Moscow, 2001), 1: 280-281 [my translation].
18. Ibid.

19. Viktor Shklovsky, *O teorii prozy* [Theory of Prose] (Moscow: Krug, 1925), 61); in my quotations from this book I made use of Benjamin Sher's competent translation (Elmwood Park, IL.: Dalkey Archive Press, 1990) which I afforded to modify but slightly.

20. *Ibid.*

21. *Ibid.* [my translation].

22. Anton Chekhov, *Sobranye sochinenii*, [Collected Works] (Moscow: 1963), 10: 493.

23. Aleksandr Rodchenko, "Puti sovremennoy fotografii," [The Paths of Contemporary Photography] *Novyi LEF* 9 [The New LEF] (1928): 33.

24. *Ibid.*, 39.

25. *Ibid.*, 38.

26. Aleksey N. Tolstoy, "Vozmozhnosti kino," [The Potential of the Cinema] *Kinonedelya* 2 (1924): 3.

27. Sergey Eisenstein, "A Lecture in Biomechanics 28 March 1935," in V.A. Shcherbakov, *Meyerkhol'dovskii sbornik* [The Meyerhold Collection] 2d ed.: *Meyerhold i drugie*, [Meyerhold and Others] ed. O.M. Feldman (Moscow: 2000), 73.

## *Ostranenie*, "The Montage of Attractions" and Early Cinema's "Properly Irreducible *Alien* Quality"

1. For a reflection on the relation of the post-war readings of Russian Formalism within the context of immanent criticism, revering the linguist Roman Jakobson and a Jakobsonian research agenda, as is suggested, see Meir Sternberg's contributions to *Poetics Today*, a journal which, over the years, devoted several specials to the topic of *ostranenie*. See for a *critique* on the (Jakobsonian) post-war reintroduction of Russian Formalism in particular Sternberg's "Telling in Time (III): Chronology, Estrangement, and Stories of Literary History," *Poetics Today* 27, 1 (2006): 125-135. See also Dominique Chateau in this volume.

2. See Lee T. Lemon and Marion J. Reis, *Russian Formalist Criticism. Four Essays* (Lincoln: University of Nebraska Press), 1965. See also Eichenbaum, "The Theory of the 'Formal Method,'" in *Russian Formalist Criticism*, eds. Lee T. Lemon and Marion J. Reis (Lincoln: University of Nebraska Press, 1965), 113. I am by far not the first to protest against the post-war structuralist version of Russian Formalism. An interesting critique is to be found in Gerald L. Bruns' "Introduction" to a 1991 translation of Shklovsky's *Theory of Prose* (trans. Benjamin Sher (Illinois State University, USA: Dalkey Archive Press, 1991).: "Russian Formalism is not Structuralism. Its method is historical research rather than the analytical construction of models. Structuralism raises itself on an opposition between system and history, structure and event; Russian Formalism defines itself not against history but against psychology. The difference between Formalism and Structuralism lies in the way the singular is preserved in the one but erased by the other. Structuralism is a method of subsumptive thinking. What matters is the totality of the system. But Shklovsky's formalism is distributed along a diachronic plane. His theory of prose is a *prose* theory of prose, not the systematic construction of a model indifferent to its examples [...]. Shklovsky's model is not the linguistics of Saussure but historical linguistics and comparative philology. He is closer to Auerbach than to Todorov. He is interested in the historicality of forms rather than in the rules

of how formal objects work." See Gerald L. Bruns, "Introduction," in *Theory of Prose*, trans. Benjamin Sher (Illinois State University, USA: Dalkey Archive Press, 1991), xii.

3. Note that the word "manifesto," most often used in these days, also by Eichenbaum, acknowledges that this term for a brash piece of writing by a group to loudly present or rather *manifest* itself was coined in the context of politics and was also used slightly earlier in the context of Italian Futurism in which the manifestos by Marinetti grew to fame in the 1910s and 1920s.

4. Eichenbaum refers to their violation of traditional notions, "which had appeared to be 'axiomatic,'" in "The Theory of the 'Formal Method,'" 104.

5. The words "brash irreverence" I took from Victor Erlich's "Russian Formalism," *Journal of the History of Ideas* 34, 4 (October – December 1973): 638. One must doubt, however, that these words are used by Erlich in a positive way. Most contemporaries and many later scholars took note of the "brashness" of the avant-garde attacks on tradition with great reserve.

6. "Formalism and Futurism seemed bound together by history," as Eichenbaum wrote in his 1926 retrospective overview of the formative years of Russian Formalism. See Eichenbaum in "The Theory of the 'Formal Method,'" 104-105: "Our creation of a radically unconventional poetics, therefore, implied more than a simple reassessment of particular problems; it had an impact on the study of art generally. It had its impact because of a series of historical developments, the most important of which were the crisis in philosophical aesthetics and the startling innovations in art (in Russia most abrupt and most clearly defined in [Futurist] poetry). Aesthetics seemed barren and art deliberately denuded – in an entirely primitive condition. Hence, Formalism and Futurism seemed bound together by history."

7. Yuri Tsivian is of course of invaluable significance in this field. See in particular his *Early Cinema in Russia and its Cultural Reception*, trans. A. Bodger, and ed. R. Taylor (London & New York: Routledge, 1994), 217. One must note that in the last two decades, interesting and highly valuable research in this area – also on the connection between early cinema and the avant-garde – mostly comes from Film Studies and so-called Early Cinema Studies in particular, and less from what is institutionally labeled as (continental) "Avant-Garde Studies."

8. See Boris Eichenbaum in "The Theory of the 'Formal Method,'" 115: "Concerning form, the Formalists thought it important to change the meaning of this muddled term. It was important to destroy these traditional correlatives and so to enrich the idea of form with new significance. *The notion of 'technique,'* [...], *is much more significant in the long-range evolution of formalism than is the notion of 'form.'*"

9. Svetlana Boym, "Poetics and Politics of Estrangement: Victor Shklovsky and Hannah Arendt," *Poetics Today* 26, 4 (winter 2005).

10. See Boris Eichenbaum in "Theory of the 'formal method'" on the crucial passages in, and impact of, Shklovsky's "The Resurrection of the Word," published in 1914.

11. For a description of Shklovsky's lecture as a freshman in 1913, see Richard Sheldon in his "Introduction" to *A Sentimental Journey* (New York: Cornell University Press, 1970).

12. On the year "the general craze for cinema reached its peak in Russia, " see Yuri Tsivian in his *Early Cinema in Russia and its Cultural Reception*, 12. For a description of Shklovsky's

lecture as a freshman in 1913, see Richard Sheldon in his "Introduction" in *A Sentimental Journey* (New York: Cornell University Press, 1970).

13. See Chapter 5 of Malte Hagener's *Moving Forward, Looking Back. The European Avant-Garde and the Invention of Film Culture 1919-1939* (Amsterdam: Amsterdam University Press, 2007).

14. See, among many others, Victor Erlich, "Russian Formalism," in *Journal of the History of Ideas*, 34, no. 4 (Oct. – Dec., 1973), 630, 634. Interesting, Erlich complains about "Art as Technique" not being more helpful in this area of interest and he states that he prefers Roman Jakobson's work for this very reason. Erlich (p. 630): "Shklovsky's key terms, e.g., "making it strange," "dis-automatization," received wide currency in the writings of the Russian Formalists. But, on the whole, Shklovsky's argument was more typical of Formalism as a rationale for poetic experimentation than as a systematic methodology of literary scholarship. The Formalists' attempt to solve the fundamental problems of literary theory in close alliance with modern linguistics and semiotics found its most succinct expression in the early, path-breaking studies of Roman Jakobson. For Jakobson, the central problem is not the interaction between the percipient subject and the object perceived, but the relationship between the "sign" and the "referent," not the reader's attitude toward reality but the poet's attitude toward language."

15. André Gaudreault, "From 'Primitive Cinema' to 'Kine-Attractography,'" in *The Cinema of Attractions Reloaded*, ed. Wanda Strauven (Amsterdam: Amsterdam University Press, 2006), 99. See also Gaudreault's and Gunning's older but influential article "Early Cinema as a Challenge to Film History" which is reprinted in the same book.

16. See Laura Mulvey, *Death 24x a Second. Stillness and the Moving Image* (London: Reaktion Books Ltd.), 2006. See also the "Conversation" with Laura Mulvey on this topic in this book.

17. See the Introduction to Tsivian's *Early Cinema in Russia and its Cultural Reception*, 1-14.

18. Ibid., 2.

19. Tom Gunning described the *stupefying* effect of early cinema on its early spectator in several places. He also described and analyzed other confrontations with the "new" in similar terms. See Tom Gunning, "Re-Newing Old Technologies: Astonishment, Second Nature, and the Uncanny in Technology from the Previous Turn-of-the-Century," in *Rethinking Media Change: The Aesthetics of Transition*, eds. David Thorburn, and Henry Jenkins (Cambridge, Mass.: MIT Press, 2003), 40-41. Here Gunning describes a typical response of "astonishment," triggered by Universal Expositions: one in which the first excited silence in the first moment of "astonishment" is followed by a typically speechless (as Kant would say) "Oh Oh oooooooo!" in the first moments of awe. See also Gunning's "The Cinema of Attractions. Early Film, Its Spectator and the Avant-Garde," in *Early Cinema. Space, Frame, Narrative*, ed. Thomas Elsaesser (London: BFI), 1990. See in particular his analysis of the first "astonishment" as part of the early viewing experience in an article in which Gunning not only touches upon the uncanny, but also on the sublime, the aesthetic experience which is known for its moment of "stupor," as Immanuel Kant has famously described in his analyses of the sublime experience: Tom Gunning, "An Aesthetic of Astonishment: Early Film and the (In)

credulous Spectator," in *Viewing Positions. Ways of Seeing Film*, ed. Linda Williams (New Brunswick, NJ.: Rutgers University Press), 1994.

20. See Laura Marcus, *The Tenth Muse: Writing about Cinema in the Modernist Period* (Oxford: Oxford UP, 2007), 102 [my italics].

21. *Ibid.*

22. Virginia Woolf and her husband, Leonard Woolf, Virginia Woolf's sister the painter Vanessa Bell, the biographer Lytton Stratchey, the painter Dora Carrington, the economist John Maynard Keynes, the art historian Roger Fry, and others.

23. For a reflection on the shared historical experience and its impact on historical thinking, see Frank Ankersmit, *Sublime Historical Experience* (Stanford, California: Stanford University Press), 2005.

24. See Ian Christie and Richard Taylor's "General Editor's Preface" to Yuri Tsivian's *Early Cinema in Russia and its Cultural Reception*, IX.

25. *Ibid.*

26. Gunning, "Foreword," in Yuri Tsivian, *Early Cinema in Russia and its Cultural Reception*, XXI.

27. Tsivian, *Early Cinema in Russia and its Cultural Reception*, 217.

28. Gunning, "Foreword," in Yuri Tsivian, *Early Cinema in Russia and its Cultural Reception*, XXI.

29. Tsivian, 5.

30. *Ibid.*, 4.

31. *Ibid.*, XIX.

32. Viktor Shklovsky, *Mayakovsky and His Circle*, trans., and ed. Lily Feiler (London: Pluto Press Ltd, 1974), 112-113. A few pages later, he added that it was explicitly "in opposition to the Symbolists, [that] the [Futurist] poets Khlebnikov, Mayakovsky and Vasily Kamensky put forward a different kind of poetics." *Ibid.*, 113-114.

33. Markov describes the cascade of Futurist groups in Russia which attacked each other as fiercely as they did the rest of the world. Vladimir Markov, "Russian Futurism and Its Theoreticians," 169. He also states that Russian and Italian Futurists were not as unrelated to each other as they often chose to pretend, yet one can safely state that they were not friends (Markov, 168.) Decisive for their more lasting impact in the field of the arts, one may argue, were the mutual relations of the Russian Futurists with OPOYAZ and their leading figure, Victor Shklovsky, who himself reaffirmed that Sergei Eisenstein would have been less significant without LEF and Mayakovsky.

34. See, apart from Tsivian, also an expert on the history of the Futurist movement in Russia, Vladimir Markov, "Russian Futurism and Its Theoreticians," in *The Avant-Garde Tradition in Literature*, ed. Richard Kostelanetz (Buffalo: Prometheus Books, 1982), 171. See also Annie van den Oever, "Een klap in het gezicht van de goede smaak. [A Slap in the Face of Public Taste] Symbolisme, avant-garde, formalisme en het probleem van de artistieke vorm," in *Avantgarde! Voorhoede?* eds Hubert van den Berg, and Gillis Dorleijn (Nijmegen: Uitgeverij Vantilt, 2002), 191-204.

35. Tsivian, 12.

36. See Vladimir Markov, "Russian Futurism and Its Theoreticians," 171. in *The Avant-Garde Tradition in Literature* (Buffalo: Prometheus Books, 1982), 171. See also Annie van den Oever, "Een klap in het gezicht van de goede smaak. [A Slap in the Face of Public

Taste] Symbolisme, avant-garde, formalisme en het probleem van de artistieke vorm," 191-204.

37. Tsivian, 12.

38. Ibid., 12.

39. See the comments on these words from Andreas Huyssen by Malte Hagener, who adopted the statement from Andreas Huyssen as a motto in his book, from which I took this quote: *Moving Forward, Looking Back. The European Avant-Garde and the Invention of Film Culture 1919-1939* (Amsterdam: Amsterdam University Press, 2007), 19.

40. Siegfried Zielinski, "Media Archeology," was originally published: 7/11/1996 Available at: www.ctheory.net. See http://www.debalie.nl/artikel.jsp?dossierid=10123&subdossierid=0&articleid=10116; INTERNET.

41. As Tsivian indicates, Nikolay Gogol was often mentioned by the Futurists in relation to the "distortions" of the seen in the cinema; see Tsivian, *Early Cinema and its Cultural Reception*, 205, 210. Gogol was the Russian 19th-century author of grotesque prose, also labeled as "strange," "distorted" and "deformed" like early cinema, but with appreciation. The distortions must have been "grotesque" to their experience. In fact, the tradition of the grotesque (or monstrous), and Gogol's grotesque prose in particular, may be said to have provided an historical model for framing the experience of the "deformed."

42. Markov, "Russian Futurism and Its Theoreticians," 171-172.

43. Many books of the period refer to Mayakovsky's memorable performances. See, among many others, memoirs by Shklovsky, (*Mayakovsky and His Circle*), Eisenstein, and see also an essay on their aggressive and vitriolic attacks, by Markov ("Russian Futurism and Its Theoreticians") and Wellek ("Russian Formalism," in *The Avant-Garde Tradition in Literature*, ed. Richard Kostelanetz (Buffalo: Prometheus Books, 1982).

44. Quote taken from Tom Gunning, *The Cinema of Attractions. Early Film, its Spectator and the Avant-Garde*. First published in *Wide Angle* vol. 8 no. 3/4 (fall 1986): 4. He cites Filippo Tommaso Marinetti, "The Variety Theater 1913" in *Futurist Manifestos*, ed. Umbro Apollonio (New York: Viking Press, 1973), 127.

45. See Tom Gunning, "An Aesthetic of Astonishment: Early Film and the (In)credulous Spectator," in *Viewing Positions. Ways of Seeing Film*, ed. Linda Williams (New Brunswick, New Jersey: Rutgers University Press), 1994.

46. See Sergej M. Ejzenstejn [Sergei Eisenstein], "Montage: The construction Principle in Art," [1923] in *The Eisenstein Reader*, ed. Richard Taylor (London: BFI, 1998), 30.

47. Viktor Shklovsky, *Mayakovsky and His Circle*, 172.

48. Ibid., 172.

49. See Sergej M. Ejzenstejn [Sergei Eisenstein], "Montage: The Construction Principle in Art," 30.

50. Shklovsky has commented on these words by Mayakovsky in his book on Eisenstein, *Ejzenštejn* [Eisenstein], trans. Manfred Dahlke (Reinbek: Rowohlt Taschenbuch Verlag GmbH, 1977), 115-116 [First published in Moscow: *Iskusstvo*, 1973]. It is an anthology of essays by Shklovsky in German translation. In the German translation, Mayakovsky's famous poem "A Cloud in Trousers" reads as follows: "Doch es wird klar – / bevor zu singen er beginnt, / geht lange man, bekommt man Schwielen vom Umherirrn, / und leise wählt im Schlamm des Herzens sich / *die dumme Plötze der Vorstellungs-*

kraft [my italics]" (p. 115). Shklovsky could much easier relate to this Futurist evocation of the unexpected ways inspiration and the imagination chose to follow than to the one evoked by the "cliché" of the classical authors, "Pegasus" (p. 116). Here, Shklovsky adds to his quote as a comment that Mayakovsky's image of the Imagination: "Schöne Worte darüber, wie schwer es ist, Bücher zu schreiben, und wie sich die <Plötze der Vorstellungskraft> hin und her wirft. Ein realeres Bild als der geflügelte Pegasus."

51. Markov, "Russian Futurism and Its Theoreticians."

52. See Tsivian, 12.

53. The qualification "brilliant" was given by Erlich, who tends to be slightly ambivalent about Shklovsky; "brilliant but brash" and "the gadfly of Opojaz" are two characterizations to be found in his contribution to The Avant-Garde Tradition in Literature, ed. Richard Kostelanetz (Buffalo: Prometheus Books, 1982), 159. The information on The Stray Dog lecture is in part taken from Benedikt Livshits, and in part from Richard Sheldon, quoted here.

54. See Richard Sheldon's "Introduction" to Viktor Shklovsky's A Sentimental Journey (New York: Cornell University Press, 1970), x. [my italics]

55. See Vladimir Markov, "Russian Futurism and Its Theoreticians."

56. See Richard Sheldon's "Introduction," x.

57. The younger Eisenstein became part of the circle surrounding Mayakovsky's LEF in 1923, ten years after Shklovsky's lecture in The Stray Dog, and Shklovsky saw him as a young man, "in wide trousers, very young, gay and with a high-pitched voice," a "versatile" person who brought to this environment of "extreme diversity" his own speciality: "he brought to LEF his ideas on eccentrism." (See Shklovsky, Mayakovsky and His Circle, 172.) The ideas on eccentrism Eisenstein presented to LEF came from the time he spent in the theater, in the years in which Meyerhold was his mentor. In fact, these two major figures and their impact on Eisenstein form an area of research in the study of Eisenstein and the "cinema of attractions" that has yet to be explored more fully.

58. See Markov, "Russian Futurism and Its Theoreticians," 171. Markov does not mention the relation to the 1914 essay by Shklovsky; The Resurrection of the Word, as both Wellek and Eichenbaum do. Factually, Sheldon described the relation in far more detail, mostly using Shklovsky's typically loose and sketchy notes that are to be found in his diaries, letters, memoirs, and novels. Sheldon points out how Shklovsky presented his lecture in The Stray Dog and worked these thoughts out into his book on The Resurrection of the Word, a year later, which he then read to his fellows at the Department of Philology – which started OPOYAZ. See Sheldon, "Introduction," xi: "In 1914 he published his paper under the title Resurrection of the Word. Shortly after its appearance, he took a copy to his teacher, Jan Baudouin de Courtenay. The famous linguist introduced Shklovsky to his most gifted students, Lev Yakubinsky and E.D. Polivanov. Although the master objected to Shklovsky's apotheosis of sound in poetry, his students responded enthusiastically. They felt that the sound patterns of poetry offered a fertile new field for linguistic analysis. Under Shklovsky's leadership, these students of Baudouin de Courtenay joined forces with the futurists in 1914. This new alliance was called OPOYAZ – Obshchestvo izucheniia poeticheskogo iazyka (Society for the Study of Poetic Language); it eventually evolved into the full-fledged critical movement known as

Russian formalism. *Resurrection of the Word* is usually considered the first document of that movement." See Sheldon, "Introduction," in Viktor Shklovsky's, *A Sentimental Journey* (New York: Cornell University Press, 1970), xi.

59. Viktor Shklovsky, *Voskresheniye slova* [The Resurrection of the Word] (Petersburg), 1914.

60. Boris Eichenbaum, "The Theory of the 'Formal Method,'" 112.

61. Victor Shklovsky, *Voskresheniye slova*, 11. See Boris Eichenbaum's "The Theory of the 'Formal Method,'" 112 for a comment and an English translation of this quote.

62. As they abducted the notion of "form" and replaced it by "technique," they obviously were against being called "Formalists" since the word carried the wrong connotations of late 19th-century aestheticism, as preached by the late 19th-century autonomists. If anything, they should have been called Russian "de-Formalists" and not "Formalists" as I have tried to explain in my 2002 article, "A Slap in the Face of Public Taste."

63. *Ibid.*,12.

64. Shklovsky, *Mayakovsky and His Circle*, 111.

65. *Ibid.* 112-113. [my italics].

66. *Ibid.*

67. *Ibid.* 113-114. [my italics].

68. Eichenbaum, "The Theory of the 'Formal Method,'" 115.

69. Tom Gunning, "Re-Newing Old Technologies: Astonishment, Second Nature, and the Uncanny in Technology from the Previous Turn-of-the-Century," in *Rethinking Media Change: The Aesthetics of Transition*, eds. David Thorburn, and Henry Jenkins (Cambridge, Mass.: MIT Press, 2003), 52.

70. See Wellek, "Russian Formalism," in *The Avant-Garde Tradition in Literature*, ed. Richard Kostelanetz (Buffalo: Prometheus Books), 1982.

71. *Ibid.*, 159.

72. Tsivian, *Early Cinema in Russia and its Cultural Impact*, 2.

73. See Wellek, "Russian Formalism," 156-159; and Markov, "Russian Futurism and Its Theoreticians," 168.

74. As Vadim Sercenevic, one of the Futurists, already stated in 1916, the Futurists were the first to create a new artistic practice, yet they could not create good theory: "It is precisely futurism that began with [poetic] practice, and it is in futurism that we find almost no theory." See Markov, "Russian Futurism and Its Theoreticians," 168.

75. *Ibid.*

76. *Ibid.*, 168-172.

77. The early avant-garde must be seen as separate from the later avant-garde. Whereas the first responded to the early cinema experience, the later avant-garde responded to the cinema in its institutional phase. As Gunning wrote, the avant-garde responded to a later phase in the development of the cinema, a phase that somewhat disappointed the high expectations of the avant-garde as it started to adopt conventional forms and patterns from the other arts as time went on. In most countries, this seems to have happened in a phase often seen as part of the years of institutionalization of the cinema. See André Gaudreault, "From 'Primitive Cinema' to 'Kine-Attractography,'" in *The Cinema of Attractions Reloaded*, ed. Wanda Strauven (Amsterdam: Amsterdam University Press, 2006), 97-99. Note that the institutionalization took place in the United States in an earlier phase from 1906 onwards, as is often said, and that the process had a

different make-up and outcome than the one in Russia and the USSR. It should also be noted that pre-revolutionary Russia and the Soviet Union after the revolution had a very self-conscious, even arrogant re-editing practice, as Hagener has argued in Chapter V of his book, and that the montage film could be seen as having been "born" from this in the 1920s, as part of the later avant-garde. All in all, the process of institutionalization both before and after the revolution followed a quite different pattern than the one in the United States, a process described by Eileen Bowser, Charles Musser, André Gaudreault, Tom Gunning, and others.

78. See Francesco Casetti, *Eye of the Century. Film, Experience, Modernity*, trans. E. Larkin, and J. Pranolo, ed. John Belton (New York: Columbia University Press, 2008), 7. Translation of Balázs' words taken from Casetti [my italics].

79. See Markov on the genre and topic: "Manifestoes in the strict sense of the word were not always concerned with theory. Most of them [by the Futurists of these days] were largely arrogant and vitriolic attacks on proceeding and contemporary literature, more often on fellow-futurists; at other times their aim was to *épater les bourgeois*, rather than declare their aesthetics." Markov, "Russian Futurism and Its Theoreticians," 169.

80. Victor Erlich, "Russian Formalism," *Journal of the History of Ideas* Vol. 34, 4 (October – December 1973), 638.

81. See for instance a critique by Eric Naiman, "Shklovsky's Dog and Mulvey's Pleasure: The Secret Life of Defamiliarization," *Comparative Literature* 50, no. 4 (autumn 1998): 333-352.

82. Viktor Shklovsky, "Art as Technique," 13.

83. See Eichenbaum, "The Theory of the 'Formal Method,'" 115.

84. Viktor Shklovsky, "Art as Technique," 13.

85. *Ibid.*, 17. [my italics]

86. *Ibid.*, 18.

87. Lemon, and Reis, "Introduction" to *Russian Formalist Criticism. Four Essays* (Lincoln: University of Nebraska Press, 1965), ix.

88. See Annie van den Oever, "Monstration and the Monstrous. The Grotesque in the Very Beginning and at the Very End," in *Proceedings of the XVI International Film Studies Conference-Permanent Seminar on History of Film Theories. In the Very Beginning, at the Very End. Film Theories in Perspective*, eds F. Casetti, and J. Gaines, V. Re. Udine: Forum, 2010.

89. These words are taken from Gunning's, "Re-Newing Old Technologies: Astonishment, Second Nature, and the Uncanny in Technology from the Previous Turn-of-the-Century," in *Rethinking Media Change: The Aesthetics of Transition*, ed. David Thorburn, and Henry Jenkins (Cambridge, Mass.: MIT Press, 2003), 49. Note that this in part is a highly interesting re-visit of Shklovsky's thinking on *ostranenie* and the experience of the newness of new technologies and techniques and their potential ("uncanny") impact.

90. Tom Gunning, "An Aesthetic of Astonishment, " 117.

91. Laura Mulvey, *Death 24x a Second. Stillness and the Moving Image* (London: Reaktion Books Ltd.), 2006.

92. See Annie van den Oever, "Monstration and the Monstrous." See also the "Conversation" with Laura Mulvey on *ostranenie* and the uncanny in this book.

93. One may argue that this period in Russia was extended by the typical *re-editing culture* it had, which rearranged and deformed the provided filmic material for its own, idiosyncratic or political purposes, thus destabilizing the film's given structure and meaning, and "alienating" it from its earlier context and purposes; see Malte Hagener, *Moving Forward, Looking Back. The European Avant-Garde and the Invention of Film Culture 1919-1939* (Amsterdam: Amsterdam University Press, 2007), Chapter V.

94. One may indeed feel that "primitive" is a useful word in this context, as Wanda Strauven has argued. See Wanda Strauven, "From 'Primitive Cinema' to "'Marvelous'" in *The Cinema of Attractions Reloaded* (Amsterdam: AUP, 2006), 105-120. She revisits the dictions between Primitive Modes of Narration and Institutional Modes of Narration, a diction which may well be made relevant in research again. See also, on the primitive, André Gaudreault, "From 'Primitive Cinema' to 'Kine-Attractography,'" in *The Cinema of Attractions Reloaded*, ed. Wanda Strauven (Amsterdam: Amsterdam University Press, 2006), 85-104.

95. Eichenbaum, "The Theory of the 'Formal Method,'" 115.

96. The term "monstration" for an introduction, or rather, demonstration of new optical techniques in culture is a valuable term which was coined by André Gaudreault. For further explanation, see Annie van den Oever, "Monstration and the Monstrous. The Grotesque in the Very Beginning and at the Very End," 2010. See also the Conversation with Laura Mulvey in this book.

97. "The history of art is, at least in part, a history of the tools and materials with which art is made." See for more information the Daniel Langlois Foundation (Canada) and its online DOCAM research initiative, which explains having been concerned with the relationship between technological invention and artistic creation "from the beginning." See http://www.docam.ca/en/technological-timeline.html

98. See Shklovsky's *Mayakovsky and His Circle*, trans., and ed. Lily Feiler (London: Pluto Press Limited, 1974), 125.

99. I took this quote from Tom Gunning, who cites Shklovsky's "Electricity and the Theme of Old Newspapers," *Podenshchina* (Leningrad: Pisatelej, 1930), 14-15. See Tom Gunning, "Re-Newing Old Technologies: Astonishment, Second Nature, and the Uncanny in Technology from the Previous Turn-of-the-Century," in *Rethinking Media Change: The Aesthetics of Transition*, eds. David Thorburn, and Henry Jenkins (Cambridge, Mass.: MIT Press, 2003), 44.

100. Gunning, "Re-Newing Old Technologies..., " 39-44.

101. See Viktor Shklovsky, *Literature and Cinematography*, [1923] trans. Irina Masinovsky. Introduction by Richard Sheldon (Champaign & London: Dalkey Archive Press, 2008), XVI-XVII. This quote is taken from *Hamburg Account* [*Gamurgskii schet*, 110. (1928)] as translated into English and cited by Richard Sheldon in his Introduction to *Literature and Cinematography*, XVI-XVII. 19 Viktor Shklovsky, *Literature and Cinematography*, VII-IX, XII-XIII, XVI-XVII; 4-6, 13-14, 27, 38, 65-66, 73. [First published by Russkoe Universal'noe izdatel'stvo, 1923.]

102. For an excellent analysis of the romantic idea of the writer or artist as Creator, see Pierre Bourdieu, *The Rules of Art* (Cambridge, UK: Polity Press), 2005. [Translation from *Les Règles de l'art* (Éditions du Seuil, 1992). Translated by Susan Emanuel.]

## *Ostranenie*, Innovation and Media History

1.  The writing of this article was supported by a fellowship at the Internationales Kolleg für Kulturtechnikforschung und Medienphilosophie in Weimar.
2.  Frank Kessler, "Ostranenie. Zum Verfremdungsbegriff von Formalismus und Neoformalismus," *Montage/AV* 5, 2 (1996): 51-65.
3.  Viktor Shklovsky, "Art as Technique," *Russian Formalist Criticism. Four Essays*, trans. Lee T. Lemon and Marion Reis (Lincoln & London: University of Nebraska Press, 1965), 12.
4.  *Ibid.*
5.  *Ibid.*
6.  *Ibid.*
7.  David Bordwell, "Lowering the Stakes: Prospects for a Historical Poetics of Cinema," *Iris* 1, 1 (1983): 14.
8.  Kristin Thompson, *Eisenstein's Ivan the Terrible: A Neoformalist Analysis* (Princeton: Princeton University Press, 1981) and *Breaking the Glass Armor: Neoformalist Film Analysis* (Princeton: Princeton University Press, 1988).
9.  Bordwell, "Lowering the Stakes: Prospects for a Historical Poetics of Cinema," 13.
10. The concept of "foregrounding" can in fact be seen as something like a variant of "*ostranenie*," as Sternberg points out. See: Meir Sternberg, "Telling in Time (III): Chronology, Estrangement, and Stories of Literary History," *Poetics Today* 27, 1 (2006): 126, 130.
11. Thompson, *Breaking the Glass Armor: Neoformalist Film Analysis*, 7-8.
12. *Ibid.*, 10.
13. *Ibid.*, 10-11.
14. *Ibid.*, 17-18.
15. Juri Tynyanov, "On Literary Evolution," in *Readings in Russian Poetics: Formalist and Structuralist View*, ed. Ladislav Matejka and Krystyna Pomorska (Cambridge, Mass.: The MIT Press, 1971), 66-78.
16. David Bordwell, *The Films of Carl Theodor Dreyer* (Berkely etc.: University of California Press, 1979), 4.
17. *Ibid.*
18. *Ibid.*, 5.
19. David Bordwell, Janet Staiger, and Kristin Thompson, *The Classical Hollywood Cinema: Mode of Production to 1960* (New York: Columbia University Press, 1985).
20. For an overview charting the interaction between the various strands of study in Bordwell's and Thompson's work and a bibliography up to 1995, see: Britta Hartmann, and Hans-Jürgen Wulff, "Vom Spezifischen des Films. Neo-formalismus – Kognitivismus – Historische Poetik," *Montage/AV* 4, 1 (1995): 5-22.
21. David Bordwell, *Poetics of Cinema* (New York & London: Routledge, 2008), 27.
22. Christian Metz, *Langage et cinéma* (Paris: Larousse, 1970), 77.
23. Thompson, *Breaking the Glass Armor: Neoformalist Film Analysis*, 49-86.
24. Thierry Kuntzel, "The film-work, 2," *Camera Obscura* 5 (1980): 6-69.
25. Thompson, *Breaking the Glass Armor: Neoformalist Film Analysis*, 50-51.
26. Peter Steiner, "Three Metaphors of Russian Formalism," *Poetics Today* 2, 1b (1981/82): 59-116.
27. Frank Kessler, "Brieven uit de verte. Een analyse van de film EEN TELEGRAM UIT MEXICO," *Jaarboek Mediageschiedenis* 8 (Amsterdam: Stichting Mediageschiedens/Stichting beheer IISG, 1997), 201-213.

28. See Frank Kessler, "L'insistance de la lettre," *Vertigo* 2 (1988): 17-23.

29. See Eileen Bowser, "Le coup de téléphone dans les films des premiers temps," *Les premiers ans du cinema français*, ed. Pierre Guibbert (Perpignan: Institut Jean Vigo, 1985), 218-224 and Tom Gunning, "Heard over the Phone. *The Lonely Villa* and the Lorde Tradition of the Terrors of Technology," *Screen* 32, 2 (1991): 184-196 and Frank Kessler, "Bei Anruf Rettung!," *Telefon und Kultur 4. Das Telefon im Spielfilm*, ed. Forschungsgruppe Telekommunikation (Berlin: Spiess, 1991), 167-173.

30. These are terms used by Barry Salt (1983, 101), though explicitly in a purely descriptive manner and without implying any value judgement.

31. Viktor Shklovsky, *Theory of Prose* (Elmwood Park, IL: Dalkey Archive Press, 1990), 190.

32. *Ibid.*

33. Sternberg, "Telling in Time (III): Chronology, Estrangement, and Stories of Literary History," 198.

34. Bordwell, *Poetics of Cinema*, 27.

35. For an analysis of the cutting rate in films by Bauer and Kuleshov, see Yuri Tsivian, "Cutting and Framing in Bauer's and Kuleshov's Films," *KINtop. Jahrbuch zur Erforschung des frühen Films* 1 (1992): 103-113.

36. Bordwell, Staiger and Thompson, *The Classical Hollywood Cinema: Mode of Production to 1960.*

37. Michèle Lagny, Marie-Claire Ropars and Pierre Sorlin, *Générique des années 30* (Paris: Presses Universitaires de Vincennes, 1986).

38. See Noël Burch, *Life of Those Shadows* (Berkeley: University of California Press, 1990).

39. See Tom Gunning, "The Cinema of Attractions. Early Film, Its Spectator and the Avant-Garde," in *Early Cinema. Space, Frame, Narrative*, ed. Thomas Elsaesser (London: BFI, 1990), 56-62.

40. See André Gaudreault, *Du littéraire au filmique. Système du récit* (Paris: Méridiens Klincksieck, 1988).

41. Stan Brakhage, *The Brakhage Lectures* (Chicago: The School of the Art Institute of Chicago, 1972).

42. One could think here, among others, of the increasing accessibility of many film archives, which enabled scholars to considerably expand the corpus they were working with. Film festivals such as Le Giornate del Cinema Muto in Pordenone or Cinémémoire in Paris had similar effects.

43. Sternberg, "Telling in Time (III): Chronology, Estrangement, and Stories of Literary History," 126.

44. *Ibid.*

45. Tom Gunning, "Re-Newing Old Technologies: Astonishment, Second Nature, and the Uncanny in Technology from the Previous Turn-of-the-Century," in *Rethinking Media Change: The Aesthetics of Transition*, ed. David Thorburn and Henry Jenkins (Cambridge, Mass.: MIT Press, 2003), 39-60.

46. *Ibid.*, 45.

47. *Ibid.*, 39.

48. *Ibid.*, 45.

49. Charles Musser, *The Emergence of Cinema: The American Screen to 1900* (New York: Scribner, 1990).

50. Gunning, "The Cinema of Attractions. Early Film, Its Spectator and the Avant-Garde," 58.

51. Jay David Bolter, and Richard Grusin, *Remediation. Understanding New Media* (Cambridge, Mass. & London: MIT Press, 1999).

52. *Ibid.*, 21.

53. One might add that the continuous presence of a channel's logo nowadays almost always (with the exception of the commercial break) introduces an element of hyper-mediacy into the televisual image.

54. Bolter and Grusin, *Remediation. Understanding New Media*, 65.

55. Gunning, "Re-Newing Old Technologies: Astonishment, Second Nature, and the Uncanny in Technology from the Previous Turn-of-the-Century," 39.

56. Isabelle Raynauld, "Le cinématographe comme nouvelle technologie: opacité et transparence," *Cinémas* 14, 1 (2003): 117-128.

57. "Nous constatons, dans la lignée des idées de Grusin, Bolter et Gunning, qu'un média en émergence traverse une période d'opacité durant laquelle sa matérialité est si visible qu'elle peut littéralement faire écran au contenu. Par contre, lorsque la compétence des récepteurs s'accroît, l'opacité du média s'atténue pour faire place à sa transparence, donnant par conséquent plus de visibilité au contenu."

58. Bolter and Grusin, *Remediation. Understanding New Media*, 65.

59. André Gaudreault, *Cinéma et attraction. Pour une nouvelle histoire du cinématographe* (Paris: CNRS Editions, 2008).

60. Gunning, "Re-Newing Old Technologies: Astonishment, Second Nature, and the Uncanny in Technology from the Previous Turn-of-the-Century," 39-45.

## Knight's Move: Brecht and Russian Formalism in Britain in the 1970s

1. Bernhard Reich, *Im Wettlauf mit der Zeit* (Berlin: Henschelverlag, 1970), 371. This recollection by the German theatre director Bernhard Reich is cited in Stanley Mitchell's article "From Shklovsky to Brecht: Some Preliminary Remarks Towards a History of the Politicisation of Russian Formalism," *Screen* 15, no. 2 (summer 1974): 80.

2. Peter, Wollen, "Some Thoughts Arising from Stanley Mitchell's Article," *Screen* 12, no. 4 (winter 1971-72): 165.

3. Zygmunt Bauman, *The Art of Life* (Cambridge: Polity, 2008), 61.

4. *Ibid.*, 62. Bauman also refers here to Ulrich Beck's "zombie concepts" and to Jacques Derrida's use of terms "*sous rapture*," with a caveat about their lack of currency.

5. André Bazin, *What Is Cinema?* Vol. 1. Essays selected and translated by Hugh Gray (Berkeley & Los Angeles: University of California Press, 1967), 36-37. The essay by Bazin, "The Evolution of the Language of Cinema," published in 1967 was in fact a composite created by Hugh Gray of three articles, the latest of which, "Editing and its Evolution" (from which these quotations come), appeared in *L'Age Nouveau* in 1955.

6. "Editorial" *Screen* 12, no. 4 (winter 1971-72): 5.

7. *Ibid.*

8. *Screen* was explicitly echoing the position announced by *Cahiers du cinéma* two years earlier: "To us the only possible line of advance seems to be to use the theoretical writings of the Russian filmmakers of the twenties..." (*Cahiers* 216 (October 1969); quoted in *Screen* 12.1: 35). The French debates and their relationship to the events of 1968 are usefully summarised in Sylvia Harvey, *May '68 and Film Culture* (London: British Film Institute), 1980.

9. Films from a wider range of countries than France and Italy lent critical mass to the international art cinema of this period, and similar tropes are apparent in such films as Alfred Hitchcock's VERTIGO (1958) and PSYCHO (1960) and Michael Powell's PEEPING TOM (1960). But these did not generate the same level of critical discussion as the New Wave.

10. Eric Hobsbawm, *The Age of Extremes: The Short Twentieth Century, 1914-1991* (London: Weidenfelf and Nicholson 1994), 300.

11. In Britain, Panther, Cape and Fontana all offered new editions of classic authors, as well as new translations of newly "discovered" writers and highly contemporary texts that drew on them.

12. The invocation of "ceux qui inventent chaque jour le langage de notre temps" appears in the series rubric of Editions Seghers *Cinéma d'aujourd'hui*, which reached eighteen titles by 1963, including volumes on Antonioni, Resnais and Godard.

13. The earliest "Formalist" texts to appear in paperback translation were two by Shklovsky and one by Eichenbaum, in a series on literary criticism (Lee T. Lemon, and Marion J. Reis, *Russian Formalist Criticism: Four Essays* (Lincoln, Nebraska University Press), 1965), which soon reached a much wider audience.

14. P. Adams Sitney, "Structural Film" in *Film Culture* (1969); reprinted in *Film Culture anthology* (New York: Anthology Film Archives, 1970), 415.

15. Hayward exhibition, Art in Revolution – Bann's Constructivist anthology?

16. Viktor Shklovsky, *Knight's Move*, [1923] trans. Richard Sheldon (Dalkey Archive), 2005.

17. New paperback imprints with radical intellectual and political ambitions, and an international perspective, were an important feature of the 1960s. In the UK, these included Cape, Fontana and Panther, and their success would also encourage established imprints to respond to a new readership. Marx's early writings of the 1840s were published in English translation in 1961 and 1963, then appeared in a popular Panther anthology with commentary by David Caute, *Essential Writings of Karl Marx*, in 1967. A selection of Benjamin's essays appeared in English translation as *Illuminations* (Fontana) in 1970, and became an immediate bestseller.

18. James Smith, "Brecht, the Berliner Ensemble, and the British Government," *New Theatre Quarterly* 22, 4 (2006): 307-323.

19. Margaret Eddershaw, *Performing Brecht: Forty Years of British Performances* (London: Routledge, 1996), 59-61.

20. John Arden, *Plays 1* (London: Methuen), 2002.

21. John Willett, *The Theatre of Bertolt Brecht* [1959] (London: Methuen, 1967), 178.

22. The other work was Martin Esslin, *Brecht: The Man and His Work* (New York: Doubleday), 1961.

23. Karl Marx, *Economic and Political Manuscripts* [1844], cited in David Caute, ed. *Essential Writings of Karl Marx* (London: Panther, 1967), 59.

24. Raymond Williams, *Keywords: A Vocabulary of Culture and Society* (London: Fontana, 1976): 29-31.

25. *Daily Express*, 30.3.1962.

26. *LA Daily News*, 15.9.1998. Available from http://www.thefreelibrary.com/LESS-THAN PERFECT+%6oTHREEPENNY+OPERA'+HAS+ITS+CHARMS-a083836726

27. Godard wrote of his two scavenging soldiers in LES CARABINIERS: "these characters are not situated psychologically or morally, and even less sociologically. Everything happens at the animal level, and this animal is filmed from a vegetable point of view, when it's actually mineral, that's to say Brechtian." Scenario des CARABINIERS (1962), (Jean Collet, 1963: 94)

28. On Brecht's distinction between "Aristotelian" and "epic" theatre, see for instance Bertolt Brecht, *Short Description of a New Technique of Acting which Produces and Alienation Effect*, at http://www.english.emory.edu/DRAMA/BrechtAlien.html (accessed 29.6.10).

29. Colin MacCabe, "Realism in the Cinema: Notes on Some Brechtian Theses, *Screen* 15. 2 (1974): 26.

30. Stanley Mitchell, "From Shklovsky to Brecht: Some Preliminary Remarks Towards a History of the Politicisation of Russian Formalism," *Screen* 15. 2 (summer 1974): 74-81.
31. Brecht quoted in: Mitchell, "From Shklovsky to Brecht," 74.
32. *Ibid.*, 76.
33. *Ibid.*, 75
34. Ben Brewster, "From Shklovsky to Brecht: A Reply," *Screen* 15.2 (summer 1974): 88.
35. Boris Eikhenbaum, "Problems of Film Stylistics," in *Russian Poetics in Translation*, ed. Richard Taylor (Oxford: RPT Publications, 1982).
36. This "new Eisenstein" was celebrated in the 1988 exhibition, *Eisenstein: Life and Art*, held at the Hayward Gallery and Museum of Modern Art Oxford, in a book based on the accompanying conference: Christie & Taylor, *Eisenstein Rediscovered* (London: Routledge and Kegan Paul, 1993), and in a new edition of Eisenstein's writings under the general editorship of Taylor.
37. Stephen Heath, "From Brecht to Film: Theses, Problems," *Screen* 16, no. 4 (1975-76): 34.
38. *Ibid.*
39. The movement that became known as "cinéma-vérité" in the early 1960s, inspired by Vertov's "kino Pravda," had become a target of attack in France by 1968, accused of merely reflecting bourgeois reality rather than exposing or criticising it.
40. Claire Johnston, and Paul Willemen, *Screen* 16, no. 4 (1975-76): 34.
41. *Ibid.*, 110-111.
42. Scenarios by Mayakovsky in the "Soviet Film 1920s" issue of *Screen* (12. 4 (1971): 122-149).
43. Peter Wollen, *Signs and Meaning in the Cinema* (London: Secker and Warburg, 1970), 124.
44. Interview with Peter Wollen in *Screen* 15. 3 (1971): 130.
45. *Blackbird Descending: Tense Alignment* (1977); *Emily, or Third Party Speculation* (1978), *Finnegan's Chin: Temporal Economy* (1981).
46. Marcellin Pleynet, "The 'Left' Front of the Arts: Eisenstein and the 'Young Hegelians,' *Cinéthique* 5 (Sept-Oct 1969), trans. Susan Bennett, *Screen* 13.1 (spring 1972). Trotsky denounced both Futurists and Formalists in his *Literature and Revolution* (1925). The dangers of giving ammunition to Cold War anti-Sovietism were stressed by *Cinéthique*.
47. Ian Christie, and John Gillet, eds, *FEKS, Formalism, Futurism: 'Eccentrism' in Soviet Cinema 1918-1935* (London: British Film Institute), 1978.
48. Although some essays from this collection of Formalist studies on cinema had already appeared in *Screen*, a full English translation of *Poetika Kino* would not appear until 1982, edited by Richard Taylor.
49. This extract from Kozintsev's memoir, *L'écran profonde* (1966), was translated from the French by Tom Milne (Christie, Gillett, 1978, 25)
50. Shklovsky quoted in (Christie, Gillett, 16).
51. Vladimir Nedobrovo quoted in (Christie, Gillett, 19).
52. Narboni quoted in (Christie, Gillett, 57-60). Narboni adds as a footnote (without giving any source): "Eisenstein underlined the following sentence in his copy of *Archaists and Innovators* (Tynyanov): 'What is important is that language does not merely convey a concept but is a way of constructing the concept.'"
53. David Bordwell, *Narration in the Fiction Film* (Madison: University of Wisconsin Press), 1985; Kristin Thompson, *Breaking the Glass Armor. Neoformalist Film Analysis* (Princeton: Princeton University Press), 1988.
54. Viktor Shklovsky, *Knight's Move* [1923], trans. Richard Sheldon (Dalkey Archive), 2005.

55. Selections from Antonio Gramsci's *Prison Notebooks* appeared in English translation in the early 1970s and had a powerful effect on the New Left of the period (Antonio Gramsci, *Selections from the Prison Notebooks*. trans. Quintin Hoare, and Geoffrey Nowell-Smith (London: Lawrence and Wishart, 1971).

56. Brecht letter to *Neues Deutschland*, 1953, quoted in Willett (1967): 205-6.

## *Ostranenie* in French Film Studies: Translation Problems and Conflicting Interests

1. Without going back to the monarchy, the French political centralism can be characterized by the "so called 1992 'Toubon law' that protects French against the use of other languages (both English and... regional languages, on occasion!)," *Les Langues régionales de France, un état des lieux à la veille du XXIe siècle*, [The Regional Languages of France: An Inventory on the Eve of the XXIst Century] eds. Philippe Blanchet, Roland J.L. Breton, Harold F. Schiffman (Louvain-la-Neuve: Peeters Publishers, 1999), 74.

2. Tzvetan Todorov, *Théorie de la littérature* (Paris: Seuil, 1965), 83.

3. *Ibid.*, 45.

4. I am indebted to my friend and colleague, Pere Salabert, who provided me with information about the Spanish translation of *ostranenie*, which helps to clarify that the difficulty of translating *ostranenie* is not restricted to a particular language or country.

5. "On aurait également tort d'identifier la découverte, voire l'essence de la théorie « formaliste », aux platitudes galvaudées sur le secret professionnel de l'art, qui serait de faire voir les choses en les désautomatisant et en le rendant surprenantes ("ostra-nénie")." Todorov, *Théorie de la littérature*, 10-11 [my translation].

6. Meir Sternberg, "Telling in Time (III): Chronology, Estrangement, and Stories of Literary History," *Poetics Today* 27, 1 (2006): 125.

7. *Ibid.*, 169.

8. *Ibid.*, 175.

9. *Ibid.*, 178.

10. "Trente ans après, la théorie de l'information ressuscite les thèses de Chklovski en expliquant que l'information apportée par un message diminue au fur et à mesure que sa probabilité augmente." Todorov, *Théorie de la littérature*, 16 [my translation].

11. Umberto Eco, *L'Œuvre ouverte*, [Opera aperta, 1962] trans. C. Roux de Bézieux (Paris: Seuil, Pierres vives, 1965), 88, 110.

12. In his essay *Das Unheimliche*, Freud wrote that "the word 'heimlich' is not unambiguous, but belongs to two sets of ideas (...): on the one hand, it means what is familiar and agreeable, and on the other, what is concealed and kept out of sight" (http://www-rohan.sdsu.edu/~amtower/uncanny.html).

13. Pierre Bourdieu, *Distinction. Critique sociale du jugement* (Paris: Minuit, Le Sens Commun, 1979).

14. *Ibid.*, 568.

15. François Albèra, *Les Formalistes Russes et le cinéma. Poétique du film*, translation of *Poetika Kino* by V. Posener, R. Gayraud and J.C. Peuch, ed. François Albèra (Paris: Nathan, 1996), 16.

16. Jean Narboni, "Introduction," in *Formalistes Russes et le cinéma. Poétique du film Poétique du film*. Translation of *Poetika Kino* by V. Posener, R. Gayraud, and J.C. Peuch. Edited by François Albèra (Paris: Nathan, 1996), 57.
    "The Formalist "jamming" could be seen in light of the absence of a unified doctrine, or consensus on how to approach the work of art, which caused difficulties, a "jam,"

in agreement as to what constituted as poetical and what as practical" [my translation]. "La rectification de Jakobson et le marquage qu'il opère du travail véritable devant porter sur le rapport signifiant/signifié, indique tout ce qui sépare le brouillage formel d'une possible pratique matérialiste."

17. *Ibid.*, 57. "L'influence des thèses de Chklovski sur la nécessité dans l'art de "désautomatiser" la perception par des effets d' "ostranénie," dont a vu plus haut la réfutation par Jakobson, et abandonnées par Chklovski lui-même (cf. entretien avec Vladimir Pozner, in "Les Lettres Françaises," 17), fut considérable en Rusie pendant les années 20 (...). Incapables de poser le rapport dynamique des signifiants aux signifiés, axées sur le seul plan des "effets stylistiques," des altérations superficielles et finalement fort peu subversives de la langue poétique, les théories shklovskiennes tombent tout à fait normalement sous le coup de l'accusation de formalisme (...)" [my translation].

18. Vladimir Pozner, "Victor Chklovski parle à Vladimir Pozner," *Les Lettres Françaises* 1206 (October 1967): Narboni's reference, 17, is fanciful.

19. Frédérique Matonti, "L'anneau de Mœbius. La réception en France des Formalistes Russes," *Actes de la recherche en sciences sociales. Engagements intellectuels. Sociologie publique* 176-177, eds. Frédérique Matonti and Gisèle Sapiro (2009): 66 [my translation].

20. Catherine Depretto, "Roman Jakobson et la relance de l'Opojaz (1928-1930)," *Littérature* 107 (October 1997). Jakobson's remark in the preface reveals he was already in dispute with Shklovsky as he preferred to side with Osip Brik instead of with Shklovsky himself.

21. Léon Robel, "Un trio prodigieux," ed. Charles Dobzynski, *Europe, Les Formalistes Russes* 911 (March 2005): 6 [my translation].

22. Matonti, "L'anneau de Mœbius. La réception en France des Formalistes Russes," 65-66.

23. Antoine Vitez, "Pour un portrait de Vsévolod Meyerhold," *Les Lettres Françaises* 1010 (2-8 June 1964), quoted by Frédérique Matonti, "L'anneau de Mœbius. La réception en France des Formalistes Russes," 67.

24. Jean-Pierre Faye, "Formalisme ou sens," *Critique* 215 (April 1965): 339.

25. "Victor Chklovski parle à Vladimir Pozner," *Les Lettres Françaises* 1206 (October 1967) [my translation].

26. *Ibid.*

27. Sigmund Freud, "The Interpretation of Dreams," [1900] in *The Standard Edition of the Complete Psychological Works*, trans. James Strachey (London: Hogarth Press and The Institute of Psycho-Analysis, 1986), 339.

28. "Victor Chklovski parle à Vladimir Pozner," *Les Lettres Françaises* 1206 (October 1967) [my translation].

29. *Ibid.*

30. Concerning his book *Zoo, or Letters Not About Love*, Shklovsky explains that it proceeded emotionally from his unhappy relationship with Elsa Triolet, and speaking about being rivals, we must bear in mind that she was Lili Brik's sister and that Jakobson considered marrying her.

31. Barthélemy Amengual, *Que viva Eisenstein* (Lausanne: L'Âge d'homme, 1981).

32. *Ibid.*, 490 [my translation].

33. François Albèra, *Les Formalistes Russes et le cinéma*, 8.

34. François Albèra, *L'Avant-garde au cinéma* (Paris: Armand Colin, 2005), 38.

35. Arthur Danto, *The Transfiguration of the Commonplace: A Philosophy of Art* (Cambridge, Mass.: Harvard University Press, 1981) [backcover].

36. *Ibid.*, 5.

37. Friedrich Hegel, *Aesthetics: Lectures on Fine Art*, trans. T. M. Knox (Oxford: Clarendon Press, 1973), 1:162-163.
38. *Ibid.*
39. *Ibid.*
40. Gérard Genette, *Figures I* (Paris: Seuil, 1966), 207.
41. "Victor Chklovski parle à Vladimir Pozner," *Les Lettres Françaises* 1206 (October 1967) [my translation].

## Christian Metz and the Russian Formalists: a "Rendez-Vous Manqué"?

1. Roland Barthes, "En sortant du cinéma," in *Le bruissement de la Langue* (Paris: Seuil, 1984), 386.
2. Christian Metz, "Sur mon travail," in *Essais Sémiotiques* (Paris: Klincksieck, 1977), 176.
3. Boris Eichenbaum, "Problems of Film Stylistics," *Screen* 15, 3 (autumn 1973): 22.
4. The history of the metaphor of the language of cinema has been studied in: Dominique Chateau, *Le cinéma comme Language* (Paris: Editions l'association Internationale pour la sémiologie du spectacle/Publication de la Sorbonne ACEV, 1986).
5. Claude Lévi-Strauss, and Roman Jakobson, "'Les Chats' de Baudelaire," *L'homme: Revue Française d'anthropologie* 2 (1962): 5-21.
6. Thomas Elsaesser, and Emile Poppe, "Film," in *The Encyclopedia of Language and Linguistics* Vol. 3, ed. Rich Asher (Oxford: Pergamon Press, 1994), 1228.
7. In Koch's *Evolutionary Cultural Semiotics* four epochs are differentiated: his formalist period from 1914 to 1920, in which R. Jakobson was both the founder of the Moscow Linguistic Circle and a member of the influential *Opayaz* group. Then a structuralist period (1920-1939), when R. Jakobson was a dominating figure of the Prague School of Linguistics and Aesthetics. In his semiotic period, from 1939 to 1949, he was associated with the Copenhagen Linguistic Circle (Brøndal, Hjelmslev), and he was active in the founding of the Linguistic Circle of New York. The interdisciplinary period began in 1949 with his teaching at Harvard (...). See: Walter Koch, *Evolutionary Cultural Semiotics* (Bochum: Brockmeyer, 1986), 225-226.
8. Christian Metz, *Le Signifiant Imaginaire* (Paris: Union Générale d'Editions, 1977).
9. Herbert Eagle, ed., *Russian Formalist Film Theory: An Introduction* (Ann Arbor: Michigan Slavic Publications, 1981), 13-14.
10. Christian Metz, *Language and Cinema*, trans. Donna Jean Umiker-Sebeok (The Hague etc: Mouton, 1974), 184-185. French original: *Langage et cinéma* (Paris: Larousse, 1970).
11. Christian Metz, "Problems of Denotation in the Fiction Film," in *Film Language. A Semiotics of the Cinema*, trans. Michael Taylor (New York: Oxford University Press, 1974), 120n; French original: "Problèmes de denotation," in *Essais sur la Significations au cinéma* (Paris: Editions Klincksieck, 1968), 122n.
12. Christian Metz, "Paradigmatic and Syntagmatic," in *Language and Cinema*, 177. Original "Paradigmatique et Syntagmatique," in *Langage et Cinéma*, 133. In a note, Metz refers to the texts of Boris Tomashevsky and J. Tynyanov, which were reprinted in Tzvetan Todorov's *Théorie de la littérature* (Paris: Seuil, 1965).
13. Boris Tomachevski "La nouvelle école d'histoire littéraire en Russie," *Revue des etudes slaves* (1928): 238-239; or J. Tynyanov in "De l'évolution littéraire"(1927), reprinted in Tzvetan Todorov ed., *Théorie de la littérature* (Paris: Seuil, 1965), 123.
14. "[...]ce n'est pas le premier ouvrage où l'on trouve des réflexions de cet ordre. Il ne faut pas oublier les divers apports des Formalistes russes, en particulier le recueil col-

lectif de 1927, Poetika Kino, auquel ont collaboré Chklovski, Tynianov, Eichenbaum. Et aussi, de façon plus diffuse, plus éparse certains passages dans les écrits des principaux critiques et/ou théoriciens du cinéma: Eisenstein, évidemment, mais aussi Arnheim, Balázs, Bazin, Laffay, Mitry dans une autre optique, Cohen-Séat, Morin. Ces auteurs (et d'autres auxquels je ne pense pas sur le moment) se posaient assez précisément divers problèmes de signification [...]." See: Raymond Bellour and Christian Metz, "Entretien sur la Sémiologie du cinéma," [1970] in *Essais sur la signification au cinéma*, Tome II (Paris: Klincksieck, 1972), 195 [my translation].

15. Roger Odin, in an article on C. Metz, sums up all the linguists and other movements in the theoretical field which had an "influence" on the work of the film semiotician: "(the great erudition of Metz is also visible here): '[...] la liste des linguistes qu'il cite (...) Charles Bally, E. Benveniste, Claire Blanche Benveniste, Charles Beaulieux, Karl Bühler, Henri Bonnard, Eric Buysssens, Jean Cantineau, André Chevel, N. Chomsky, Marcel Cohen, Dubois, la commentatrice de Hjlemslev, Mme E. Fischer-Jorgensen, les formalistes russes, Gougenheim, A. Julien Greimas, Guillaume, Pierre Guiraud, Harris, Louis Hjelmslev, Jakobson, Kurylowicz et la notion de "catégories isofonctionnelles," Labov et l'école "variationniste," Samuel R. Levin, André Martinet, Matoré, Antoine Meillet [...]' and this is just part of a long list of names." See: Roger Odin, "Christian Metz et la linguistique," in *Christian Metz et la théorie du cinéma* [numéro spécial], eds. M. Marie and M. Vernet (Paris, Méridiens: Klincksieck, 1990), *Iris* 10 (April 1990): 90.

16. "Je retoucherais aujourd'hui sur deux points cette estimation intuitive des importances. Les travaux de Jean Epstein, malgré leur intelligence si vive, me semblent en définitive brouillons, exaltés, terriblement idéalistes (...). D'autre part les Formalistes Russes, dont on ne connaissait rien à l'époque, ont consacré au cinéma des études de grand poids, dont certaines ont été traduites entre-temps grâce à la politique systématique d'"éditions" qu'ont suivie les Cahiers du Cinéma." See: Christian Metz, "Une étape dans la réflexion sur le cinéma," in *Essais sur la signification au cinéma*, Vol. 2, 14.

17. With the Russian Formalists, the recourse to linguistic notions was part of a cultural strategy: to help break down the division of high culture and popular or folk culture, by developing methods of analysis which could be seen to apply to both with equal success. This agenda may well explain why their writings were "rediscovered" in the 1960s, when thanks to the pervasive influence of structuralism in the fields of mass-cultural artefacts, a similar agenda took shape. Thomas Elsaesser and Emile Poppe, "Film," 1228.

18. The term in fact has the character of a comprehensive result of an already realized semiosis. For a semiotician, the term poses more or less the same problem as the notion of style. See A.J. Greimas: "Il paraît difficile, (...) de transformer la notion de "style" en un concept opératoire (...) La difficulté, tient sans doute à la puissance intégrative de cette notion. À son caractère de résultante globale et totalisatrice de la sémiosis réalisée." A.J. Greimas and J. Courtés, *Sémiotique: dictionnaire raisonné de la théorie du langage*, Vol. 2 (Paris: Hachette, 1986), 213.

## Should I See What I Believe?

1. "A biocultural perspective can explain how evolution has made knowledge possible, albeit imperfectly, and how it has made the quest for better knowledge possible." Brian Boyd, "Getting It All Wrong: Bioculture Critiques Cultural Critique," *American Scholar*

75 (autumn 2006): 24. On a similar topic, see another "bridge-essay": Katherine Thomson-Jones, "Inseparable Insight: Reconciling Cognitivism and Formalism in Aesthetics," *The Journal of Aesthetics and Art Criticism* 63, no. 4 (autumn 2005): 375-384.

2. Hugo Münsterberg, *The Photoplay: A Psychological Study and Other Writings* [1916] (London & New York: Routledge, 2002).

3. Laurent Jullier, "L'esprit, et peut-être même le cerveau. La question psychologique dans la *Revue Internationale de Filmologie*, 1947-1962," *CinémaS* 19, no. 2 (spring 2009): 143-168. [in press].

4. To put it more precisely, the beginnings were far more "Cognitive" than "Evolutionary." For example, the seminal essay by David Bordwell, "A Case for Cognitivism" (first published in *Iris* 9 (spring 1989): 11-40), uses more cognitive tools (especially from the modular-constructivist theory) than ecological or adaptationist ones. Besides, something remains unchanged in both cases: the misconstrual of these "naturalistic" views by their "culturalist" opponents: see the defense by Bordwell himself: "A Case for Cognitivism: Further Reflections," *Iris* 11 (summer 1990): 107–112.

5. See for instance: Uri Hasson et al., "Intersubject Synchronization of Cortical Activity During Natural Vision," *Science* 303 (March 2004): 1617-1618.

6. Dan Sperber, "Why Rethink Interdisciplinarity?," available from http://www.interdisciplines.org/interdisciplinarity/ papers/1/; INTERNET. In this essay, Sperber tells the story of "psychologists invited to present their work at an anthropology conference. The disappointment is strong on both sides." One can wonder what it would have been if we tell a comparable story replacing "anthropology" by "aesthetics" or "Cultural Studies." To see how it could be, cf. Brian Boyd, "Getting It All Wrong: Bioculture Critiques Cultural Critique." Boyd explains how Literary Studies see "as a bargain with the devil (...) the idea that the sciences, the humanities and the arts should be connected with each other, so that science (most immediately, the life sciences) can inform the humanities and the arts, and vice versa" (p. 18; this idea is called *consilience* in biologist E.O. Wilson's book of that name).

7. Henry Jenkins, *Textual Poachers: Television Fans & Participatory Culture. Studies in Culture and Communication* (New York: Routledge 1992).

8. J. J. Gibson, *The Ecological Approach to Visual Perception* (Mahwah, NJ.: Lawrence Erlbaum Associates, Inc., 1986).

9. William Epstein, "Perceiving, Reasoning, and Imagining," *The American Journal of Psychology* 118, no. 2 (summer 2005): 320.

10. Joseph D. Anderson, *The Reality of Illusion: An Ecological Approach to Cognitive Film Theory* (Carbondale, IL.: Southern Illinois University Press, 1996). See also: Joseph D. Anderson, Barbara Fisher Anderson, and David Bordwell, *Moving Image Theory: Ecological Considerations* (Carbondale, IL.: Southern Illinois University Press, 2007). Note there is a link between Filmology (see note 3) and J. J. Gibson's ecological approach, cf. Georges Thines, Alan Costall and George Butterworth, eds., *Michotte's Experimental Phenomenology of Perception* (Hillsdale, NJ.: Erlbaum, 1991).

11. Zenon Pylyshyn, *Seeing and Visualizing: It's Not What You Think* (Cambridge, MA.: MIT Press, 2003), 181.

12. Even zoom-in and zoom-out do not provoke any trouble. "The fact that nonetheless zooms do not look strange or unnatural is remarkable. It might be explained by the familiarity with binoculars or – more likely – by the failure of observers to discriminate the subtle differences between zoom and actual approach." Our visual system is extremely flexible and plastic: "Gibson may not have realized the dissolving power that movies could have on his realist position." Heiko Hecht, "Film as Dynamic Event Per-

ception: Technological Development Forces Realism to Retreat," *Image: Journal of Interdisciplinary Image Science* 3 (January 2006): 17, 21.

13. David Cahan, ed., *Hermann Ludwig Ferdinand von Helmholtz and the Foundations of Nineteenth Century Science* (Los Angeles: University of California Press, 1994).

14. Irvin Rock, *Indirect Perception* (Cambridge, MA.: MIT Press, 1997).

15. William Epstein, "Perceiving, Reasoning, and Imagining," *The American Journal of Psychology* 118, no. 2 (summer 2005): 319.

16. Robert Schwartz, "Vision and Cognition in Picture Perception," *Philosophy and Phenomenological Research* 62, no. 3 (May 2001): 707.

17. *Ibid.*

18. Joel Norman, "Two Visual Systems and Two Theories of Perception: An Attempt to Reconcile the Constructivist and Ecological Approaches," *Behavioral and Brain Sciences* 24, 6 (2001).

19. Ulrich Neisser, *The Perceived Self: Ecological and Interpersonal Sources of Self Knowledge* (New York: Cambridge University Press, 1993). Howard Gardner, *The Mind's New Science: A History of the Cognitive Revolution* (New York: Basic Books, 1985).

20. Putnam quoted by Melinda Szaloky, "Making New Sense of Film Theory Through Kant. A Novel Teaching Approach," *New Review of Film and Television Studies* 3, no. 1 (May 2005): 37.

21. Francisco Varela, Evan Thompson, and Eleanor Rosch, *L'inscription corporelle de l'esprit: Sciences cognitives et expérience humaine* (Paris: Le Seuil, 1993), 234.

22. "Evolution has equipped us with fast and frugal heuristics, rough ways of knowing that are sufficient for our mode of life. We can expect imprecision and even systematic error in our "knowledge" if they help us to survive. We therefore have, for instance, a systematic bias toward overinterpreting objects as agents, in case that thing moving on the ground is a snake." (Boyd, "Getting It All Wrong: Bioculture Critiques Cultural Critique," 23).

23. "Suppose that you wish to describe the relationships between two objects in a room (a chair and a table) and your body. One way of encoding these relationships is to relate everything to yourself, to estimate the distance and the angle of each of these objects in relation to your body. This polar type of encoding is typically egocentric. A second means of encoding is to use the relationships between the objects themselves or relate them to a frame of references external to your body. Take as reference point the door of the room, and this time evaluate the position of the chair and the table with respect to the door. There is no reference to your body. This encoding is called allocentric [or exocentric], centered elsewhere than your own body." Alain Berthoz, *The Brain's Sense of Movement. Perspectives in Cognitive Neuroscience* (Harvard: Harvard University Press, 2002), 99-100.

24. Richard A. Shweder, and Jonathan Haidt, "The Cultural Psychology of the Emotions," in *Handbook of Emotions*, eds. M. Lewis and J. Haviland (New York: Guilford Press, 2000), 397-414.

25. David Marr, *Vision: A Computational Investigation into the Human Representation and Processing of Visual Information* (New York: Freeman, 1982).

26. "The small central fovea, with a high density of color sensitive cone cells, is responsible for detailed vision, while the surrounding periphery, containing a significantly lower density of cones and a large number of monochromatic rod cells, is responsible for, among other things, detecting motion." (Stephen Gould et al., "Peripheral-Foveal Vision for Real-time Object Recognition and Tracking in Video," *20th International Joint Conference on Artificial Intelligence*, available from http://ai.stanford.edu/~sgould/vision; INTERNET.

27. This is called *change-blindness*: J.K. O'Regan, R.A. Rensink, and J.J. Clark, "Change-Blindness as a Result of 'Mudsplashes,'" *Nature* 398 (1999): 34.
28. Timothy A. Salthouse and Cecil L. Ellis, "Determinants of Eye-Fixation Duration," *The American Journal of Psychology* 93, no. 2 (June 1980): 207.
29. John Dilworth, "Dual Recognition of Depth and Dependent Seeing," available from http://www.interdisciplines.org/ artcognition/papers/8; INTERNET.
30. Gibson, *The Ecological Approach to Visual Perception*, 283. Anderson acknowledges this position, saying film creates "two incompatible sets of information." Anderson, *The Reality of Illusion: An Ecological Approach to Cognitive Film Theory*, 48.
31. Thomas Stoffregen, "On the Nature and Perception of Depictions," available from http://www.interdisciplines.org/ artcognition/papers/14; INTERNET.
32. Ibid.
33. Szaloky, "Making New Sense of Film Theory Through Kant. A Novel Teaching Approach," 44.
34. The authors conclude: "The final acceptance of a statement as "true" or its rejection as "false" appears to rely on more primitive, hedonic processing in the medial prefrontal cortex and the anterior insula. Truth may be beauty, and beauty truth, in more than a metaphorical sense." Sam Harris et al., "Functional Neuroimaging of Belief, Disbelief, and Uncertainty," *Annals of Neurology* 62, no. 12 (December 2007): 141. Of course, two epistemological reproaches can be done: (1) the sharing of a same brain area does not mean the identity of the psychological processings; (2) as written in a review of this experience, "there are different kinds of belief: simple statements whose truth can be checked [vs.] forms of belief which we call "faith" or conviction, where assent is given to transcendent propositions which lie beyond the realm of evidence." Oliver Sacks et al., "A Neurology of Belief," *Annals of Neurology* 63, no. 2 (February 2008): 130.
35. Julian Hochberg, "Representation of Motion and Space in Video and Cinematic Displays," in *Handbook of Perception and Human Performance*, vol.1. eds. K.R. Boff, L. Kaufman, and J.P. Thomas (New York: John Wiley and Sons, 1986), 1-64.
36. Th. Stoffregen adds "a pan (the filmic approximation of a head turn) leads to changes in the orientation and position of the head relative to portions of the visible environment, and relative to portions of the audible environment, but not relative to the environment of forces, or relative to the rest of the body" (Thomas Stoffregen, "On the nature and perception of depictions", available from http://www.interdisciplines.org/ artcognition/papers/14; INTERNET). Gibson underestimated here the weight of his own theory. See for example this Gibsonian account by G. J.F. Smets: "when a pilot lands his aircraft, there will be a coupling between his movements and the layout that expands from the point he is aiming at. Now the pilot does not notice this expanding optical pattern, but he nevertheless uses it while landing. The end product of the perception process is not a representation of the world that is continually recognized by comparing it with what is already stored in our memories; rather, it is the detection of the affordance: whether and/or to what extent something is "landable," for example." G.J.F. Smets, "Perceptual Meaning," *Design Issues* 5, no. 2 (MIT Press, spring 1989): 96.
37. Hecht, "Film as Dynamic Event Perception: Technological Development Forces Realism to Retreat," 10-11, resuming Bürki-Cohen et al., "Simulator Fidelity: The Effect of Platform Motion," in *Proceedings of the Royal Aeronautical Society, International Conference on Flight Simulation - The Next Decade* (London, May 2000), 23.1-23.7. Hecht adds, "This also explains such illusions as vection, which you might have experienced in a train when you cannot tell whether your train is departing or whether the train on the adjacent platform is moving." (Hecht, "Film as Dynamic Event Perception: Technological Development Forces Realism to Retreat," 11).

38. Alva Noë, "Art as Enaction," *Art and Cognition Virtual Conference*, available from http://www.interdisciplines.org/ artcog/papers/8; INTERNET.

39. Of course, this example involves *generic knowledge* (see below): nobody would have been noticing the estrangement in a cartoon.

40. Pierre Jacob, and Marc Jeannerod, "The Motor Theory of Social Cognition. A Critique," *Trends in Cognitive Sciences* 9, 1 (January 2005): 21-25. The role of mirror neurons stops here in the bottom-up controlled part of perception, because "simulating an agent's observed movements is not sufficient (and not even necessary) for representing either an agent's prior intention or his social intention" (*Ibid.*).

41. It is even easier when the "principle of kinematic specification of dynamics" is applied. In fact, "[the single shot] of an actor lifting a box of unknown weight provides the observer with remarkably accurate judgments of dynamic facts, such as the approximate weight of the box. Thus, the kinematic information in a simple movie is sufficient to let us perceive whether the actor used an empty or a filled suitcase." Heiko Hecht, "Film as Dynamic Event Perception: Technological Development Forces Realism to Retreat," *Image: Journal of Interdisciplinary Image Science*, available from www.image-online.info; INTERNET.

42. Peter Wuss speaks of "the visual turbulence caused by the camera's attempts to find an orientation" ("Analyzing the Reality Effect in Dogma Films," *The Journal of Moving Image Studies* 1 (2002): 36, available from http://www.avila.edu/journal/index1.htm; INTERNET.

43. Hecht, "Film as Dynamic Event Perception: Technological Development Forces Realism to Retreat," 9.

44. Berthoz, *The Brain's Sense of Movement. Perspectives in Cognitive Neuroscience*.

45. Richard Dawkins, *The Selfish Gene* (Oxford: Oxford University Press), 1976.

46. Marcel Mauss, "Les techniques du corps," *Journal de Psychologie* XXXII, no. 3-4 (March – April, 1936).

47. For an intertextual analysis of sequences of KILL BILL and SHREK 2, see Laurent Jullier and Michel Marie, *Lire les images de cinema* (Paris: Larousse, 2007).

48. See for example a demonstration about music: Situngkir Hokky, "Conjectures to the Memes of Indonesian Songs," Bandung Fe Institute, Technical Department Papers 2008, available from http://cogprints.org/6099/; INTERNET.

49. Susan Blackmore, "Evolution and Memes. The Human Brain as a Selective Imitation Device," in *Cybernetics and Systems* 32, no. 1 (Philadelphia: Taylor and Francis, 2001), 225-255.

50. For a detailed analysis, see Laurent Jullier, *Abécédaire des Parapluies de Cherbourg* (Paris: L'Amandier, 2007).

51. See for the beginning of an answer: John R. Searle, "Rationality and Realism, What is at Stake?" *Daedalus* (autumn 1993): 55-83. Also: John Tooby, and Leda Cosmides, "The Psychological Foundations of Culture," in *The Adapted Mind: Evolutionary Psychology and the Generation of Culture*, eds. Barkow, Cosmides and Tooby (Oxford & New York: Oxford University Press, 1992), 19-136. And to understand how natural sciences can become "one of the 'Others' that we construct these days to haunt us with their sheer alterity," see James H. Tully and Daniel M. Weinstock, eds., "The Strange Estrangement: Taylor and the Natural Sciences," in *Philosophy in an Age of Pluralism: The Philosophy of Charles Taylor in Question* (Cambridge: Cambridge University Press, 1994), 83-95.

52. "Human minds are as they are because they evolved from earlier forms. Being ultimately biological, knowledge is likely to be imperfect, affording no firm foundation, no 'originary' moment, in Derrida diction." (Boyd, "Getting It All Wrong: Bioculture Critiques Cultural Critique," 23).

53. See Laurent Jullier, "To Cut or Let Live. The Soundtrack According to Jean-Luc Godard," in *Sound and Music in Film and Visual Media: A Critical Overview*, ed. Graeme Harper (New York: Continuum, 2009), 352-362.

54. Edward Branigan, *Narrative Comprehension and Film* (London & New York: Routledge, 1992), 61.

55. Viktor Shklovsky, "Art as Technique," *Russian Formalist Criticism. Four Essays*, trans. Lee T. Lemon, and Marion Reis (Lincoln & London: University of Nebraska Press, 1965). One can find a good resume of this turn in a quotation of the American installation artist Robert Irwin: "The act of art has turned to a direct examination of our perceptual processes." Robert Irwin, "Reshaping the Shape of Things, Part 2," *Arts* 47, no. 1 (September-October 1972): 30.

56. Nicolas Bullot, "L'attention esthétique et les objets," *Art and Cognition Virtual Conference*, available from http://www.interdisciplines.org/artcog/papers/5; INTERNET.

57. "It is through the notion of aesthetic judgement, elaborated in the *Critique of Judgement*, that Kant undertakes to solve the philosophical conundrum of how to render mental mediation (what grounds reality) transparent to itself in a meaningful but non-conceptual way, avoiding the circularity and tautology of self-reference. [After that], the Romantic intuitionist aesthetic [will appear as] the 'royal' road to the rationally impenetrable structure of subjectivity." Szaloky, "Making New Sense Of Film Theory Through Kant. A Novel Teaching Approach," 38.

58. Linking Shklovsky's "Art as Device" and the cinematic apparatus raises some epistemological problems, see: Eric Naiman, "Shklovsky's Dog and Mulvey's Pleasure: The Secret Life of Defamiliarization," *Comparative Literature* 50, no. 4 (autumn 1998): 333-352.

59. "The Venus effect occurs every time the observer sees both an actor (eg Venus) and a mirror, not placed along the observer's line of sight, and concludes that Venus is seeing her reflection at the same location in the mirror that the observer is seeing." Marco Bertamini, Richard Latto and Alice Spooner, "The Venus Effect: People's Understanding of Mirror Reflections in Paintings," *Perception* 32, 5 (May 2003): 596.

60. Szaloky, "Making New Sense of Film Theory Through Kant. A Novel Teaching Approach," 39.

61. According to Eric Naiman, Shklovsky is "completely ignoring Tolstoy's aesthetic views" (Naiman, "Shklovsky's Dog and Mulvey's Pleasure: The Secret Life of Defamiliarization," 343). In addition, "for all its rhetorical power, *Art as Device* is a confusing and contradictory article, so confusing, in fact, that the authors of studies of Formalism have kindly more or less refrained from dealing with it as a single utterance. Yet the work seems so contradictory and even haphazard that it begs for close attention to its own strangeness." (Ibid., 339).

62. Charles Taylor, *Sources of the Self: The Making of the Modern Identity* (Cambridge, MA.: Harvard University Press, 1989). The second one is the significance modern age attaches to ordinary life – it matches too, since we see the typist at work.

63. For an account opposing reflectionism, see David Bordwell, *Poetics of Cinema* (New York: Routledge, 2008), 30-32.

64. Ellen Dissanayake, *What is Art For?* (Seattle: University of Washington Press, 1988).

65. "Today it is recognized that the human species has had an evolutionary history of about four million years. Of that timespan, 399/400ths is disregarded when it is assumed that 'human history' or the 'history of art' begins, as it does in our textbooks, about 10,000 B.C. Unless we correct our lens and viewfinder, our speculations and pronouncements about human nature and endeavor 'in general' can hardly escape being limited and parochial. If we presume to speak about art, we should try to take

into account the representatives of this category created by all persons, everywhere, at anytime. Modern aesthetic theory in its present state is singularly unable and unwilling to do this." Dissanayake, What is Art For?, 5.

66. Universal devices of art include [among other things] "innovatory tendencies (exploration, originality, creation, invention, seeing things a new way, revising the old order, surprise) and the immediate fullness of sense experience (as opposed to habituated unregarded experience)." Dissanayake, What is Art For?, 36.

67. Queer theoreticians would agree to this particular point, since the politics of queer theory include ideas of "subversive repetition" and "transgressive reinscription."

## On Perception, *Ostranenie*, and Specificity

1. As is already clear from the brief introduction, contemporary film theory must address the issue of digitally synthesized motion picture images as well as television, computer games, webcam, etc. Thus, the proper term for the theory should be "moving image theory" rather than the classical "film theory." However, for sake of simplicity, in this paper I will mostly use the shorter term but with the meaning of the longer one.

2. A detailed analysis of such "puzzling" pictures can be found in James Elkin, Why are Our Pictures Puzzles? On the Modern Origin of Pictorial Complexity (New York & London: Routledge, 1999).

3. Thus, digitally synthesized images appear no less "realistic" to our perceptual system than a Neo-realist movie or a classical photograph, because they are both processed by the same cognitive mechanism we have developed during evolution. Digitally synthesized images draw their appeal precisely from their perceptual similarity or – in the case of simulation games – perceptual sameness with perceiving natural scenes or real individuals.

4. See Paul Virillo, The Aesthetics of Disappearance (New York: Semiotext(e), 1991) and Vilém Flusser, Für eine philosophie der fotografie (Göttingen, European Photography, 1983), and Flusser, Towards a Philosophy of Photography, trans. Martin Chalmers (London: Reakton Books, 2000).

5. Michel Polanyi in his book Personal Knowledge makes a distinction between focal vs. subsidiary awareness, which he applies to the perception of visual images in Michel Polanyi, "What Is a Painting?" British Journal of Aesthetics 10 (1970): 225-236. The gist of the argument revolves around the idea that for aesthetic perception the viewer should have a subsidiary awareness of the surface (i.e. the canvas) over and above the focal awareness of the painted scene. The subsidiary awareness of the surface amounts to being conscious of the way the painting or, in our case, the image has been made, that is the scene is not fully transparent but opaque: it is seen – as Wollheim (Richard Wollheim, "Seeing-as, Seeing-in and Pictorial Representation," in Art and its Objects (Cambridge: Cambridge UP, 1980), 205-226) and Walton (Kendall Walton, "Transparent Pictures. On the Nature of Photographic Realism," Critical Inquiry 12 (1984): 246-277) put it – in the picture and not through.

6. In concluding his article Benjamin makes a distinction between the masses who seek distraction when watching a movie, and art which demands concentration from the spectator. He claims that "distraction and concentration form polar opposites," and the film is most adept to provide a sort of immediacy for distraction. Bolter and Grusin (Jay David Bolter and Richard Grusin, Remediation. Understanding New Media (Cambridge, Mass. & London: MIT Press, 1999), 21) claim the purpose of virtual reality is "immersive" in that it distracts the viewers' attention from the technology which

makes its perception possible, so that the medium itself becomes transparent. I will argue that, in contrast to the medium's transparency, art and aesthetic perception imply its opaqueness, or what amounts to the same, the viewer comes to be aware of its mediating role. The proper viewer of art, according to Benjamin, is the critic who pays attention to and examines how the given work of art is made. Whereas the film, he claims, requires no attention, and its "proper" public is an "absent-minded" one. While I embrace Benjamin's analysis of the aura, I will attempt to go beyond the scope of his conclusion and contest his overall characterization of the film as distraction. I demonstrate with examples that, despite its reproducibility, film does not stand a lesser chance of being specific than an autographic art like painting. By autographic art, theorists mean that a work of art cannot be wholly codified or scored down in a symbolic language, hence it is sensitive to forgery. In contrast, allographic works of art like musical compositions can be scored, hence they cannot be forged. And the reason is that the specificity is an inherent property of objects including art, and as such it cannot be reproduced entirely mechanically, but it can and in fact is sometimes perceived as a singular and unique property of objects by means of which they can be unambiguously identified. That means that the reception of art, i.e. the distinction between attention and distraction, is primarily a perceptual problem, whereas Benjamin in the first part of his article uses aura and its core element, distance, as if they were ontological concepts. Film would then demand a different ontology from autographic arts. While not denying this, I would remind the reader of the fact that visual technology has significantly widened the scope of human perception.

7. For a counter-example, think of goofs (e.g. misuse of props, shadow of camera, part of audio cable seen in the image, etc.) in films which reveal the use of audio-visual technology by means of which they have been shot and put together.

8. Three decades later Susan Sontag reflects upon the effect of the photograph (see Susan Sontag, *On Photography* (New York: Anchor Books), 1973). She observes, although not entirely unequivocally, that the photograph penetrates the world, eliminates distance, gets very close to the thing itself; however, the photograph's presence is only a fake presence: it can never totally abolish the distance that opens up between the photographer and the photographed object. With this claim Sontag implicitly restores Benjamin's aura into its own right even in an age of mechanical reproduction. She sets a lower bound to artfulness as a form of perception. Finally it is today's phenomenological film theory which in my view can explain most consistently why and when the aura is lost: it is *not* lost during the reception of the film, but it dissolves during the use of digital media, especially the digital internet space. In my discussion, however, I limit myself to a few remarks about Vivian Sobchack's seminal book, *The Address of the Eye*, and her approach to digital media (Vivian Sobchack, *The Address of the Eye: a Phenomenology of Film Experience* (Princeton: Princeton UP), 1992). Instead of elaborating the phenomenological point further, I introduce some ideas from my own research in cognitive aesthetics and cognitive film theory.

9. Viktor Shklovsky, "Art as Technique," *Russian Formalist Criticism. Four Essays*, trans. Lee T. Lemon, and Marion Reis (Lincoln & London: University of Nebraska Press, 1965), 12.

10. Ibid., 9.

11. It does not so much inaugurate a norm/deviation model; rather it calls for a functional description of formal features within a given style. Kristin Thompson uses the concept of *ostranenie* in this sense for the analysis of artistic form.

12. Shklovsky, "Art as Technique," 12.

13. Note that in the case of *Kubla Khan*, remaining in half-truth is the result of a fictional story. In the preface prefixed to the poem, Coleridge admits that he wrote his verse as *a dim recollection* of a dream from which he was woken up by an unexpected visitor. The loss of meaning is due to the opaque boundary between waking up and sleeping, being half-awake and half-asleep as he was. We could say he was one of the first artists who was writing while taking drugs.

14. The relevance of the main ideas appearing in *The Critique of Pure Reason* on the idea of the Sublime, which gets only a passing treatment, is important to note. The third critique is still controversial, despite the famous Kantian dictum about the starry sky above and the moral law inside man. Moreover, many philosophers and scholars have pointed out that there are a couple of terms in the two critiques which are closely related. Respect may be the most important one. (See Immanuel Kant, *Critique of Practical Reason (Cambridge Texts in the History of Philosophy)* (Cambridge: Cambridge UP, 1997) It should be applied both to transcendental laws and to finite objects of Nature and man himself as a social being. Sublime objects may be the best means to awaken man to ethical consciousness. The connection of the two books is a common topic, especially in modern French thought, as it is attested by the unorthodox treatment of the Sublime in Lyotard (See Jean-François Lyotard, *Leçons sur l'Analitique du Sublime* (Paris: Galilée, 1991)). But for film studies, it is Deleuze's approach to critical thinking that can be the most relevant. To put it succinctly, for Deleuze critical thinking means that each human faculty should be pushed to its very limits in order to arrive at a form of thinking which becomes productive, creative, experimenting and even artistic.

15. On the Deleuzian and the romantic element, see previous note.

16. Walter Benjamin, *The Work of Art in the Age of Mechanical Reproduction* [Das kunstwerk im zeitalter seiner technischen reproduzierbarkeit (1936)], trans. Harry Zohn. in *Illuminations: Essays and Reflections*, ed. Hannah Arendt (New York: Shocken Books, 1968), 240.

17. Shklovsky, "Art as Technique," 9.

18. Or in Sontag's terminology, between informative value and aesthetic distance, i.e. time's signature in the photograph.

19. Benjamin, *The Work of Art in the Age of Mechanical Reproduction*, 240.

20. Ibid., 248.

21. See László Tarnay and Tamás Pólya, *Specificity Recognition and Social Cognition* (Frankfurt a/M & New York & Oxford: Peter Lang, 2004).

22. Our contention in the book is that specificity recognition was crucial in social evolution: species which live in groups or families need to recognize their fellow family members individually as this-and-this, and not only categorically as so-and-so. Nest-leaving bird parents, for example, would not feed others but only their own young ones, and vice versa, the young would not accept food from other conspecifics but their parents. Among primates and humans the upper limit of recognizing individual group or family members is said to be around 160. This seems to be a cognitive (brain size) limit to distinguish among individuals. Beyond that limit categorical perception overtakes the function of specificity recognition, and we identify people as "the man with the Martini," "the king of France" or "the most intelligent person in the class."

23. This is the reason why newer and newer forms of individual recognition have been introduced at custom check-ins in the past years, from facial recognition systems, through fingerprint recognition, to iris recognition.

24. This means that many forms of individual recognition, which are very developed in other species, have regressed in humans. Dogs and cheetahs identify even a single pheromone by smelling, whales identify their conspecific's individual sound, nest-leaving birds recognize the heads of their family members, etc. Probably the only bio-

logically hard-wired human capacity to individuate is the mothers' ability to identify their newborn babies by their smells, even without having ever touched them. (See Marsha Kaitz, A. Good, A.M. Rokem, and A.I. Eidelman, "Mother's Recognition of their Newborns by Olfactory Cues," *Developmental Psychobiology* 20 (1987): 587-591.) And it works the other way round as well: babies prefer their mothers' perfume. (See Benoist Schaal, "Presumed Olfactory Exchanges between Mother and Neonate in Humans," in *Ethology and Psychology*, eds. J. LeCamus and J. Cosnier (Toulouse: Privat-IEC, 1986), 101-110.)

25. No wonder that in his letters to his brother, Van Gogh praises the Dutch painter Frans Hals of making use of 20 different shades of black, while at the end of his career van Gogh himself insisted upon using more than 20 different shades of white. To add an example from film history, Gilles Deleuze, the film philosopher, praises Abel Gance for composing his images "white on white."

26. See especially J.D. Anderson, *The Reality of Illusion: An Ecological Approach to Cognitive Film Theory* (Carbondale: Southern Illinois UP, 1996) and James Patterson, "Is a Cognitive Approach to the Avant-Garde Cinema Perverse?" in *Post-theory: Reconstructing Film Studies*, eds. David Bordwell and Noël Caroll (Madison: University of Wisconsin Press, 1996), 108-129.

27. See Alexander Veselovsky, *Sobranie Sochinenii* (St. Petersburg, 1913) and Herbert Spencer, *Philosophy of Style* [1852] (Whitefish, MT.: Kessinger Publishing, 2004 ), as quoted by Shklovsky in "Art as Technique," 9-10.

28. Dan Sperber and Deirdre Wilson, *Relevance: Communication and Cognition* (Oxford: Basil Blackwell, 1986).

29. It is along the same line that Noël Carroll (See Noël Carroll, "A Note on Film Metaphor," in *Theorizing the Moving Image* (Cambridge: Cambridge UP, 1996), 212-223) incorporates the core concept of *ostranenie* into his approach to the film metaphor, where he defines the core of film metaphors "[t]he physical noncompossibility of the homospatially fused but disparate elements" encountering which "the spectator is encouraged to search or to explore some other way in which the symbol before her may be taken in order to make sense" (215). From the fact that there is no automatic answer to the noncompossibility of the image (or accordingly to the strangeness or newness of a poetic metaphor), it does not follow that "deautomatization" is possible only if the principle of relevance runs off-line. When the viewer tries to understand the noncompossible figure of Moloch devouring the workers as an entrance to the factory in Fritz Lang's METROPOLIS and rakes her brain for a "proper" meaning within the film's fiction, she may well follow the principle of relevance to understand most with the least effort.

30. Shklovsky, "Art as Technique," 12.

31. See László Tarnay, and Tamás Pólya, "Reprezentáció és specificitás," *Passim* 7 (2005): 67-100.

32. Vilayanur S. Ramachandran, and William Hirstein, "The Science of Art," *Journal of Consciousness Studies* 6.6-7 (1999): 15-41.

33. See D. Gamboni, *Potential Images. Ambiguity and Indeterminacy in Modern Art* (London: Reaktion Books, 2002), 28-35.

34. We use the term "modulation" for its musical overtones. In music, modulation refers to the specific (singular and unique) manner in which the different qualities of sound or singing shift almost imperceptibly between moods, pitches, singing and speech (recitative) or rhythmic patterns (rubato). In all these cases the term expresses the spontaneous, uncontrollable aspect of the changes. Thus, it is a near synonym of improvisation, yet it is more general than the latter. A reference must be made here to

David Bordwell's use of the term in David Bordwell, *Figures Traced in Light* (Berkeley & Los Angeles: University of California Press), 2005, where he applies it to the small, hardly perceptible changes within the film image or, I would say, texture of the image. Understood in this latter sense, modulating images highlighted by Bordwell in the films of Hou, Angelopulos, Misoguchi, etc. would indeed belong to our fourth level.

35. Shklovsky, "Art as Technique," 12.
36. Benjamin, *The Work of Art in the Age of Mechanical Reproduction*, 248.
37. No wonder that even in the digital age, film makers frequently reproduce digitally. By re-recording the film on celluloid or tape, the over-magnifying creates a granular structure in the photographic substance. By making their otherwise digitally made films look granular – sometimes also considered to be "noisy" – they refer to the "old" tradition of shooting films on 35 mm footage, or they would like to add a touch of the documentary.
38. It is widely accepted in cognitive aesthetics and film theory that in most cases the spectators see the represented scene directly, i.e., they "see through" the surface or the plane of representation (the canvas or the projected image plane), even if the surface is noisy to a certain extent. That means the surface of representation is transparent for them. They are primarily aware of the represented scene, while they are secondarily aware of the surface of representation. BLOWUP toys with our cognitive "tolerance" concerning the quantity of noise in the image. We as spectators can still see through its "messy" texture and recognize the figure.
39. See Gilles Deleuze and Félix Guattari, *What is Philosophy?* trans. Janis Tomlinson and Graham Burchell III (1991; reprint, New York: Columbia UP, 1996).
40. See Gilles Deleuze, *Difference and Repetition*, trans. Paul Patton (1968; reprint, London: Athlone Press, 1994).
41. Manola Antonioli, *Deleuze et l'Histoire de la Philosophie* (Paris: Klimé, 1999), 85.
42. At least a passing reference must be made here to the Deleuzian project of philosophy. According to him, it is in the sensible that the radically new appears. It follows that one cannot think but at the expense of pulling down or bypassing all its existing categories and concepts and creating new concepts. At least this is how Deleuze conceives the task of philosophy. The Deleuzian project is not totally irrelevant for the present investigation. When Deleuze in his cinema books argues that modern film blocks the working of the sensorimotor scheme which is so typical of classical movies, he suggests – although not explicitly – that traditional narrative interpretation relies on the "seamless" action-reaction scheme, once again a form of "automatized" perception. What is needed for "new" thought or the thought of the new is *perceptually* new stimuli. It is only the senses which provide the intellect with radically new materials and thus provoke it, ignite it, and carry it onto never trodden paths far away from conceptual categories. The senses act as the source of the Sublime *for* the intellect (for a brief and lucid survey, see Antonioli, *Deleuze et l'Histoire de la Philosophie*).

## Estrangement and the Representation of Life in Art

1. Viktor Shklovsky, "Art as Technique," *Russian Formalist Criticism. Four Essays*, trans. Lee T. Lemon and Marion Reis (Lincoln & London: University of Nebraska Press, 1965), 3-57. For recent contributions on the concept of estrangement in Shklovsky and Russian Formalism, see *Poetics Today* 26, 4 (2005) and 27, 1 (2006).
2. Shklovsky, "Art as Technique," 11.
3. Ibid.

4.  For a recent ode to habit see Alva Noë, *Out of Our Heads. Why You Are Not Your Brain, and Other Lessons from the Biology of Consciousness* (New York: Hill and Wang, 2009), 97-128.
5.  Shklovsky, "Art as Technique," 11.
6.  For a more elaborate treatment of semiotic cognition, see Van Heusden, "A Bandwidth Model of Semiotic Evolution," in *Semiotic Evolution and the Dynamics of Culture*, eds. M. Bax, B. van Heusden and W. Wildgen (Bern: Peter Land, 2004), 1-28, Van Heusden, "Dealing with Difference: From Cognition to Semiotic Cognition," in *Cognitive Semiotics* 4 (2009): 117-133, and Van Heusden, "Semiotic Cognition and the Logic of Culture," in *Pragmatics and Cognition* 17, 3 (2009) [in press].
7.  Shklovsky, "Art as Technique," 12.
8.  The term "algebraic" stems from Bergson (cf. James M. Curtis, "Bergson and Russian Formalism," *Comparative Literature* 28, 2 (1976): 109-121).
9.  Shklovsky, "Art as Technique," 11.
10. *Ibid.*, 12 [italics in the original].
11. Douglas Robinson, *Estrangement and the Somatics of Literature. Tolstoy, Shklovsky, Brecht* (Baltimore: The Johns Hopkins University Press, 2008).
12. Shklovsky, "Art as Technique," 12 [italics added].
13. See Van Heusden, *Why literature? An Inquiry into the Nature of Literary Semiosis* (Tübingen: Stauffenburg Verlag, 1997) for a theory of literature as mimetic semiosis.
14. Robinson, *Estrangement and the Somatics of Literature. Tolstoy, Shklovsky, Brecht*, 99. Shklovsky takes a much broader and also a more neutral view on art than Brecht. The "truth" revealed is a different one: for Shklovsky it is the truth of experience, of life. For Brecht it is a discursive, ideological truth. From my point of view, Shklovsky is the one who got it right. Brecht mixes up the artistic with a non-artistic, rhetorical or political function. Which does not mean of course that art could not be political. It often is, but the political should not be confused with the artistic function.
15. From "Vyshla" 1915, a review of Mayakovsky's "A Cloud in Trousers," translated and quoted by Robinson, *Estrangement and the Somatics of Literature. Tolstoy, Shklovsky, Brecht*, 86.
16. Shklovsky gave a heart-breaking personal account of his "life and times" in his autobiographical *Sentimental Journey* (Ithaka New York: Cornell University Press, 1984). For the original work, see *Sentimental'noe putesestvie* (Moskow: Gelikon, 1923).
17. As Robinson (Robinson, *Estrangement and the Somatics of Literature. Tolstoy, Shklovsky, Brecht*, 79) points out, estrangement is one of the central ideas of German and English Romanticism and German idealism (Rousseau, Hegel, Novalis, Shelley, Schlegel, Wordsworth and others). It is a direct consequence of the suspicion of the modern world view towards tradition and "idées reçues" (what Wordsworth, in the 1798 advertisement to the *Lyrical Ballads*, calls the "gaudiness and inane phraseology" of many modern writers). The autonomous individual, relying on his or her own intellectual capacities, must see the world anew again and again. The discovery of the world as being separated from habits of perception is thus one of the effects of an enlightened world view, although it is questionable whether the romantic poets would themselves have acknowledged this.

## The Perception of Reality as Deformed Realism

1.  Jarmo Valkola, *Cognition and Visuality* (Jyväskylä: University of Jyväskylä, 2004), 179.
2.  Viktor Shklovsky, "Art as Technique" [1919] *Russian Formalist Criticism: Four Essays*, ed. and trans. Lee T. Lemon and Marion J. Reis (Lincoln: University of Nebraska Press,

1965), 12. The distinction between "perceived" and "known" materializes through the trope of *ostranenie* as an intentional defamiliarizing, deautomatizing, estranging action of an artist.

3. Hugo Münsterberg, *The Film: The Psychological Study* [1916] (New York: Dover Publications, 1970). The goal of Münsterberg's masterwork was to get film across as an independent, separate art form. It highly correlates with Shklovsky's (first published in 1919), and the Russian Formalism's theoretical efforts (which is to define *literaturnost* (*literariness*) in general, a contemporary term of Roman Jakobson); see Boris Eichenbaum's "historical summation" of the "formal method," which is more about the "struggle for a science of literature" rather than providing a definitive methodology. Boris Eichenbaum: "The Theory of the 'Formal Method,'" [1926] eds. Lee T. Lemon and Marion J. Reis, 99.

4. The construction process of induction, from the parts towards the whole, is similar to the *bottom-up* interpretative root, while the deductive – from the whole towards the parts, narrative approach imitates the *top-down* perceptive attitude. Serial, bottom-up inductivity believes in the priority of direct, distinct stimuli (typically activated at the recognition of colors, or at tracking moving objects), while the direction of deductive top-down, which is influenced by previous knowledge, is activated, for example, by recognizing faces (the case of selecting the familiar from the crowd).

5. Mark D. Seddon, *Investigating the Effect on Attention of Action Continuity* (MSc thesis in Cognitive Science and Natural Language: University of Edinburgh, 2003), 21.

6. For example, Stephen E. Palmer confirms that about 150-200 milliseconds pass between the idea to move the eye and the execution of the movement, and the eye needs an average of 300 milliseconds to fix on the object of seeing. Stephen E. Palmer, *Vision Science: Photons to Phenomenology* (Cambridge: MIT Press, 1999).

7. This still has nothing to do with short- or long-term memories: according to Eugene Zechmeister and Stanley Nyberg, the role of the *sensory store* is restricted to the physiological process of the visual decoding of the eye. Eugene B. Zechmeister, and Stanley E. Nyberg, *Human Memory: An Introduction to Research and Theory* (Monterey, CA.: Thomson Brooks / Cole, 1982).

8. Seddon, 22.

9. Within the film history of narrative representation from around 1910 onward, the narrative-centered rules keep developing into norms. The most important aim of this, still evolving, set of "formal and stylistic norms" (Bordwell, Staiger, and Thompson 1985, xiv) – which was named "Classical Narration" by David Bordwell (1985, 156-204) and "Institutional Mode of Representation" by Noël Burch (1990) – is accessibility, the maintenance of comprehensibility through film language (that is, about linearity, causality, seamlessness, transparency, redundancy, limited consciousness, the working mechanisms of the camera identified with the ideal viewer, etc.). In order to deliver these, it employed the help of narrative, psychological, and cognitive theories of the last hundred years. Its final goal is to perfect the deduction, as Bordwell (1997a, 95) claims, "Filmmakers had to create psychologically convincing representations." In accordance with my present interest, it is important to highlight that this is not about the presentation of reality but rather about its psychologically based representation, which utilizes strategies of "convincing/persuasiveness." David Bordwell, Janet Staiger, and Kristin Thompson, *The Classical Hollywood Cinema: Film Style and Mode of Production to 1960* (London: Routledge & Paul Kegan; New York: Columbia UP, 1985). David Bordwell, *Narration in the Fiction Film* (Madison: University of Wisconsin Press, 1985). Noël Burch, *Life to Those Shadows*. ed. and trans. Ben Brewster (Berkeley: University of

California Press, 1990). David Bordwell, *On the History of Film Style* (Cambridge, Mass., & London: Harvard UP, 1997a).

10. Meir Sternberg, "Telling in Time (III): Chronology, Estrangement, and Stories of Literary History," *Poetics Today* 27, 1 (spring 2006): 138.

11. Bordwell, *Narration in the Fiction Film*, 33.

12. *Schemata*: Top-down structured sets of knowledge that form the information of the perceptual input into coherent mental representations. The term is from Ernst Gombrich, meaning "ready" knowledge groups helping reception through categorization. To interpret "ready" is the goal of the cognitive analysis of the notion.
    *Template schemata*: Cognitive systems for storing data, bigger structures, which develop from adequately ordered hierarchy of schemes. Accordingly, these are culture-specific units building on stronger knowledge and learning compared to schemata. Bordwell, *Narration in the Fiction Film*, 31, 34-35. Ernst Gombrich, *Art and Illusion: A Study in the Psychology of Pictorial Representation* (Princeton: Princeton UP, 1961), 146-178.

13. Bordwell, *On the History of Film Style*, 155.

14. Warren Buckland, *The Cognitive Semiotics of Film* (Cambridge: Cambridge UP, 2000), 124-131.

15. In connection with the latter, category [c], Christian Metz adds with a little cognitive malignity that notwithstanding their aims, not even avant-garde filmmakers can realize this category, as their socialization based on a cognitive film basis does not allow them to disobey the rules of film grammar. Christian Metz, *Film Language: A Semiotics of the Cinema*, trans. Michael Taylor (New York: Oxford UP, 1974), 211.

16. Buckland, 127.

17. Buckland, 129.

18. Bordwell, *Narration in the Fiction Film*, 318. In another comprehensive film theoretical study, Bordwell examines this scene maintaining his point, "Such manipulation of editing blocks our normal expectations about story and forces us to concentrate on the very process of piecing together the film's narrative action." David Bordwell, *Film Art. An Introduction*, [1979] 5th ed. (New York: McGraw-Hill, 1997b), 305.

19. To make a difference is a cardinal question: the theory of neo-formalism and constructivism does not reconstruct the fabula anymore than in the Tynjanovian or Proppian sense, but rather, it constructs it. Following András Bálint Kovács's recapitulation, "In the original terminology, *fabula* (tale, story) is a chronological and causal sketch what the *syuzhet* (plot) 'dresses' with concrete characters, twists, settings, etc. The viewers' task is to construct a tale from the procedures of the syuzhet (narration tricks, *prijom* by Viktor Shklovsky) and stylistic elements. Wording is important here. Bordwell does not talk about *reconstruction*, he does not say that the viewers understand and re-complete an already existing story in their head. Bordwell thinks that the story is not 'hidden' anywhere 'behind' the syuzhet. [...] The tale is the mental construction of the viewer based on those signals that the formal elements of the film offer for them." András Bálint Kovács, *A film szerint a világ* (Budapest: Palatinus, 2002), 20 [my translation].

20. Buckland, 127. Buckland's struggle expressed talkatively by his parentheses around the word "*back*" (supposedly the quotation mark has the same role in Bordwell's "'*correct*' *chronology*").

21. According to Barry Salt's *Cinemetrics* measurements, while the entire film's average shot length (ASL) is 21.3 seconds, the analyzed scene's ASL is approximately only 2 seconds. Barry Salt, "Cinemetrics on *Pierrot le Fou*" (29-03-2007), available from http://www.cinemetrics.lv/movie.php?movie_ID=617 [06-08-2009]; INTERNET.

22. Shklovsky, "Art as Technique," 18.

23. András Bálint Kovács, *Metropolis, Párizs*, (Budapest: Képzõmõvészeti Kiadó, 1992), 177 [my translation].
24. Thus eases Shklovsky's dejection: "we have lost our awareness of the world. [...] Only the creation of new forms of art can restore to man sensation of the world, can resurrect things and kill pessimism." Viktor Shklovsky, "The Resurrection of the Word," [1914] *Russian Formalism. A collection of Articles and Texts in Translation*, ed. Stephen Bann, and John E. Bowlt (Edinburgh: Scottish Academic Press,1973), 46.
25. Shklovsky, "Art as Technique," 11-12.
26. Shklovsky's poetical and Godard's political narrative-estranging aims against the classical norms are seemingly identical: however, both their intended conclusions and the actual appearances of these intentions point in different directions. In order to gain poetical increments, Shklovsky wanted to wedge the divisive deautomatization of *ostranenie* into the course of the perception of reality.
27. David Bordwell, *Poetics of Cinema* (New York: Routledge, 2008), 93.
28. Deductive top-down processes are "influenced by the individual's knowledge and expectations rather than simply by the stimulus itself" and do not take the information coming from the object of reception as the sole decisive factor. Michael W. Eysenck, and Mark Keane, *Cognitive Psychology. A Student's Handbook*, 5th ed. (Hove: Psychology Press Ltd., 2005), 2.
29. Thus, the estrangement's manifestation is not only a structural or narrative question, not only a simple category concerning the perception's automatisms, it also is a question of shaping an indirect, emotional, somatic, sometimes even unconscious domain of the experience. Closely following and quoting Dewey's progressive thoughts, Shusterman concludes that "the roots of art and beauty lie in the 'basic vital functions,' 'the biological commonplaces [where] 'formal conditions...are rooted deep in the world itself,' in our own biological rhythms and the larger rhythms of nature, which gradually get reflected and elaborated into the rhythms of myth and art." As a matter of fact, in order to grasp these "roots of art," Shusterman pursues his own definition of *literariness*, merging Shklovsky's formal investigations of the physical appearances of artifacts with the receivers' biocultural, somatic character.
    Considering the fact that Joseph D. Anderson's pioneering book on the ecological approach of film theory was first published in 1996, Shusterman's work – first published in 1992 – is not only highly inspiring but highly progressive as well. Joseph D. Anderson, *The Reality of Illusion – An Ecological Approach to Cognitive Film Theory* [1996] (Carbondale & Edwardsville: Southern Illinois UP, 1998). Richard Shusterman, *Pragmatist Aesthetics. Living Beauty, Rethinking Art* (Oxford & Cambridge: Blackwell, 1992).
30. Pier Paolo Pasolini, "Cinema di Poesia" (paper presented at the Festival of the New Film, Pesaro, Italy, June 1965). Published in the *Cahiers du Cinéma*, October 1965. Paul Beers, trans., "De poëtische film," *De Revisor* 1, no 9 &10 (December 1974): 74 [my translation].

## *Conversation* with András Bálint Kovács

1. András Bálint Kovács, "Tarkovsky," in *The Routledge Companion to Philosophy and Film*, eds. Paisley Livingstone and Carl Plantinga (New York: Routledge, 2009). Kovács,"Openness of the Work of Art: Deleuze and Eco," in *Afterimages of Gilles Deleuze's Film Philosophy*, ed. David Rodowick (Minneapolis: University of Minnesota Press, 2009 (he was the Hungarian translator of Deleuze's *Cinema* I-II). See also: Kovács, "Sartre, the

Philosophy of Nothingness and the Modern Melodrama," in *The American, Journal of Aesthetics and Art Criticism* Vol. 64. no.1 (2006) 135-145.

2. See for instance the papers András Bálint Kovács presented at SCSMI conferences: "Causal Inference During Filmviewing"(2009), "Causal Cues in Narratives" (2008), "Situations and Narrative Comprehension" (2004).

3. András Bálint Kovács, "The Sokal-Briqmond Affair," 2000 (February 1998): 53-61.

4. Remember, for example, the way René Clair in his *Entr'acte* [1924] uses Dutch shots, blurred images, dissolving stills, etc. to frame the church of La Madeleine and the Place de l'Opéra.

5. See the essay by Laurent Jullier in this book.

6. András Bálint Kovács, "Things that Come After Another," *New Review of Film and Television Studies* 5, no.2 (August 2007): 157-73.

7. *Ibid.*

8. Richard Allen, and Murray Smith, "Introduction" in *Film Theory and Philosophy*, (Oxford & New York: Oxford University Press, 1999), 12.

9. Jacques Derrida, "Différance," trans. Alan Bass, in *Margins of Philosophy* (Chicago: University of Chicago Press, 1982), 3-27.

10. See for instance Anne Campbell, *A Mind of Her Own. The Evolutionary Psychology of Women* (Oxford & New York: Oxford University Press, 2002).

11. Dan Sperber, *Why rethink interdisciplinarity?* Text discussed in the virtual seminar "Rethinking interdisciplinarity," available from www.interdisciplines.org; INTERNET.

12. *Ibid.*

13. See for example: Torben Grodal, *Embodied Visions* (New York: Oxford University Press, 2008), or Robert Hanna, and Michelle Maiese, *Embodied Minds in Action* (Oxford & New York: Oxford University Press, 2009).

14. Walter J. Freeman, "Consciousness, Intentionality and Causality," in *Does Consciousness Cause Behavior?* eds. Susan Pockett, William P. Banks, and Shaun Gallagher (Cambridge, MA.: MIT, 2006), 73-105.

15. See for example: David Wegner, *The Illusion of the Conscious Will* (Cambridge, MA.: MIT Press, 2002).

16. Torben Grodal, *Embodied Visions* (Copenhagen: Department of Film and Media, University of Copenhagen, 2006), 27.

## *Conversation* with Laura Mulvey

1. Laura Mulvey, *Death 24x a Second. Stillness and the Moving Image* (London: Reaktion Books Ltd., 2006), 52.

2. *Ibid.*

3. André Gaudreault, "From 'Primitive Cinema' to 'Kine-Attractography,'" in *The Cinema of Attractions Reloaded*, ed. Wanda Strauven (Amsterdam: Amsterdam University Press, 2006), 99.

4. For a description of Shklovsky's lecture as a freshman in 1913, see Richard Sheldon in his "Introduction" in *A Sentimental Journey* (New York: Cornell University Press, 1970).

5. Sigmund Freud, "The Uncanny," in *The Standard Edition of the Complete Psychological Works of Sigmund Freud*, Vol. XIV ed. James Stratchey (London, 1953-74).

6. Laura Mulvey, *Death 24x a Second*, 34.

7. Ernst Jentsch, "On the Psychology of the Uncanny," [1906] *Angelaki* 2, no. 1 (1995): 7-16. In her article (lecture) "A Sudden Gust of Wind (after Hokusai): from After to Before the Photograph," Laura Mulvey discusses the work of photographer Jeff Wall

in relation to the "question of technology and the conceptual space which Wall himself describes as 'improbable.'" Interestingly, Mulvey approaches Wall's work in terms of a "technological uncanny" and refers to Jentsch's 1906 essay "On the Psychology of the Uncanny" to indicate that Jentsch located "the uncanny in the disorientation experienced by the most rational mind when faced with an illusion that is, if only momentarily, inexplicable. This sense of 'intellectual uncertainty' could be aroused, for instance, by automata or wax works that seem to be almost alive." See: Laura Mulvey, "A Sudden Gust of Wind (after Hokusai): from After to Before the Photograph," *Oxford Art Journal* 30, no. 1. (2007): 31-32.

8. Stephen Heath, "Cinema and Psychoanalysis," in *Endless Night. Cinema and Psychoanalysis. Parallel Histories*, ed. Janet Bergstrom (University of California Press, 1999), 30, and Virginia Woolf, "The Cinema," [1926] in *Collected Essays II* (Hogarth Press, 1966).

9. Marcel Proust, *À la recherche du temps perdu*, Vol. 2, 1913-1927.

10. Vladimir Nabokov, *Speak, Memory* (New York: Penguin Books, 1982), 19.

11. *Ibid.*, 17-18.

12. *Ibid.*, 18.

13. Viktor Shklovsky, "Art as Technique," *Russian Formalist Criticism. Four Essays*, trans. Lee T. Lemon and Marion Reis (Lincoln & London: University of Nebraska Press, 1965), 3-57.

14. Sigmund Freud, "Letter to Romain Rolland (A Disturbance of Memory on the Acropolis)," ed. Adam Phillips in *The Penguin Freud Reader* (London: Penguin Books Ltd, 2006), 68-76.

15. Sigmund Freud, "The Uncanny," in *The Standard Edition of the Complete Psychological Works of Sigmund Freud*, Vol. XIV ed. James Stratchey (London, 1953-74).

16. *Ibid.*

17. Wolfgang Kayser, *Das Groteske. Seine Gestaltung in Malerei und Dichtung* (Tübingen: Stauffenburg Verlag, 2004).

18. *Ibid.*, 199.

19. See David Summers, *Michelangelo and the Language of Art* (Princeton, N.J.: Princeton University Press, 1981).

20. Arthur Danto, *The Transfiguration of the Commonplace: A Philosophy of Art* (Cambridge, Mass.: Harvard University Press, 1981).

21. See Shklovsky on Eisenstein: *Ejzenštejn*, trans. Manfred Dahlke (Reinbek: Rowohlt Taschenbuch Verlag, 1977), 125. [First published in Moscow: Iskusstvo, 1973.]

22. Boris Eichenbaum, "Problems of Cinema Stylistics," in *Formalist Film Theory* (Michigan: University of Michigan, 1981), 57. [First published in *Poetika Kino* (Moscow, Leningrad: Kinopečat' 1927).]

23. Frank Ankersmit, *Sublime Historical Experience* (Stanford, Ca.: Stanford University Press, 2005).

24. Annette Michelson, "The Man with the Movie Camera: From Magician to Epistemologist," *Artforum* 10, no. 7 (March 1972): 60-72.

25. Laura Mulvey, "Visual Pleasure and Narrative Cinema," in *Screen* (autumn 1975): 6-18.

26. Laura Mulvey, *Fetishism and Curiosity* (London: BFI, 1996).

27. Eric Naiman, "Shklovsky's Dog and Mulvey's Pleasure: The Secret Life of Defamiliarization," *Comparative Literature* 50, no. 4 (autumn 1998): 333-352.

28. Scott Bukatman, "Spectacle, Attractions and Visual Pleasure," in *The Cinema of Attractions Reloaded*, ed. Wanda Strauven (Amsterdam: Amsterdam University Press, 2006), 71-83.

# General Bibliography

This bibliography, compiled in collaboration with Viola ten Hoorn, is not exhaustive. It is general in the sense that it is not limited to studies on Russian Formalism, bringing together references from various disciplines and research areas. Partly a selection of studies cited or referred to by the different contributors, it lists works that specifically relate to the notion of "ostranenie" (or "alienation" in general) as well as studies that are relevant for the contextualization and the theory formation of the concept and its reception in the post-war era.

Albera, François. *Les formalistes russes et le cinéma. Poétique du film.* Translation of *Poetika Kino* by V. Posener, R. Gayraud, and J.C. Peuch. Edited by François Albera. Paris: Nathan, 1996.

—. *L'Avant-Garde au cinéma.* Paris: Armand Colin, 2005.

Albright, Daniel. *Untwisting the Serpent: Modernism in Music, Literature and the Other Arts.* Chicago: University of Chicago Press, 2000.

Allen, Richard, and Murray Smith. "Introduction." In *Film Theory and Philosophy.* Oxford & New York: Oxford University Press, 1999.

Amengual, Barthélemy. *Que viva Eisenstein.* Lausanne: l'Âge d'homme, 1981.

Anderson, Joseph D. *The Reality of Illusion: An Ecological Approach to Cognitive Film Theory.* Carbondale, IL.: Southern Illinois University Press, 1996.

Anderson, Joseph D., Barbara Fisher, and David Bordwell. *Moving Image Theory: Ecological Considerations.* Carbondale, IL.: Southern Illinois University Press, 2007.

Ankersmit, Frank. *Sublime Historical Experience.* Stanford, California: Stanford University Press, 2005.

Antonioli, Manola. *Deleuze et l'histoire de la philosophie.* Paris: Klimé, 1999.

Arden, John. *Plays 1.* London: Methuen, 2002.

Arnheim, Rudolph. *Film as Art.* [1932] Berkeley & London: University of California Press, 1957.

Barthes, Roland. "En sortant du cinéma." In *Le bruissement de la langue.* Paris: Seuil, 1984.

Bauman, Zygmunt. *The Art of Life.* Cambridge: Polity, 2008.

Bazin, André. *What Is Cinema?* Vol. 1. Edited and translated by Hugh Gray. Berkeley & Los Angeles: University of California Press, 1967.

Beilenhoff, Wolfgang (ed.). *Poetika Kino. Theorie und Praxis des Films im russischen Formalismus.* Frankfurt am Main: Suhrkamp, 2005.

Bellour, Raymond, and Christian Metz. "Entretien sur la sémiologie du cinéma." [1970] In *Essais sur la signification au cinéma,* Tome II. Paris: Klincksieck, 1972.

Benjamin, Walter. *The Work of Art in the Age of Mechanical Reproduction*. [Das kunstwerk im zeitalter seiner technischen reproduzierbarkeit (1936)]. Translated by Harry Zohn. In *Illuminations: Essays and Reflections*, ed. Hannah Arendt. New York: Shocken Books, 1968.

—. *Illuminations*. Edited and Translated by Harry Zohn. London: Cape, 1970.

Bertamini, Marco, Richard Latto, and Alice Spooner. "The Venus Effect: People's Understanding of Mirror Reflections in Paintings." *Perception* 32, 5 (May 2003).

Berthoz, Alain. *The Brain's Sense of Movement. Perspectives in Cognitive Neuroscience*. Harvard: Harvard University Press, 2002.

Blackmore, Susan. "Evolution and Memes. The Human Brain as a Selective Imitation Device." In *Cybernetics and Systems* 32, no. 1, 225-255. Philadelphia: Taylor and Francis, 2001.

Blanchet, Philippe, Roland J.L. Breton, and Harold F. Schiffman, eds. *Les langues régionales de France, un état des lieux à la veille du XXIe siècle*. [The Regional Languages of France: An Inventory on the Eve of the XXI[st] Century] Louvain-la-Neuve: Peeters Publishers, 1999.

Bolter, Jay David, and Richard Grusin. *Remediation. Understanding New Media*. Cambridge, Mass. & London: MIT Press, 1999.

Bordwell, David. *The Films of Carl Theodor Dreyer*. Berkeley etc.: University of California Press, 1979.

—. "Lowering the Stakes: Prospects for a Historical Poetics of Cinema." *Iris* 1, 1 (1983): 5-18.

—. *Narration in the Fiction Film*. Madison: University of Wisconsin Press, 1985.

—. "A Case for Cognitivism." *Iris* 9 (spring 1989): 11-40.

—. "A Case for Cognitivism: Further Reflections." *Iris* 11 (summer 1990): 107-112.

—. *Film Art: An Introduction*. [1979] 5th ed. New York: McGraw-Hill, 1997.

—. *On the History of Film Style*. Cambridge, Mass. & London: Harvard University Press, 1997.

—. *Figures Traced in Light*. Berkeley & Los Angeles: University of California Press, 2005.

—. *Poetics of Cinema*. New York & London: Routledge, 2008.

Bordwell, David, Janet Staiger, and Kristin Thompson. *The Classical Hollywood Cinema: Mode of Production to 1960*. New York: Columbia University Press, 1985.

Bourdieu, Pierre. *Distinction. Critique sociale du jugement*. Paris: Le Sens Commun, Minuit, 1979.

—. *The Rules of Art*. Cambridge, UK: Polity Press, 2005.

Bowser, Eileen. "Le coup de téléphone dans les films des premiers temps." *Les premiers ans du cinéma français*. Edited by Pierre Guibbert. Perpignan: Institut Jean Vigo (1985): 218-224.

—. *History of the American Cinema: The Transformation of Cinema 1907-1915*. New York: Charles Scribner's Sons, 1990.

Boyd, Brian. "Getting It All Wrong: Bioculture Critiques Cultural Critique." *American Scholar* 75 (autumn 2006).

Boym, Svetlana. "Poetics and Politics of Estrangement: Victor Shklovsky and Hannah Arendt." *Poetics Today* 26, 4 (winter 2005).

Brakhage, Stan. *The Brakhage Lectures*. Chicago: The School of the Art Institute of Chicago, 1972.

Branigan, Edward. *Narrative Comprehension and Film*. London & New York: Routledge, 1992.

Brecht, Bertolt. *Short Description of a New Technique of Acting which Produces an Alienation Effect.* Available from http://www.english.emory.edu/DRAMA/BrechtAlien.html; INTERNET.

Brewster, Ben. "From Shklovsky to Brecht: A Reply." *Screen* 15, no. 2 (summer 1974): 82-102.

Bruns, Gerald L. "Introduction." In *Theory of Prose.* [Viktor Shklovsky] Translated by Benjamin Sher. Illinois State University, USA: Dalkey Archive Press, 1991.

Buckland, Warren. *The Cognitive Semiotics of Film.* Cambridge: Cambridge University Press, 2000.

Bukatman, Scott. "Spectacle, Attractions and Visual Pleasure." In *The Cinema of Attractions Reloaded,* ed. Wanda Strauven, 71-83. Amsterdam: Amsterdam University Press, 2006.

Bullot, Nicolas. "L'attention esthétique et les objects." *Art and Cognition Virtual Conference.* Available from http://www.interdisciplines.org/artcog/papers/5; INTERNET.

Burch, Noël. *Life to Those Shadows.* Edited and translated by Ben Brewster. Berkeley: University of California Press, 1990.

Burke, Peter. *What is Cultural History?* Cambridge, Malden: Polity, 2008.

Bürki-Cohen et al. "Simulator Fidelity: The Effect of Platform Motion." In *Proceedings of the Royal Aeronautical Society International Conference on Flight Simulation – The Next Decade.* London (May 2000): 23.1-23.7.

Cahan, David, ed. *Hermann Ludwig Ferdinand von Helmholtz and The Foundations of Nineteenth Century Science.* Los Angeles: University of California Press, 1994.

Caldwell, John, ed. *Theories of the New Media.* London: Athlone, 2000.

Campbell, Anne. *A Mind of Her Own. The Evolutionary Psychology of Women.* Oxford & New York: Oxford University Press, 2002.

Carroll, Noël. "A Note on Film Metaphor." In *Theorizing the Moving Image,* 212-223. Cambridge: Cambridge University Press, 1996.

—. "The Grotesque Today. Preliminary Notes Toward a Taxonomy." In *Modern Art and the Grotesque,* edited by F.S. Connelly. Cambridge: Cambridge University Press, 2003.

Casetti, Francesco. *Eye of the Century. Film, Experience, Modernity.* Translated by E. Larkin, and J. Pranolo. Edited by John Belton. New York: Columbia University Press, 2008.

Chateau, Dominique. *Le cinéma comme language.* Paris: Editions l'association internationale pour la sémiologie du spectacle/publication de la Sorbonne ACEV, 1986.

Chekhov, Anton. *Sobranye Sochinenii.* [Collected Works] Vol. 10. Moscow, 1963.

Christie, Ian, and John Gillett eds. *FEKS, Formalism, Futurism: 'Eccentrism' in Soviet Cinema 1918-1935.* London: British Film Institute, 1978.

Christie, Ian, and Richard Taylor. *Eisenstein Rediscovered.* London: Routledge and Kegan Paul, 1993.

Collet, Jean. *Jean-Luc Godard: Cinema d'aujourd'hui 18.* Paris: Editions Seghers, 1963.

Crawford, Lawrence. "Viktor Shklovskij: Differance in defamiliarization." *Comparative Literature* 36, 3 (summer 1984): 209-219.

Curtis, James M. "Bergson and Russian Formalism." *Comparative Literature* 28, 2 (1976): 109-121.

Danto, Arthur. *The Transfiguration of the Commonplace: A Philosophy of Art.* Cambridge, Mass.: Harvard University Press, 1981.

Dawkins, Richard. *The Selfish Gene.* Oxford: Oxford University Press, 1976.

Deleuze, Gilles, and Félix Guattari. *What is Philosophy?* [1991] Translated by Janis Tomlinson, and Graham Burchell III. New York: Columbia University Press, 1996.

Deleuze, Gilles. *Difference and Repetition.* [1968] Translated by Paul Patton. London: Athlone Press, 1994.

—. *Kant's Critical Philosophy.* [1963] Translated by Hugh Tomlinson, and Barbara Habberjam. London: Althone Press, 1983.

Depretto, Catherine. "Roman Jakobson et la relance de l'opojaz (1928-1930)." *Littérature* 107 (October 1997).

Derrida, Jacques. "Différance." In *Margins of Philosophy.* Translated by Alan Bass. Chicago: University of Chicago Press, 1982.

Dewey, John. *Late Works of John Dewey.* [1934] Carbondale: Southern Illinois University Press, 1987.

Dilworth, John. "Dual Recognition of Depth and Dependent Seeing." Available from http://www.interdisciplines.org/ artcognition/papers/8; INTERNET.

Dissanayake, Ellen. *What Is Art For?* Seattle: University of Washington Press, 1988.

Eagle, Herbert, ed. "Russian Formalist Film Theory: An Introduction." In *Formalist Film Theory.* Michigan: University of Michigan, 1981.

Eco, Umberto. *L'Œuvre Ouverte.* [Opera aperta, 1962] Translated by C. Roux de Bézieux. Paris: Seuil, 1965.

Eddershaw, Margaret. *Performing Brecht: Forty Years of British Performances.* London: Routledge, 1996.

Eichenbaum, Boris. "The Theory of the 'Formal Method.'" In *Russian Formalist Criticism,* edited by Lee T. Lemon, and Marion J. Reis. Lincoln: University of Nebraska Press, 1965.

—. "Problems of Film Stylistics." *Screen* 15, 3 (autumn 1973).

—. "Problems of Cinema Stylistics." In *Formalist Film Theory,* edited by H. Eagle. Michigan: University of Michigan, 1981. [First published in *Poetika Kino.* Moscow & Leningrad: Kinopečat, 1927.]

—. "Problems of Film Stylistics." In *Russian Poetics in Translation,* ed. Richard Taylor. Oxford: RPT Publications, 1982.

Eisenstein, Sergej M. "Montage: The Construction Principle in Art." [1923] In *The Eisenstein Reader,* ed. Richard Taylor. London: BFI, 1998.

—. "The Montage of Attractions." In *The Eisenstein Reader,* ed. Richard Taylor. London: British Film Museum, 1998.

—. "The Montage of Film Attractions." In *The Eisenstein Reader,* ed. Richard Taylor. London: British Film Museum, 1998.

—. "A Lecture in Biomechanics 28 March 1935." In V.A. Shcherbakov, *Meyerkhol'dovskii sbornik* [The Meyerhold Collection] 2d ed.: *Meyerhold i drugie* [Meyerhold and Others]. Edited by O.M. Feldman. Moscow, 2000.

Elkin, James. *Why Are Our Pictures Puzzles? On the Modern Origin of Pictorial Complexity.* New York & London: Routledge, 1999.

Elsaesser, Thomas, and Emile Poppe. "Film." In *The Encyclopedia of Language and Linguistics.* Vol. 3. Edited by Rich Asher. Oxford: Pergamon Press, 1994.

Elsaesser, Thomas. "Early Film History and Multi-Media. An Archeology of Possible Futures?" In *New Media, Old Media*, eds. Hui Kyong Chun, and Thomas W. Keenan. New York & London: Routledge, 2005.

Epstein, Jean. "Grossissement." In *Bonjour Paris*. Paris: Editions de la Sirene, 1921.

—. "Magnification and Other Writings." *October*, no. 3 (1977): 21-24.

Epstein, William. "Perceiving, Reasoning, and Imagining." *The American Journal of Psychology* 118, no. 2 (summer 2005).

Erlich, Victor. "Russian Formalism." *Journal of the History of Ideas* 34, 4 (October – December 1973).

—. "Russian Formalism." In *The Avant-Garde Tradition in Literature*, ed. Richard Kostelanetz. Buffalo: Prometheus Books, 1982.

Esslin, Martin. *Brecht: The Man and His Work*. New York: Doubleday, 1961.

Eysenck, Michael W., and Mark Keane. *Cognitive Psychology. A Student's Handbook*. 5$^{th}$ ed. Hove: Psychology Press Ltd., 2005.

Faye, Jean-Pierre. "Formalisme ou sens." *Critique* 215 (April 1965).

Flusser, Vilém. *Für eine Philosophie der Fotografie*. Göttingen: European Photography, 1983.

—. *Towards a Philosophy of Photography*. Translated by Martin Chalmers. London: Reakton Books, 2000.

Freeman, Walter J. "Consciousness, Intentionality and Causality." In *Does Consciousness Cause Behavior?* eds. Susan Pockett, William P. Banks, and Shaun Gallagher, 73-105. Cambridge, MA.: MIT, 2006.

Freud, Sigmund. "The Uncanny." In *The Standard Edition of the Complete Psychological Works of Sigmund Freud*. Vol. XIV. Edited by James Strachey. London, 1953-74.

—. "The Interpretation of Dreams." [1900] In *The Standard Edition of the Complete Psychological Works*. Translated by James Strachey. London: Hogarth Press and The Institute of Psycho-Analysis, 1986.

—. "Letter to Romain Rolland (A Disturbance of Memory on the Acropolis)." In *The Penguin Freud Reader*, ed. Adam Phillips, 68-76. London: Penguin Books Ltd, 2006.

Gamboni, D. *Potential Images. Ambiguity and Indeterminacy in Modern Art*. London: Reaktion Books, 2002.

Gardner, Howard. *The Mind's New Science: A History of the Cognitive Revolution*. New York: Basic Books, 1985.

Gaudreault, André. *Du littéraire au filmique. Système du récit*. Paris: Méridiens Klincksieck, 1988.

—. "Early Cinema as a Challenge to Film History." In *The Cinema of Attractions Reloaded*, edited by Wanda Strauven, 365-380. Amsterdam: Amsterdam University Press, 2006.

—. "From 'Primitive Cinema' to 'Kine-Attractography.'" In *The Cinema of Attractions Reloaded*, edited by Wanda Strauven, 85-104. Amsterdam: Amsterdam University Press, 2006.

—. *Cinéma et attraction. Pour une nouvelle histoire du cinématographe*. Paris: CNRS Editions, 2008.

Genette, Gérard. *Figures I*. Paris: Seuil, 1966.

Gibson, J.J. *The Ecological Approach to Visual Perception*. Mahwah, NJ.: Lawrence Erlbaum Associates, Inc., 1986.

Gombrich, Ernst. *Art and Illusion: A Study in the Psychology of Pictorial Representation*. Princeton: Princeton University Press, 1961.

—. *The Sense of Order*. Ithaca: Cornell University Press, 1979.

Gould, Stephen et al. "Peripheral-Foveal Vision for Real-time Object Recognition and Tracking in Video." *20th International Joint Conference on Artificial Intelligence*. Available from http://ai.stanford.edu/~sgould/vision; INTERNET.

Gramsci, Antonio. *Selections from the Prison Notebooks*. Translated by Quintin Hoare and Geoffrey Nowell-Smith. London: Lawrence and Wishart, 1971.

Greimas, A.J., and J. Courtés. *Sémiotique: dictionnaire raisonné de la théorie du langage*. Vol. 2. Paris: Hachette, 1986.

Grodal, Torben. *Embodied Visions*. Copenhagen, Department of Film and Media: University of Copenhagen, 2006.

—. *Embodied Visions*. New York: Oxford University Press, 2008.

Gunning, Tom. "The Cinema of Attractions. Early Film, Its Spectator and the Avant-Garde." In *Early Cinema. Space, Frame, Narrative*, edited by Thomas Elsaesser. London: BFI, 1990.

—. "Heard over the Phone. THE LONELY VILLA and the Lorde Tradition of the Terrors of Technology." *Screen* 32, 2 (1991): 184-196.

—. "An Aesthetic of Astonishment: Early Film and the (In)credulous Spectator." In *Viewing Positions. Ways of Seeing Film*, edited by Linda Williams. New Brunswick, New Jersey: Rutgers University Press, 1994.

—. "Foreword." In *Early Cinema in Russia and its Cultural Reception*. Yuri Tsivian. Translated by A. Bodger. Edited by R. Taylor. London & New York: Routledge, 1994.

—. "The Whole Town's Gawking. Early Cinema and the Visual Experience of Modernity." *Yale Journal of Criticism* 7, 2 (1994): 189-201.

—. "Re-Newing Old Technologies: Astonishment, Second Nature, and the Uncanny in Technology from the Previous Turn-of-the-Century." In *Rethinking Media Change: The Aesthetics of Transition*, edited by David Thorburn, and Henry Jenkins, 39-60. Cambridge, Mass.: MIT Press, 2003.

—. *Chaplin and the Body of Modernity*. Presented at the BFI Charles Chaplin Conference July 2005. Available from http://chaplin.bfi.org.uk/programme/ conference/pdf/tom-gunning.pdf; INTERNET.

Hagener, Malte. *Moving Forward, Looking Back. The European Avant-Garde and the Invention of Film Culture 1919-1939*. Amsterdam: Amsterdam University Press, 2007.

Hanna, Robert, and Michelle Maiese, *Embodied Minds in Action*. Oxford & New York: Oxford University Press, 2009.

Harpham, Geoffrey Galt. *On the Grotesque. Strategies of Contradiction in Art and Literature*. Aurora: The Davies Group, Publishers, 2006.

Harris, Sam et al. "Functional Neuroimaging of Belief, Disbelief and Uncertainty." *Annals of Neurology* 62, no. 12 (December 2007).

Hartmann, Britta, and Hans-Jürgen Wulff. "Vom spezifischen des Films. Neo- formalismus – Kognitivismus – Historische Poetik." *Montage/AV* 4, 1 (1995): 5-22.

Harvey, Sylvia. *May '68 and Film Culture*. London: British Film Institute, 1980.

Hasson, Uri, et al. "Intersubject Synchronization of Cortical Activity During Natural Vision." *Science* 303 (March 2004): 1617-1618.

Heath, Stephen. "From Brecht to Film: Theses, Problems." *Screen* 16, no. 4 (1975-76): 34.

—. "Cinema and Psychoanalysis." In *Endless Night. Cinema and Psychoanalysis. Parallel Histories*, ed. Janet Bergstrom. University of California Press, 1999.

Hecht, Heiko. "Film as Dynamic Event Perception: Technological Development Forces Realism to Retreat." *Image: Journal of Interdisciplinary Image Science* 3 (January 2006).

Hegel, Friedrich. *Aesthetics: Lectures on Fine Art*. Vol. 1. Translated by T.M. Knox. Oxford: Clarendon Press, 1973.

Heusden, Barend van. *Why Literature? An Inquiry into the Nature of Literary Semiosis*. Tübingen: Stauffenburg Verlag, 1997.

—. "A Bandwidth Model of Semiotic Evolution." In *Semiotic Evolution and the Dynamics of Culture*, edited by M. Bax, B. van Heusden, and W. Wildgen, 1-28. Bern: Peter Land, 2004.

—. "Dealing with Difference: From Cognition to Semiotic Cognition." In *Cognitive Semiotics* 4 (2009): 117-133.

—. "Semiotic Cognition and the Logic of Culture." In *Pragmatics and Cognition* 17 (2009), 611-627.

Hobsbawm, Eric. *The Age of Extremes: The Short Twentieth Century, 1914-1991*. London: Weidenfelf and Nicholson, 1994.

Hochberg, Julian. "Representation of Motion and Space in Video and Cinematic Displays." In *Handbook of Perception and Human Performance*, edited by K.R. Boff, L. Kaufman, and J.P. Thomas. Vol. 1. 1-64. New York: John Wiley and Sons, 1986.

Hokky, Situngkir. "Conjectures to the Memes of Indonesian Songs." Bandung Fe Institute, Technical Department Papers 2008. Available from http://cogprints.org/6099/; INTERNET.

Irwin, Robert. "Reshaping the Shape of Things, Part 2." *Arts* 47, no. 32 (September-October 1972): 2-48.

Jacob, Pierre, and Marc Jeannerod. "The Motor Theory of Social Cognition. A Critique." *Trends in Cognitive Sciences* 9, 1 (January 2005): 21-25.

Jenkins, Henry. *Textual Poachers: Television Fans & Participatory Culture. Studies in Culture and Communication*. New York: Routledge 1992.

Jentsch, Ernst. "On the Psychology of the Uncanny." [1906] *Angelaki* 2, no. 1 (1995): 7-16.

Johnston, Claire, and Paul Willemen. *Screen* 16, no.4 (1975-76).

Jullier, Laurent. *Abécédaire des parapluies de Cherbourg*. Paris: L'Amandier, 2007.

—. "To Cut or Let Live. The Soundtrack According to Jean-Luc Godard." In *Sound and Music in Film and Visual Media: A Critical Overview*, edited by Graeme Harper. 352-362. New York: Continuum, 2009.

—. "L'esprit, et peut-être même le cerveau. La question psychologique dans la *revue internationale de filmologie*, 1947-1962." *CinémaS* 19, no. 2 (spring 2009): 143-168 [in press].

Jullier, Laurent, and Michel Marie. *Lire les images de cinéma*. Paris: Larousse, 2007.

Kaitz, Marsha, et al. "Mother's Recognition of their Newborns by Olfactory Cues." *Developmental Psychobiology* 20 (1987): 587-591.

Kandinsky, Vasily. "Kuda idet 'novoye iskusstvo'?" [Where is the 'new art' heading?] In *Izbranye trudy po teorii iskusstva*. [Selected Writings on the Theory of Art] Vol 1. Moscow: 2001.

—. "Stupeni. Tekst khudozhnika." [Steps. An Artist's Text] In *Selected Writings on the Theory of Art*. Vol. 1 Moscow: 2001.

Kant, Immanuel. *Critique of Practical Reason. (Cambridge Texts in the History of Philosophy)*. Cambridge: Cambridge University Press, 1997.

Kayser, Wolfgang. *Das Groteske. Seine Gestaltung in Malerei und Dichtung.* Tübingen: Stauffenburg Verlag Brigitte Narr GmbH, 2004.

Kessler, Frank. "L'insistance de la lettre." *Vertigo* 2 (1988): 17-23.

—. "Bei Anruf Rettung!" *Telefon und Kultur 4. Das Telefon im Spielfilm.* Edited by Forschungsgruppe Telekommunikation. Berlin: Spiess (1991): 167-173.

—. "Ostranenie." In *New German Critique. An Interdisciplinary Journal of German Study* 68, edited by David B. Bathrick et al. (spring-summer 1996).

—. "Ostranenie. Zum Verfremdungsbegriff von Formalismus und Neoformalismus." *Montage/AV* 5, 2 (1996): 51-65.

—. "Brieven uit de verte. Een analyse van de film EEN TELEGRAM UIT MEXICO." *Jaarboek Mediageschiedenis* 8, 201-213. Amsterdam: Stichting Mediageschiedens/Stichting beheer IISG, 1997.

—. "The Cinema of Attractions as Dispositif." In *The Cinema of Attractions Reloaded*, ed. Wanda Strauven. Amsterdam: Amsterdam University Press, 2006.

Koch, Walter. *Evolutionary Cultural Semiotics.* Bochum: Brockmeyer, 1986.

Kovács, András Bálint. *Metropolis, Párizs.* Budapest: Képzõmõészeti Kiadó, 1992.

—. "The Sokal-Briqmond Affair." 2000 (Februari 1998): 53-61.

—. *A film szerint a világ.* Budapest: Palatinus, 2002.

—. "Things that Come After Another." *New Review of Film and Television Studies* Vol. 5, 2 (August 2007): 157-173.

—. "Openness of the Work of Art: Deleuze and Eco." In *Afterimages of Gilles Deleuze's Film Philosophy*, edited by David Rodowick. Minneapolis: University of Minnesota Press, 2009.

—. "Sartre, the Philosophy of Nothingness and the Modern Melodrama." *The American Journal of Aesthetics and Art Criticism* Vol. 64, 1 (2009).

—. "Tarkovsky." In *The Routledge Companion to Philosophy and Film*, edited by Paisley Livingstone and Carl Plantinga. London & New York: Routledge, 2009.

Kuntzel, Thierry. "The film-work, 2." *Camera Obscura* 5 (1980): 6-69.

Lagny, Michèle, Marie-Claire Ropars, and Pierre Sorlin. *Générique des années 30.* Paris: Presses Universitaires de Vincennes, 1986.

Lemon, Lee T., and Marion J. Reis. *Russian Formalist Criticism. Four Essays.* Lincoln: University of Nebraska Press, 1965.

Lévi-Strauss, Claude, and Roman Jakobson. "'Les chats' de Baudelaire." *L'homme: Revue Française d'Anthropologie* 2 (1962): 5-21.

Levitan, Isaak. "Pis'ma. Dokumenty.Vospominaniya." [Letters, Documents, Reminiscences] Moscow, 1956.

Lyotard, Jean-François. *Leçons sur l'analytique du sublime.* Paris: Galilée, 1991.

MacCabe, Colin. "Realism in the Cinema: Notes on Some Brechtian Theses. *Screen* 15. 2 (1974): 26.

Marcus, Laura. *The Tenth Muse: Writing about Cinema in the Modernist Period.* Oxford: Oxford UP, 2007.

Marinetti, Filippo Tommaso. "The Variety Theater 1913." In *Futurist Manifestos*, ed. Umbro Apollonio. New York: Viking Press, 1973.

Markov, Vladimir. "Russian Futurism and Its Theoreticians." In *The Avant-Garde Tradition in Literature*, edited by Richard Kostelanetz. Buffalo: Prometheus Books, 1982.

Marr, David. *Vision: A Computational Investigation into the Human Representation and Processing of Visual Information*. New York: Freeman, 1982.

Marx, Karl. *Essential Writings of Karl Marx*. Edited by David Caute. London: Panther, 1967.

Matonti, Fréderique. "L'anneau de Mœbius. La réception en France des formalistes russes." *Actes de la recherche en sciences sociales, Engagements intellectuels. Sociologie publique*, 176-177, eds. Frédérique Matonti, and Gisèle Sapiro (March 2009): 52-68.

Mauss, Marcel. "Les techniques du corps." *Journal de Psychologie XXXII*, no. 3-4 (March-April 1936).

McLuhan, Marshall. *Understanding Media. The Extensions of Man*. London & New York: Routledge, 2008.

Metz, Christian. *Langage et cinéma*. Paris: Larousse, 1970.

—. "Une étape dans la réflexion sur le cinéma." In *Essais sur la signification au cinéma*. Vol. 2. Paris: Klincksieck, 1972.

—. *Film Language: A Semiotics of the Cinema*. Translated by Michael Taylor. New York: Oxford University Press, 1974.

—. *Language and Cinema*. Translated by Donna Jean Umiker-Sebeok. The Hague: Mouton, 1974.

—. "Problems of Denotation in the Fiction Film." In *Film Language: A Semiotics of the Cinema*. Translated by Michael Taylor. New York: Oxford University Press, 1974.

—. *Le Signifiant Imaginaire*. Paris: Union Generale D'Editions, 1977.

—. "Sur mon travail." In *Essais Sémiotiques*. Paris: Klincksieck, 1977.

Michelson, Annette. "The Man with the Movie Camera: From Magician to Epistemologist." *Artforum* 10, no. 7 (March 1972): 60-72.

Mitchell, Stanley. "From Shklovsky to Brecht: Some Preliminary Remarks Towards a History of the Politicisation of Russian Formalism." *Screen* 15, no. 2 (summer 1974): 74-81.

Molidor, Christian, and Mike Harter. "Sontag On Photography. Two Views." *Center for Media Literacy* (spring 1980). Available from http://www.medialit.org/reading_room/article355.html#bio; INTERNET.

Mulvey, Laura. "Visual Pleasure and Narrative Cinema." *Screen* (autumn 1975): 6-18. Available from http://screen.oxfordjournals.org; INTERNET.

—. *Fetishism and Curiosity*. London: BFI, 1996.

—. *Death 24x a Second. Stillness and the Moving Image*. London: Reaktion Books Ltd., 2006.

—. "A Sudden Gust of Wind (after Hokusai): from After to Before the Photograph." *Oxford Art Journal* 30, no. 1. London: Oxford University Press, (2007): 27-37.

Münsterberg, Hugo. *The Film: The Psychological Study*. [1916] New York: Dover Publications, 1970.

—. *The Photoplay: A Psychological Study and Other Writings*. [1916] London & New York: Routledge, 2002.

Musser, Charles. *The Emergence of Cinema: The American Screen to 1900*. New York: Scribner, 1990.

Nabokov, Vladimir. *Invitation to a Beheading*. Great Britain: Weidenfeld and Nicolson, 1963.

—. *Speak, Memory*. New York: Penguin Books, 1982.

—. *Het origineel van Laura, Hfst. Twee*. Translated by Rien Verhoef. Amsterdam: De Bezige Bij, 2009.

Naiman, Eric. "Shklovsky's Dog and Mulvey's Pleasure: The Secret Life of Defamiliariza-tion." *Comparative Literature* 50, no. 4 (autumn 1998): 333-352.

Narboni, Jean. "Introduction." In *Les Formalistes russes et le cinéma. Poétique du film*. Francois Albera. Paris: Nathan, 1996.

Neisser, Ulrich. *The Perceived Self: Ecological and Interpersonal Sources of Self Knowledge*. New York: Cambridge University Press, 1993.

Noë, Alva. "Art as Enaction." *Art and Cognition Virtual Conference*. Available from http://www.interdisciplines.org/ artcog/papers/8; INTERNET.

—. *Out of Our Heads. Why You Are Not Your Brain, and Other Lessons from the Biology of Conscious-ness*. New York: Hill and Wang, 2009.

Norman, Joel. "Two Visual Systems and Two Theories of Perception: An Attempt to Recon-cile the Constructivist and Ecological Approaches." *Behavioral and Brain Sciences* 24 (2001): 6.

Odin, Roger. "Christian Metz et la linguistique." In *Christian Metz et la théorie du cinéma* [nu-méro spécial]. Edited by M. Marie and M. Vernet. *Iris* 10 (April 1990). Paris: Klincksieck, 1990.

Oever, Annie van den. "Een klap in het gezicht van de goede smaak. Symbolisme, avant-garde, formalisme en het probleem van de artistieke vorm." In *Avantgarde! Voorhoede?* edited by Hubert van den Berg, and Gillis Dorleijn, 191-204. Nijmegen: Uitgeverij Van-tilt, 2002.

—. *Fritzi en het groteske*. Amsterdam: De Bezige Bij, 2003.

—. *Life Itself. Louis Paul Boon as Innovator of the Novel*. Translated by Annette Visser. Elmwood Park, IL.: Dalkey Archive Press, 2008.

—. "Monstration and the Monstrous. The Grotesque in the Very Beginning and at the Very End." In *Proceedings of the XVI International Film Studies Conference-Permanent Seminar on His-tory of Film Theories. In the Very Beginning, at the Very End. Film Theories in Perspective*. eds F. Casetti, and J. Gaines, and V. Re. Udine: Forum, 2010.

O'Regan, J.K., R.A. Rensink, and J.J. Clark. "Change-Blindness as a Result of 'Mud-splashes.'" *Nature* 398 (1999).

Palmer, Stephen E. *Vision Science: Photons to Phenomenology*. Cambridge: MIT Press, 1999.

Pasolini, Pier Paulo. "Cinema di Poesia," [De poëtische film, 1965] In *De Revisor* 1, 9 &10 (December 1974): 70-77.

Patterson, James. "Is a Cognitive Approach to the Avant-Garde Cinema Perverse?" In *Post-Theory: Reconstructing Film Studies*, eds. David Bordwell, and Noël Carroll, 108-129. Madi-son: University of Wisconsin Press, 1996.

Pleynet, Marcellin. "The 'Left' Front of the Arts: Eisenstein and the 'Young Hegelians.'" [*Cinéthique* 5 (fall 1969)] Translated by Susan Bennett. *Screen* 13, no. 1 (spring 1972): 101-119.

Polanyi, Michel. "What Is a Painting?" *British Journal of Aesthetics* 10 (1970): 225-236.

Pozner, Vladimir. "Victor Chklovsky parle à Vladimir Pozner." *Les Lettres Françaises* 1206 (Oc-tober 1967).

Proust, Marcel. À *la recherche du temps perdu*. Vol. 2. 1913-1927.

Pylyshyn, Zenon. *Seeing and Visualizing: It's Not What You Think*. Cambridge, MA.: MIT Press, 2003.

Ramachandran, Vilayanur S., and William Hirstein. "The Science of Art." *Journal of Consciousness Studies* 6.6-7 (1999): 15-41.

Raynauld, Isabelle. "Le Cinématographe comme nouvelle technologie: Opacité et transparence." *Cinémas* 14, 1 (2003): 117-128.

Reich, Bernhard. *Im Wettlauf mit der Zeit*. Berlin: Henschelverlag, 1970.

Robel, Leon. "Un Trio Prodigieux." In *Europe, Les Formalistes Russes* 911, ed. Charles Dobzynski (March 2005).

Robinson, Douglas. *Estrangement and the Somatics of Literature. Tolstoy, Shklovsky, Brecht*. Baltimore: The Johns Hopkins University Press, 2008.

Rock, Irvin. *Indirect Perception*. Cambridge, MA.: MIT Press, 1997.

Rodchenko, Aleksandr. "Puti sovremennoy fotografii." [The Paths of Contemporary Photography] *Novyi LEF* 9 [The New LEF] (1928).

Rodowick, D.N. "An Elegy for Theory." *October* 122 (autumn 2007): 91-109.

Routt, William. "Demolishing a Wall." *Senses of Cinema*. Available from http://archive.sensesofcinema.com/contents/01/14/demolishing_a_wall.html; INTERNET.

Sacks, Oliver et al. "A Neurology of Belief." *Annals of Neurology* 63, no. 2 (February 2008).

Salt, Barry. *Film Style & Technology: History & Analysis*. London: Starword, 1983.

—. "Cinemetrics on PIERROT LE FOU" (29-03-2007). [cited 6 August 2009]. Available from //www.cinemetrics.lv/movie.php?movie_ID=617; INTERNET.

Salthouse, Timothy A., and Cecil L. Ellis. "Determinants of Eye-Fixation Duration." *The American Journal of Psychology* 93, no. 2 (June 1980): 207-234.

Schaal, Benoist. "Presumed Olfactory Exchanges between Mother and Neonate in Humans." In *Ethology and Psychology*, eds. J. LeCamus, and J. Cosnier, 101-110. Toulouse: Privat-IEC, 1986.

Scheunemann, Dietrich, ed. *European Avant-Garde: New Perspectives*. Amsterdam, Atlanta: Rodopi, 2000.

Schwartz, Robert. "Vision and Cognition in Picture Perception." *Philosophy and Phenomenological Research* 62, no. 3 (May 2001): 707-719.

Searle, John R. "Rationality and Realism, What is at Stake?" *Daedalus* (autumn 1993): 55-83.

Seddon, Mark D. *Investigating the Effect on Attention of Action Continuity*. M.Sc. thesis in Cognitive Science and Natural Language: University of Edinburgh, 2003.

Sheldon, Richard. "Introduction." In *A Sentimental Journey*. New York: Cornell University Press, 1970.

Sher, Benjamin. *Translator's Introduction to Theory of Prose* [Shklovsky]. Elmwood Park, IL.: Dalkey Archive Press, 1990.

—. "Nature vs. Art. A Note on Translating Shklovsky." *Poetics Today* 26, 4 (winter 2005): 640. Available from http://www.google.com/search?q=cache: JN4XARAb-74J:www.websher.net/srl/tran.html+Shklovsky's+Art+as+ Device+ostranenie; INTERNET.

Shklovsky, Viktor. *Voskresheniye slova*. [The Resurrection of the Word] Petersburg, 1914.

—. *Sentimental`noe putesestvie*. [Sentimental Journey] Moskow: Helikon, 1923.

—. "Electricity and the Theme of Old Newspapers." In *Podenshchina* Leningrad: Pisatelej, 1930.

—. "Art as Technique." In *Russian Formalist Criticism. Four Essays*. [1917] Translated by Lee T. Lemon, and Marion J. Reis, 3-57. Lincoln & London: University of Nebraska Press, 1965.

—. *A Sentimental Journey*. New York: Cornell University Press, 1970.

—. "The Resurrection of the Word." [1914] In *Russian Formalism. A Collection of Articles and Texts in Translation*, edited by Stephen Bann, and John E. Bowlt, 41-47. Edinburgh: Scottish Academic Press, 1973.

—. *Mayakovsky and his Circle*. Translated and edited by Lily Feiler. London: Pluto Press Limited, 1974.

—. *Ejzenštejn*. [1973] Translated by Manfred Dahlke. Reinbek: Rowohlt Taschenbuch Verlag GmbH, 1977.

—. *O teorii prozy* [Theory of Prose]. Moscow: Krug, 1983.

—. "On Poetry and Trans-Sense Language." [1916] Translated by Gerald Janacek and Peter Mayer. *October* 34 (autumn 1985).

—. *Theory of Prose*. Elmwood Park, IL.: Dalkey Archive Press, 1990.

—. *Zoo, or Letters Not about Love*. Translated by Richard Sheldon. London: Dalkey Archive Press, 2001.

—. *Knight's Move*. Translated by Richard Sheldon. [1923] Springfield IL.: Dalkey Archive, 2005.

—. *Literature and Cinematography*. [1923] Translated by Irina Masinovsky. Introduction by Richard Sheldon. Champaign & London: Dalkey Archive Press, 2008.

Shusterman, Richard. *Pragmatist Aesthetics. Living Beauty, Rethinking Art*. Oxford & Cambridge: Blackwell, 1992.

Shweder, Richard A., and Jonathan Haidt. "The Cultural Psychology of the Emotions." In *Handbook of Emotions*, eds. M. Lewis, and J. Haviland, 397-414. New York: Guilford Press, 2000.

Sitney, P. Adams. "Structural Film." In *Film Culture* [1969]; reprinted in *Film Culture Reader*. New York: Anthology Film Archives, 1970.

Smets, G.J.F. "Perceptual Meaning." *Design Issues* 5, no. 2. (MIT Press, spring 1989): 86-99.

Smith, James. "Brecht, the Berliner Ensemble, and the British Government." *New Theatre Quarterly* 22, no. 4 (2006): 307-323.

Sobchack, Vivian. *The Address of the Eye: A Phenomenology of Film Experience*. Princeton: Princeton University Press, 1992.

—. "The Scene of the Screen: Envisioning Cinematic and Electronic 'Presence.'" In *Materialities of Communication*, eds. Hans Ulrich Gumbrecht, and K. Ludwig Pfeffer, 83-106. Stanford: Stanford University Press, 1994.

—. "What My Fingers Knew: The Cineasthetic Subject, or Vision in the Flesh." In *Carnal Thoughts: Embodiments and Moving Image Culture*, 53-84. Berkeley: University of California Press, 2004.

—. "'Cutting to the Quick': *Techne*, *Physis*, and *Poiesis* and the Attractions of Slow Motion." In *Cinema of Attractions Reloaded*, edited by Wanda Strauven, 337-351. Amsterdam: Amsterdam University Press, 2006.

Sontag, Susan. *On Photography*. New York: Anchor Books, 1973.

Spencer, Herbert. *Philosophy of Style*. [1852] Whitefish, MT.: Kessinger Publishing, 2004.

Sperber, Dan. "Why Rethink Interdisciplinarity?" Available from http://www.interdisciplines.org/interdisciplinarity/ papers/1/; INTERNET.

Sperber, Dan, and Deirdre Wilson. *Relevance: Communication and Cognition*. Oxford: Basil Blackwell, 1986.

Staiger, Janet. *Perverse Spectators: The Practices of Film Reception*. New York: New York University Press, 2000.

Steiner, Peter. "Three Metaphors of Russian Formalism." *Poetics Today* 2, 1b (1981/82): 59-116.

Sternberg, Meir. "Telling in Time (III): Chronology, Estrangement, and Stories of Literary History." *Poetics Today* 27, 1 (2006): 125-135.

Stoffregen, Thomas. "On the Nature and Perception of Depictions." Available from http://www.interdisciplines.org/ artcognition/papers/14; INTERNET.

Strauven, Wanda, ed. *The Cinema of Attractions Reloaded*. Amsterdam: Amsterdam University Press, 2006.

Striedter, J. *Russischer Formalismus*. München: Wilhelm Fink Verlag, 1969.

Summers, David. *Michelangelo and the Language of Art*. Princeton, N.J.: Princeton University Press, 1981.

—. "The Archeology of the Modern Grotesque." In *Modern Art and the Grotesque*, edited by F.S. Connelly. Cambridge: Cambridge University Press, 2003.

Symons, James M. *Meyerhold's Theatre of the Grotesque*. Cambridge: Rivers Press Limited, 1973.

Szaloky, Melinda. "Making New Sense of Film Theory Through Kant. A Novel Teaching Approach." *New Review of Film and Television Studies* 3, no. 1 (May 2005): 33-58.

Tarnay, László. "On the Metaphysics of Screen Violence and Beyond." In *Apertura* 3, 4 (2008). Available from htttp://www.apertura.hu/2008/nyar/tarnay; INTERNET.

Tarnay, László, and Tamás Pólya. *Specificity Recognition and Social Cognition*. Frankfurt a/M & New York & Oxford: Peter Lang, 2004.

—. "Reprezentáció és specificitás." *Passim* 7 (2005): 67-100.

Tatar, Maria M. "The Houses of Fiction. Toward a Definition of the Uncanny." *Comparative Literature* 33, 2 (spring 1981): 167-182.

Taylor, Charles. *Sources of the Self: The Making of the Modern Identity*. Cambridge, MA.: Harvard University Press, 1989.

Taylor, Richard, ed. *The Poetics of Cinema*. [Translation of *Poetika Kino*, 1927] Oxford: Russian Poetics in Translation, 1982.

Thines, Georges, Alan Costall, and George Butterworth, eds. *Michotte's Experimental Phenomenology of Perception*. Hillsdale, NJ.: Erlbaum, 1991.

Thompson, Kristin. *Eisenstein's Ivan the Terrible: A Neoformalist Analysis*. Princeton: Princeton University Press, 1981.

—. *Breaking the Glass Armor: Neoformalist Film Analysis*. Princeton: Princeton University Press, 1988.

Thomson, Philip. *The Grotesque*. Methuen Critical Idiom Series, 1972. Available from http://davidlavery.net/grotesque/Major_Artists_Theorists/; INTERNET.

Thomson-Jones, Katherine. "Inseparable Insight: Reconciling Cognitivism and Formalism in Aesthetics." *The Journal of Aesthetics and Art Criticism* 63, no. 4 (autumn 2005): 375-384.

Thorburn, David, and Henry Jenkins. *Rethinking Media Change. The Aesthetics of Transition*. Cambridge MA. & London: The MIT Press, 2003.

Todd, Jane Marie. "The Veiled Woman in Freud's 'Das Unheimliche.'" *Signs* Vol. 11, 3 (spring 1986): 519-528.

Todorov, Tzvetan. *Théorie de la littérature*. Paris: Seuil, 1965.

Tolstoy, Aleksey Nikolaevich. "Vozmozhnosti kino." [The Potential of the Cinema] *Kinonedelya* [Cinema Weekly] no. 1, 2, 3, 8 (1924).

Tomachevski, Boris. "La nouvelle école d'histoire littéraire en Russie." *Revue des Etudes Slaves* (1928): 238-239.

Tooby, John, and Leda Cosmides. "The Psychological Foundations of Culture." In *The Adapted Mind: Evolutionary Psychology and the Generation of Culture*, eds. Barkow, Cosmides, and Tooby, 19-136. Oxford & New York: Oxford University Press, 1992.

Tsivian, Yuri. "Cutting and Framing in Bauer's and Kuleshov's Films." *KINtop. Jahrbuch zur Erforschung des Frühen Films* 1 (1992): 103-113.

—. *Early Cinema in Russia and its Cultural Reception*. Translated by A. Bodger. Edited by R. Taylor. London & New York: Routledge, 1994.

—. "Turning Objects, Toppled Pictures: Give and Take Between Vertov's Films and Constructivist Art." *October* 121 (summer 2007): 92-110.

Tully, James H., and Daniel M. Weinstock., eds. "The Strange Estrangement: Taylor and the Natural Sciences." In *Philosophy in an Age of Pluralism: The Philosophy of Charles Taylor in Question*, 83-95. Cambridge: Cambridge University Press, 1994.

Tynjanov, Jurij. "On Literary Evolution." In *Readings in Russian Poetics: Formalist and Structuralist View*, edited by Ladislav Mateijka, and Krystyna Pomorska, 66-78. Cambridge, Mass.: The MIT Press, 1971.

Valkola, Jarmo. *Cognition and Visuality*. Jyväskylä: University of Jyväskylä, 2004.

Varela, Francisco, Evan Thompson, and Eleanor Rosch. *L'inscription corporelle de l'esprit: sciences cognitives et expérience humaine*. Paris: Seuil, 1993.

Veselovsky, Alexander. *Sobranie sochinenii*. St. Petersburg, 1913.

Virillo, Paul. *The Aesthetics of Disappearance*. New York: Semiotext(e), 1991.

Walton, Kendall. "Transparent Pictures. On the Nature of Photographic Realism." *Critical Inquiry* 12 (1984): 246-277.

Wegner, David. *The Illusion of the Conscious Will*. Cambridge, MA.: MIT Press, 2002.

Wellek, René. "Russian Formalism." In *The Avant-Garde Tradition in Literature*. Edited by Richard Kostelanetz. Buffalo: Prometheus Books, 1982.

Willett, John. *The Theatre of Bertolt Brecht*. London: Methuen, 1967.

Williams, Raymond. *Keywords: A Vocabulary of Culture and Society*. London: Fontana, 1976.

Wollen, Peter. *Signs and Meaning in the Cinema*. London: Secker and Warburg, 1970.

—. "Some Thoughts Arising from Stanley Mitchell's article." *Screen* 12, no. 4 (winter 1971-72): 162-167.

Wollheim, Richard. "Seeing-as, Seeing-in and Pictorial Representation." In *Art and its Objects*. Cambridge: Cambridge University Press, 1980.

Woolf, Virginia. "The Cinema." [1926] In *Collected Essays II*. Hogarth Press, 1966.

Wuss, Peter. "Analyzing the Reality Effect in Dogma Films." *The Journal of Moving Image Studies* 1 (2002): Available from http://www.avila.edu/journal/index1.htm; INTERNET.

Zechmeister, Eugene B., and Stanley E. Nyberg. *Human Memory: An Introduction to Research and Theory*. Monterey, CA.: Thomson Brooks / Cole, 1982.

# Notes on Contributors

**Dominique Chateau** is professor at the UFR d'arts plastiques et sciences de l'art at the Panthéon-Sorbonne University (Paris 1). He teaches aesthetics and film studies. He is the author of *La Question de la question de l'art* (1994), *Arts plastiques: archéologie d'une notion* (1999), *Qu'est-ce que l'art?* (2000), *Cinéma et Philosophie* (2003), *Sartre et le cinéma* (2005), *Esthétique du cinéma* (2006), *Introduzione all'estetica del cinema* (2007), *Qu'est-ce qu'un artiste?* (2008), *Philosophie d'un art moderne: le cinéma* (2009), *L'Art comptant pour un* (2009).

**Ian Christie** is professor of film and media history at Birckbeck College, University of London. He has worked at the British Film Institute as head of Distribution, Exhibition, Video Publishing and Special Projects, and is co-founder and Vice President of Europe Cinemas. His current research interests include early cinema and related media, British cinema and television, Russian cinema, from the pre-Soviet Russian cinema to contemporary Russian cinema, and the digital revolution. His books include *The Last Machine: Early Cinema and the Birth of the Modern World* (1994), *Gilliam on Gilliam* (1999), *A Matter of Life and Death* (2000).

**Barend van Heusden** is professor of Culture and Cognition in the Department of Arts, Culture, and Media Studies at the University of Groningen, the Netherlands. His research focuses on the cognitive semiotics of culture and the arts. Since 2008 he has been leading the Dutch national research project 'Culture in the Mirror' (2008-2012), which aims to develop a theoretical framework for an integrated culture education curriculum for children and youngsters from 4 to 18 years old.

**Laurent Jullier** is director of research at the Institut de Recherches sur le Cinéma et l'Audiovisuel (IRCAV) at the University of Sorbonne Nouvelle (Paris III) and professor of film studies at the Institut Européen de Cinéma et d'Audiovisuel (IECA) at the University of Nancy II. He received his PhD. from Sorbonne Nouvelle in 1994. He has written several articles for *Esprit* and for *Encyclopædia Universalis*, as well as a number of books on cinema, among which several were translated in Spanish, Portuguese, Italian, German, Chinese and Korean.

**Frank Kessler** is professor of media history at the University of Utrecht. His main reseach interests lie in the field of early cinema and the history of film theory. He is a co-founder and co-editor of KINtop. *Jahrbuch zur Erforschung des Frühen Films* and the KINtop-*Schriften* series. From 2003 to 2007 he was the president of DOMITOR, an international association to promote research on early cinema. Currently a research fellow at the Internationales Kolleg für Kulturtechnikforschung und Medienphilosophie in Weimar, he works on a project on the concept of *dispositif*. Together with Nanna Verhoeff he edited *Networks of Entertainment. Early Film Distribution 1895-1915* (2007).

**Miklós Kiss** teaches film studies in the Department of Arts, Culture, and Media Studies at the University of Groningen, the Netherlands. He has been an assistant and researcher at Jyväskylän Yliopisto, Finland, where he received his PhD. His research interests include narrative and cognitive film theory, film-induced tourism, and the questions of orientation in the film-diegetic world. He is the author of *Between Narrative and Cognitive Approaches. Film Theory of Non-linearity Applied to Hungarian Movies* (2008), and co-editor of *Narratívák 7* (2008).

**András Bálint Kovács** is professor at the Institute of Art & Communication, ELTE (Budapest), where he holds the Chair of the Department of film studies. He is fellow of the Society for Cognitive Studies of the Moving Image (SCSMI). His research interests include narrative universals, and the psychology of causality and cinematic narrative. Known for his writings on Tarkovsky and Gilles Deleuze, he is also the author of *Metropolis, Paris: On German Expressionism and the French New Wave* (1992), *Film and Narration* (1997), *Trends in Modern Cinema* (2005), and his most recent book *Screening Modernism: European Art Cinema 1950-1980*, (2009).

**Laura Mulvey** is professor of film and media studies at Birkbeck College, University of London. As part of the 1970s generation of British film theorists and filmmakers, she is best known for her seminal article "Visual Pleasure and Narrative Cinema" (*Screen*, 1975) that helped shift the direction of film theory towards feminist film theory. Her current research interests include rethinking technology and aspects of technological change in film and television, and the aesthetics of stillness in the moving image: avant-garde and fiction. Her latest book *Death 24x a Second. Stillness and the Moving Image* (2006), addresses the role new technologies play in the viewing experience and re-evaluates the nature of the filmic medium.

**Annie van den Oever** is the initiator and director of the ICEC research project Mutations and Appropriation in European Film Studies in the Groningen Research School for the Study of the Humanities. She is also director of the MA Program in Film Studies in the Dept. of Arts, Culture, and Media at the University of Groningen, and leads the international Minor Program Film in Culture. She chairs the Board of the Groningen University Film Archive. Having worked in the fields of literature and film, she has published on the grotesque and the avant-gardes in both disciplinary fields. Her current research interests include the study of the perceptual impact of new optical and visual techniques on the viewer, the grotesque as a dominant format in our mediated culture and transformational moments in the history of film. Her publications include Fritzi en het groteske (2003), Life Itself (2008), "Monstration and the Monstrous. The Grotesque in the Very Beginning and at the Very End" (2009).

**Emile Poppe** is currently attached to the Cinémathèque Royale de Belgique. He studied Philosophy and Communication in Brussels and Semiotics with A.J. Greimas and R. Barthes in Paris where he obtained his PhD. He was associated professor of film studies at the University of Nijmegen. As editor in chief of the film journal Versus, he founded the illustrious film archives, Vrienden van het Nijmeegs Filmarchief, a valuable collection consisting of over 2000 films, film equipment, film posters and critical writings on film, now in possession of the University of Groningen. Since 2005 he is associated member of the Groningen Research School for the Study of the Humanities. He has published extensively on issues of film narratology, semiotics, new media, and theater, and is co-founder of the on-line review journal E-View.

**László Tarnay** is currently associate professor at the Centre for the Study of the Moving Image at the University of Pécs, Hungary. He teaches aesthetics, film theory and philosophy. His main research interests are French phenomenology, cognitive studies and argumentation theory. He is the co-author of The Recognition of Specificity and Social Cognition (2004). He has published articles in Apertura. Degrés, Journal of Cinema Studies, and Metropolis. He has also translated two books by the French philosopher, Emmanuel Lévinas, into Hungarian.

**Yuri Tsivian**, William Colvin professor in the Humanties at the University of Chicago, received his PhD in film studies from the Institute of Theater, Music, and Cinema, Leningrad, 1984. He is the author of Silent Witnesses: Russian Films, 1908-1919 (1989), Early Cinema in Russia and its Cultural Reception (1991) and, in collaboration with Yuri Lotman, Dialogues with the Screen (1994), Ivan the Terrible (2002), Lines of Resistance: Dziga Vertov and the Twenties (2004). Also known for his video-commenting on DVD-released films, such as Dziga Vertov's MAN WITH A MOVIE CAMERA (1995), he received an award from the British Academy of Film and Television Arts in 2001 for developing the best interactive learning project with his CD ROM Immaterial Bodies: Cultural Anatomy of Early Russian Films (USC, 2000).

# Index of Names

# Index of Film Titles

# Index of Subjects

conceptual, semantic content  99
conceptualism  94
    constructivism  27, 31, 139, 151, 237
    constructivist approach  122, 135
    constructivist artists  89
    constructivist groups  89
    constructivist photography  24
    constructivist psychology  121
    culturalists-constructivists  139
continuity
    continuity principles, editing  70-71
    continuity thesis  121
    linear continuity  165
conventions  77
criticism (political, psychoanalytical, feminist)  177
cultural conceptions of vision  143
cultural studies  177, 181
culturalist approaches  121
    culturalist approach (political use of)  183

# D

Dada  151
Darwinian disciplines  180
deautomatization  12, 17, 152, 166, 171, 233
    cognitive deautomatization  166
deconstructionism  103
deduction  142
deep-focus staging  70
defamiliarization  12, 15, 26-27, 31, 50, 54, 62, 64, 66-67, 69, 71, 73-75, 77-79, 99, 119-121, 123-126, 128-140, 145-146, 150-151, 153, 155, 158, 175-177, 179-180, 187, 196
    audiovisual defamiliarization  139
    defamiliarization as deautomatized perception  145
    defamiliarization as the prolongation of perception  155
    defamiliarization (the theory of)  49
    defamiliarization through external mutation  132

    defamiliarization through internal mutation  132
    formal defamilarization  63
    narrative defamiliarization  17, 177
    perceptive defamiliarization  124
deformation, narrative deformation  166, 171
device  13, 23, 62, 64, 70-71, 74, 82, 93-94, 100, 106, 166, 178
    artistic device  76, 179
    canonized devices  71
    defamiliarizing device  78, 138
    device of displacement  107
    device of ostranenie  103, 105-106
    distancing and framing devices  87
    estranging device  160
    formal device(s)  77, 103, 107-108
    formalist device  106
    narrative device  65
    poetic (narrative) devices  178
    postmodern device  128
    prosthetic devices  143
    stylistic device  65
    technological device  77
    the problem of devices  115
diachronicity  61
    diachronic development  63
    diachronic dimension  73
    diachronic perspective  69, 72
    diachronic process  62, 77
    diachronic process of familiarization  77
différance  17, 134, 180
differenciation  99
digital technology  143
distance (from the perceiver)  144-149, 155, 231
distanciation  103, 188
Dogma films  130, 138
duality of information  124

# E

early cinema  11, 13, 33, 72-73, 77, 185, 189

## Forthcoming titles in this Series

*Subjectivity and Film Form*, by Dominique Chateau (ed.)

*The Film Audience and Spectatorship*, by Ian Christie (ed.)

## Academic Advisory Board

Francesco Casetti
Laurent Creton
Jane Gaines
Frank Kessler
András Bálint Kovács
Eric de Kuyper
Laura Mulvey
Roger Odin
Patricia Pisters
Emile Poppe
Pere Salabert
Heide Schlupmann
Vivian Sobchack